COUNTERFEIT OR COUNTERPART

BY: JOSHUA EZE

Counterfeit or Counterpart
Published by Casting Seeds Publishing

Scripture quotations unless otherwise indicated are from the ESV ® Bible (The Holy Bible, English Standard Version), Copyright © 2001 by Crossway. Used by permission. All rights reserved.

Copyright © 2020 by Joshua Eze
Cover design by Joshua Eze

All Rights Reserved. No Part of this book may be reproduced or transmitted in any form or by any means, electronic or mechanical, including photocopying and recording, or by any information storage and retrieval system, without permission in writing from the publisher.

Published in the United States by Casting Seeds Publishing an extension and aid to UNPLUGGED.

***

Websites and Social Media sites:
Website: IAMUNPLUGGED.COM
Social Media: **@MYCOACHJOSH**

COACH JOSH

TABLE OF CONTENTS

- **INTRODUCTION**: WHY TESTING MATTERS – 5
- **SECTION ONE**: WHAT IS THE DIFFERENCE? – 11
- **SECTION TWO**: SPIRITUAL MATHEMATICS – 35
- **SECTION THREE**: HOW TO DISCERN/HOW GOD CONFIRMS – 57
- **SECTION FOUR**: HOW TO PROPERLY TEST EVERYTHING – 91
- **SECTION FIVE**: SCRIPTURAL SUPPORT – 185

THIS ICON WILL BE THROUGHOUT THE BOOK HIGHLIGHTING VIDEOS THAT WILL SUPPORT THE BOOK. MAKE SURE TO REGISTER NOW AT LIFEWORK.TEACHABLE.COM/COURSES FOR ACCESS!

TO EVERYONE WHO DESIRES TO BE IN GOD'S WILL!

WHY TESTING MATTERS

It is possible to know and fulfill the will of God for your life. God is a God that desires to be known. He is not hidden; he is present. Life is more serious than most take it. The more seriously you take your life, the more you will examine its potential parts. We must test what's in front of us. Testing matters because purpose matters. Not everything in front of you is for you and from God. God created you for a purpose and desires to guide you through each phase of it, but you must know how to test.

God commands us in His word to test what's behind everything; He says in 1 John 4:1

> "Beloved, do not believe every spirit but test the spirits to see whether they are from God."

Just about everything in your life was sent to it, whether sent from the kingdom of God or sent from the realm of Satan. I say just about everything because I'm sure both groups didn't purposely send every single little thing, but everything accepted or welcomed by you could be intentionally used by them. The main word in this verse is the word, beloved. For us to be-come, we must be-loved. To become who God has created us to be and to impart our gift to the world, we must first be loved. Those who know that God loves them limit themselves and have limits on everyone else. God loves you and only wants what's best for you. Love is powerful; it builds confidence and creates boundaries. Do you truly know how much God loves you? God's love for us has no limits, but unfortunately, we put limits on how His love works on us.

I'm not sure if you heard of this formula, but there are three B's that reveal a lot about how we operate and they are; belong, believe and behave. Both non-equal groups, (God being supreme and Satan being second-class) desire to affect your behaviors. Behaviors are very influential and contagious due to their ability to attract consequences and inspire others to behave and receive accordingly. See, your choices are valuable due to the consequences that follow them. God desires for your behaviors to be like His so that true virtue can be shown and shared throughout the world. In contrast, Satan wants for your behaviors to be inspired by rebellion so that rebellion can be spread abroad. That's why Satan is after the fathers because if he can taint how we view our earthly fathers, then he can taint the way we view our Heavenly Father.

For these behaviors to be influenced, they first must belong somewhere. Both you and I desire to belong. We both want to belong to a group and to belong to a cause. Our enemy knows this and aims to taint how we view God and His love so that we won't learn how to test thoroughly. He wants us to see God from one of these two extremes. He wants us to either believe that God doesn't love us or that God overly loves us. God loves us sufficiently, not excessively. God's love for us is balanced, tender, and true, true being the most important one. God's love is honest and helpful. It loves you but hates your sin. It loves you where you are but will not leave you where you are. His love is not brutal, perverted, or absent like some fathers are but warm, authentic, and thoughtful. Satan doesn't want you to view God this way. He wants you to see God as either an absentee father or a father that allows anything. He wants you to have the wrong image of God in your mind so that you won't belong to him and believe correctly.

Many people's attitudes and actions toward God are directly affected by their image of Him in their minds. When your mind knows that he loves you, you live for Him, but when your mind is unsure about him, your life becomes unstable and unguarded. Love guards. Love limits. Whoever you belong to directly affects your beliefs. They affect the way you see yourself and the world around you.

God is true and must not be created into a graven image. It's a grave mistake to make a graven image of God.

Many people cannot test what is in front of them due to how they see God. In order to see what's in front of you correctly, you must see God correctly. When you know God, you will know what is from God.

Another scripture that helps us to understand better why we should test is Romans 12:1-2 let's take some time to break it down it says

> I appeal to you; therefore, brothers, by the mercies of God, to present your bodies as a living sacrifice, holy and acceptable to God, which is your spiritual worship. 2 Do not be conformed to this world but be transformed by the renewal of your mind, that by testing you may discern what is the will of God, what is good and acceptable and perfect

The key phrase in this verse is

> that by testing, you may discern the will of God, what is good, acceptable, and perfect. (testing and discern being the most important words.)

We must never forget that we are pilgrims passing through with a purpose. Those who know who they are understand the importance of purpose and pilgrimage. This is not our home. We must live **UNPLUGGED** from here. When eternity is your focus, you take your time to test and discern. Only through the Holy Spirit's empowerment will you be able to discern the will of God, what is good, acceptable, and perfect in every situation. Let's break down each briefly.

The will of God is your sanctification. Salvation has three parts, and they are justification, sanctification, and glorification. The justification phase is where the goodness of God draws you to a place of repentance, and you recognize your depraved state and your desperate need for a savior. This recognition leads to faith in Jesus for your salvation. It is when you become adopted into the Kingdom of God not of your own doing but solely by God's grace. Sanctification is the process where your patterns of life begin to match your position in Christ. At the moment of salvation, Jesus' righteousness was imputed on you, sealing you forever as sons and daughters of God. When God looks at us, He sees his seal, His Spirt, sealing us until we are home with Him forever. Right now, we are sealed from hell and God's wrath and set apart as his children. We are positionally righteous but not righteous in pattern.

Sanctification is not us needing more of the Holy Spirit but the Holy Spirit desiring more of us. He embodies our spirit but endeavors to renew our soul and refresh our bodies. The more we allow Him to restore the locked areas of our lives, the more our patterns will match our position—lastly, glorification. Glorification is when we have passed from this life to the next, and we are connected to our new bodies and live forever in a perfect state with God. His will is for us to be like him. Right now, we all bear His image, but not all of us bear his likeness. When you are like God in character, you can distinguish between the characters in front of you.

Next is testing and discerning what is good. God doesn't look at what we do but how and why we do it. He looks at our motives. The more we are like God, the more we can judge well. When we judge ourselves and take out the beam in our eyes, we will clearly see the specks in others. We must know what is truly good for us. Not everything good for someone else is good for you. What may be good for another may be bad for you. Not everyone is good with money, good with responsibilities, promotion, etc. So it's essential to trust the spirit of God to let you know who and what is right for you. God's view of goodness is different than the world's picture of it. In these days people are making bad things good, and good things bad the bible says in Isaiah 5:20

> Woe to those who call evil good and good evil, who put darkness for light and light for darkness, who put bitter for sweet and sweet for bitter!

We are seeing this right now, and if you are not discerning, you will be thinking you are doing good, but in all, actuality you are doing badly. It's better to go against the grain doing good than following the crowd, confused about what good is.

Next is what is acceptable. Life is not about doing what's acceptable to man but doing what's acceptable to God. We are to work unto the Lord and not to man. God is the one that promotes us that's why the word says in Colossians 3:23-24

> 23 Whatever you do, work heartily, as for the Lord and not for men, 24 knowing that from the Lord, you will receive the inheritance as your reward. You are serving the Lord Christ.

It says that in whatever you do work whole-heartedly as for the Lord and not for men. People's expectations are often far below the expectations of God. We are to always do everything with God in mind. It's crazy how we hide our sins from others but do them openly before God as if His eyes are not everywhere. God sees all, and it should be our mission to do everything as he would. See, when you work unto the Lord, you will have exceptional favor with men because your integrity will bring them prosperity. Those who harbor God's likeness may not be likable due to their beliefs but will be likable due to their work ethic. Look at Daniel and Joseph; they were top people in kingdoms that were prejudice and didn't worship their God. In every situation, there is an acceptable way, and God wants you to engage it because, like in verse 24, those who work in excellence unto the Lord will from the Lord receive an inheritance.

Lastly, is the word perfect. Obedience leads to perfect outcomes. Our goal should be to operate at peak obedience. When we are in tune with the Spirit of God and our fellowship with Him is flourishing, we will function in continuous obedience leading us to produce perfect outcomes even in imperfect situations. We are not perfect at all, but we can, through obedience, be spot on, creating a favorable outcome not only for God but for those involved with our obedience.

In this life, you will face counterfeit wills, goodness, acceptableness, and perfections, and we must be in tune with God so that we can recognize the differences. Now how do we get to this place where we are testing and discerning at a high level where we can in a moment's notice, notice the will of God, what's good, acceptable, and perfect? Let's look at the top half of the scripture it says

> I appeal to you; therefore, brothers, by the mercies of God, to present your bodies as a living sacrifice, holy and acceptable to God, which is your spiritual worship. 2 Do not be conformed to this world but be transformed by the renewal of your mind.

The first part of this formula is to present our bodies as living sacrifices holy and acceptable unto God, which is our spiritual worship or reasonable service. It's unfortunate how many people are "presenting" on behalf of a God they don't know. Many of these people are false prophets who speak on behalf of a God they aim to defame. Others are the people who follow these individual's teachings and are not living under God. We must present our whole selves as a living, dying breed. At every moment, we should present ourselves as a product of God that allows their spirit to live and their flesh to die. This becomes possible when we recognize the holiness of God. God is holy, and he said to us in his word to be Holy as he is holy. Holiness means being set apart in every area and in every way, meaning that I will only do what I see my heavenly father do. I will embody his mindset and move as he would move. I will be a tool with only His fingerprints on them. Holiness leads to wholeness. When we allow ourselves to be set apart from the world, we become whole and able to hold. Our mission should be to be whole enough to properly hold God's stuff, and this comes from being holy as He is Holy.

The next part of the verse says,

> which is our spiritual worship or reasonable service,

meaning this is a reasonable request from God. This is not something we should look for brownie points for but something we do simply because of how great His love is towards us. This will keep you in the pilgrimage mindset. It will keep you flowing in the Holy Ghost flow, producing his fruit to help your fellow man.

The next part of the formula is in verse 2. It says do not be conformed to this world but be transformed by the renewing of your mind. To properly test and discern, your mind must be renewed. Right now, your mind is either being ruined or being renewed. Whatever or whomever you allow to influence, you will pull you towards its ideologies. Which way is your mind going? Your mind is a muscle, and it must be molded and prepped to navigate through life. Many people's minds haven't been developed in years. They have allowed their minds to be hijacked and thought for by others. Whoever controls the masses' minds controls how they move and spend their money. When people become lazy mentally, they hand over their thinking to other entities that will produce the fruit they desire out of their subjects through the thoughts they sow. The more we understand God's word, the more we can determine what is in front of us.

Testing matters, my friend and your life must be lived slowly and sensitively. We are just pilgrims passing through. This is not our home. Those who make this place their home will fall for countless counterfeits, but those who live heading home will be mission-minded and take their time to test and discern.

In this book, you will learn the differences between a counterfeit and a counterpart, how to do spiritual mathematics, what discernment is, and how God confirms. You will also learn the formula on how to properly test everything from family, friends, foes, and fruit. This book will be a resource I believe you will use throughout your life and pass down for generations. I pray it helps you see what is in front of you. Let's head to the next chapter and learn the difference between a counterfeit and a counterpart.

WHAT IS THE DIFFERENCE?

In this chapter, we are going to discuss the differences between a counterfeit and a counterpart. We will also break down how each ends up on the counter of our lives. But before we do, let's establish some definitions and some key points.

Definitions:

- Counterfeit: made in exact imitation of something valuable or important with the intention to deceive or defraud. A fraudulent imitation of something else.

- Counterpart: a person or thing holding a position or performing a function that corresponds to another person or thing in another place.

- Counter: a level surface (such as a table, shelf, or display case) over which transactions are conducted, or food is served or on which goods are displayed, or work is conducted.

Key Points:

1. What is a counterfeit? pg: 11
2. What is a counterpart? pg: 16
3. What CLOUDS our judgment? pg: 22
4. How they affect your money, diet, goods, and work pg: 31
5. Why leveling up mentally is vital. pg: 34

What is a counterfeit?

A counterfeit is a fraudulent imitation of something valuable and important. It is a fraudulent item or individual that is being forced to fit where it wasn't created to belong. Nothing with God is forced. Everything with Him flows. He has created everything beautiful for its time. Satan wants to thwart this process through deception. His system was designed to make imitations and have them delivered or presented to us before God's perfect pieces are manifested. Our foolishness funds Satan's factory. The less discerning we are, the more his imitations are developed. His corporation is built on deception. Deception only works when its appearance is similar to the truth it opposes. The less of the truth you know, the more of a lie you will receive. God is not making new items and individuals for your life; they have already been made; they are just waiting for their timely release. Satan knows this and wants to occupy your time with influences that will lure your freewill from fellowshipping with God and fulfilling your purpose to being face to face with his counterfeits.

Satan, his demons, and his system have seen your kind before and can, to a degree, predict your gifting, personality, potential desires, etc. They know you better than you know yourself. Their knowledge of you stems from the tending of your family tree. They are familiar with your great, great grandparents and the mental, emotional, and physical traumas and curses that they've passed down. They orchestrate with outcomes in mind. They want to make sure you know nothing about the true and living God and His love for you, and they do this by affecting the home and connecting its history. He wants you to be invisibly connected to the dark sides of your family's history through the habits and false hopes that were prevalent in the home you were brought up in. It is no coincidence that many people today are surrounded by the same consequences that surround those from their families' past. This is by design. They want the same counterfeits that were in front of your great, great grandparents to be in front of you. That is why he has developed a system that produces specific pressures that produce specific patterns that produce specific problems that produce specific pains keeping people dependent on the system with no desire to turn to God. Most homes were filled with pressure stemming from internal pain.

Many of our parents parented through their pain, putting pressure on us, leading us to develop particular patterns, setting us up to becoming more invested in Satan's system. All we were told was go to school, get a degree, get a job, work all your life, retire, and die or do what thou wilt. Nothing in Satan's system advertises or advocates for individuality, originality, creativity, purpose, fulfillment, or joy rooted in one's thriving relationship with God. It only focuses on sensuality, lust, and curiosity. It boasts of broadness but has a tight rope. It doesn't want you to be free in Christ and see all the parts God has for you to enjoy. He wants us to look at everything created with perverted eyes.

Satan hates the image you bear. He hates that you look just like God. He hates that you replaced him. He was by far one of if not the best angel created, and many believed he was the angel over music. He didn't know that after his demise, what would rise from the dirt would be his replacement. See, everything about us was created to worship God. Our voices are like horns; our hands and feet are like drums; everything about us points to praising God. That is why Satan wants you and me to use our instruments to worship him and feed his system. He doesn't want you dependent on God destroying his kingdom. That is why we are bombarded with counterfeit ideas, items, and individuals every day, aiming to get our attention putting us in detention. This is why you must live UNPLUGGED from this world and become PLUGGED into God so that you won't be caught by any of the tentacles of this system. Let's continue.

Fraudulent things are made quicker and are made of weaker material. You either get what you paid for, or you get what Christ paid for. Satan wants us to purchase impulsively. He wants us to quickly buy his counterfeit parts with our time, energy, and resources. He knows that a person who is desperate and not dependent on God will not wait for the proper time for the delivery of God's durable parts. So Satan sells them, shiny and quickly made parts that will only hold them up temporarily. They will feel, taste, sound, smell, and look good but will not be durable. God's parts for your life are durable, and they will last forever. His love, joy, peace, goodness, etc. are the immaterial durable parts you need to hold anything significant. Without His Spirit released to do His will in our lives, we will not be held up. See a Rolls Royce will always be more valuable than a Hyundai due to the parts used to make it. Hand-made/ custom made cars will always be more expensive than machine-made vehicles. Most machine-made cars are made in factories where all the parts are made and readily accessible. Hand made cars like Rolls Royce's are made in factories where not all parts are made and readily available. Most of their parts are imported. Therefore lengthening the time of its production and depending on the imported parts increasing its value. God has a set time for your parts to be imported into your life and for a good reason. He wants to make sure your frame is well-built and mature enough to carry his luxury. What do you want to be? Do you want to be a Hyundai or a Rolls Royce? Do you want parts that will hold you up or hold you back?

Satan loves to leverage against us our lust for valuable and important things. There is nothing wrong with desiring to be married, to have kids, to be successful, etc. but when these things become idols, we become rivals or enemies of God. His glue for this outcome is our lust. Lust, by definition, is an overbearing desire for something without the discipline to sustain it properly. The Bible says in James 1:13-15

13 Let no one say when he is tempted, "I am being tempted by God," for God cannot be tempted with evil, and he himself tempts no one. **14** But each person is tempted when he is lured and enticed by his own desire. **15** Then desire when it has conceived gives birth to sin, and sin, when it is fully grown, brings forth death.

The Bible clarifies that God doesn't tempt anyone and that He is incapable of being evil or releasing evil. The scripture follows that statement with the formula of how lust lures us to the consequences of accepted counterfeits. It says that each person is tempted when he or she is lured and enticed by their own desires, keyword's own desires. We can only be drawn by what is drawn on our hearts. Whatever is in our hearts will be used to connect with Satan's counterfeits. If God's Spirit hasn't filled the hole in your heart, you will naturally build emotions and desires for that hole to be filled. And when the right idea, item, or individual is presented in front of you, you will immediately accept it. That's why Satan wants you to incubate in dysfunction and sin so that your carnal desires will mature to the level of meshing or mixing. The Bible says that desires, when conceived or, in other words, have become intimate with an ideal will birth sin.

Satan wants you to commit, and the only way to commit is through a sinful act. He knows the effects of sin. He knows that sin has two predominant effects; it has an immediate effect and a delayed effect. Most of our initial engagements with sin produced immediate effects. Satan doesn't want you to see the consequences of sin at the moment of peak lust, so he hides them in enjoyment and pleasure; this then makes a person comfortable with the sin and still high off their own lust; which over time sets them up to collapse into a state of condemnation, and the same one that tempted them into the sin will be the same one to torment them with condemnation. He knows that most people are not mature or knowledgeable enough about God's love and his gift of repentance. He wants us to think that God hates us and for us to never recognize his goodness that will draw us to repentance. What follows this is the delayed effects of sin, which is death. It says that when lust and ideals are intimate and produce sin, and sin has become fully grown, it will bring forth death. Satan wants sin in your life for an extended period of time so that at the appointed time, it will bring destruction to your family, purpose, goals, and life. See, all sins have a set time for death to be released. These set times are determined by your history, misery, chemistry, and or curiosity. Not all sins have the same set times. That's why it is never wise to play with sin. You can't win with practicing sin. Let's continue.

Satan has an exact imitation of everything God created. He has perverted everything pure. He has an exact imitation of love, marriage, parenting, sexuality, etc. you name it; he has an exact imitation of it. His goal is to get as close to God's way as possible. Deception is dense, my friend. You and I are, to some degree, up under some form of deception. The Bible says that the truth is what sets us free. Jesus said that He is the way the truth and the life and that the Spirit of truth his Spirit will lead and guide us to all truth. Every day for the believer is an opportunity for them to be set free in a hidden area. Those who flow with the Spirit will always find themselves experiencing greater freedom. But those who become stagnant or connected to this world system will find themselves continuously deceived thinking they are free, but in all actuality, they are greatly bound.

God wants us to see the things of life how He sees them. He is the one that holds the definition, meaning, and value of everything. If you want to know the value of love, marriage, sex, parenting, singleness, etc. you must seek it through God. When people are dramatically affected and have no ideas of how or where to be delivered from these demonic ideals and entities, they will settle for counterfeits. The two structures Satan is after is the family and the church. Suppose he can keep houses from becoming homes and buildings from becoming churches. In that case, he can keep people enslaved and tormented. It's unfortunate how perverted the modern-day church has become, and I'm not talking about God's glorious church, His body, but the institutionalized and popularized church of today. These churches are stripping away what it means to be a church. They have become cult-like and control centers for Satan to keep babes from being mature and the non-converted from being converted. He has hired men and women to preach a diluted and partial gospel that has no power to save, creating synagogues of Satan that doesn't focus on discipleship and deliverance. To be discerning in this life, you must be delivered by Jesus and a disciple of Jesus. Many people are walking around with ancestral demonic spirits with nowhere to be set free. The church was designed to be a hospital and a gym. It was designed to heal and build. But when the house that opened you up to demonic influences and the church that pacifies the demon's influence is not built well, neither will its offspring.

Everything we value must be in the order of value. That is why God must be number one and at the center of everything in our lives. We must welcome God in every area of our lives to be delivered and held accountable. Many people do not want God to have access to every room in their souls. They don't want God to have access to their memory bank, or their thought patterns or their emotions or world views. They want to think, feel, and live the way they want despite their internal pain and obvious consequences. God must be valued because when He is, we will recognize our value. It's hard to appreciate a thing without understanding its importance. Only the creator of a thing can determine its value. Whatever we connect ourselves to ultimately is what will determine our worth. When the dollar was removed from the gold standard, it began to lose value. The same happens to us when we are removed from the God standard. That's what makes repentance so beautiful. At any given moment of dipping or sinning, we can genuinely repent and be brought up to where we were created to be. Satan doesn't want you to be backed by God or recognize your value and worth in him. He knows the impenetrable effects of a soul that is content in God. That is why he wants your list of importance to be out of order.

Counterfeits have caused a ton of damage within the family unit. It has made many wives, husbands, kids compete with things that are below them. Satan has used counterfeit ambitions and expectations to cause problems in families. Many men and women are pursuing careers at a pace that God never intended for them to pursue. Look at our world today. The family is continuously being ran over by ambition. The work structure of society has people working long hours, leaving scraps of minutes for their families to try and get their full. Satan has reordered a lot of people's list of importance. He wants us not to be able to perceive accurate value. A job or career will never be more valuable than a family. In every arena, family in the eyes of God will always be more important. But society in many areas subtly advertises that a job or career is more valuable than a family. A job or career will never be more valuable than your health. But in our society, it is advertised to spend your health to get wealth and spend your wealth to gain health. It is essential to have your list of priorities in order because one thing or person in the wrong place could drastically affect the others on that list.

Questions to think on:

- What are your top priorities right now?
- In which areas of your life does God not have access to and why?

Satan's intentions for you will never be in your favor. His intention is to deceive you until you are destroyed. He hates you and will through your insecurities, fears, and identity issues lure you in front of his counterfeits that will cause you to compromise and plummet into condemnation and into cycles of addiction. He will sell you a dream and with that dream steal your time, energy and leave you empty-handed. There is no good return from sin and engaging with things that were not created for you. He is a fraud, a scammer and he is no one to trust. That's why we must be content and sensitive to the spirit so that we are not fooled. Satan is a master manipulator the ultimate conman. He is in the deceiving business. He cannot be trusted.

Throughout this life, you will have many items, ideals, and individuals placed on the counter of your life, asking you to make a deal. Anyone or anything, including yourself that tries to force a thing or a person to fit your life, is a counterfeit.

<u>What is a counterpart?</u>

A counterpart is a person or a thing holding a position or performing a function that corresponds to God's calling for your life. God has a specific calling for you but it's hard to know what it is if you keep ignoring his calls or just keeping his text on read with no desire to apply it. God has key parts to play key parts in your life. These parts are durable parts, parts that will hold you up forever. Like I mentioned in the section above God's immaterial and impenetrable parts which are the fruits of the spirit are key to being sustained and sustaining anything in life. The greatest counterpart is The Holy Spirit and it is through Him that we are able to hold anything significant. The fruits of the spirit are found in Galatians 5:22-23 which says

> 22 But the fruit of the Spirit is love, joy, peace, patience, kindness, goodness, faithfulness, 23 gentleness, self-control; against such things, there is no law.

Notice in the text it says the fruit of the spirit not the fruits of the spirit meaning you can't have one without the other. Without love, there is no joy. Without joy, there is no peace. Without peace, there is no patience. Without patience, there is no kindness. Without kindness, there is no goodness. Without goodness there is no faithfulness, gentleness, or self-control. They all flow in that order. For us to be faithful, gentle, and self-controlled we must first know God as love. Love is the chief cornerstone of our countenance and character. The word even says that amongst the others love is the greatest (1 Cor 13:13). Without God's perfect love in your life fear will run rampant. The bible says in 1 John 4:18

> 18 There is no fear in love, but perfect love casts out fear. For fear has to do with punishment, and whoever fears has not been perfected in love.

When a person is not being perfected by God's love their fears will affect their joy, peace, patience, kindness, goodness, faithfulness, gentleness, and self-control. Fear is a tormentor and it doesn't torment alone it will open the door for its friend's anxiety, stress, and depression to aid in the torment. We must know that God loves us and we must let Him love us. We must let him love us thoroughly which includes both his tender and tough love. Once we investigate and embrace God's love we are then able to understand joy and what it means to be content. Where God's love is known his timing is trusted. Those who know they are loved by God trust His timing and are not pressed by anything because they are only impressed by God. Joy is essential for holistic success. Joy is not based on conditions like happiness is it is based on all conditions being met in Christ. Once the mind and heart are content in God and they find their strength in Him it opens the door for peace. It's hard to have peace without joy. Those who are joyful have a firm peace. They are at peace because they know all of their needs are met in Christ and that God's timing is perfect. They are settled in the will of God therefore they know they are safe.

Love that creates a joy that creates peace automatically creates patience. See love and joy are foundational perspectives. Once acquired they automatically create peace and patience. A person that is at peace doesn't mind being patient because they know they are in the flow of God which always leads to the favor of God. They don't lean on their own understandings because they know it will never hold them up they instead rest in the peace that surpass all understanding powerful enough to keep their hearts from failing and their minds from illness. Patience is key to everything in life. Everything in life requires a certain amount of patience to engage and manage it. Like I've said in many videos you don't have the grace or patience for everyone and everyone doesn't have the grace or patience for you. That is why it is important to only accept what God has for you. Any time you are connected with someone or something that wasn't built for you; you will end up unbalanced and frustrated. The patience that is birth from peace which is birth from joy which is birth from love produces kindness. It's easy to be kind when you are fine. Kindness is the fruit of Patience. The more you are aware of God's flow and trust His timing the more open you are to be kind. How can we help the blind if we are not kind? Kindness is essential for outreach and soul winning. It is important to renew the minds of the ignorant. The bible says that kindness will heap coals of fire on people's heads meaning it will help renew their minds. This doesn't mean you open your heart to abusers it means walk in love and forgiveness and in doing so you will help set captives free.

Kindness when applied though forgiveness opens the door for you to be a person that continuously does good. Good deeds have a tendency of helping people who are doing bad deeds. The more good that is done the more lives that can be saved. No little deed goes unnoticed and being loved by God and being content in his joy and being peaceful, patient, and kind really create space for the goodness of God to draw others to repentance. When a person is at this state of doing good continuously they can't help but be faithful to God, their wives, husbands, and children. They can't help but be gentle where they once were irritable and frustrated. They can't help but be self-controlled mentally, emotionally and physically. These immaterial parts are the parts that really help us to truly hold up marriages, persecution, family, purpose, friends, ministries, etc. Without these things we and the things connected to us will fall apart!

At the core of our being, like I mentioned in the previous chapter, we desire to belong or to be apart. The ramifications of Adams and Eve's decision in the garden is really having a toll on a lot of people today. Before the fall everything in creation was in perfect harmony, each part of it was connected. But when Eve broke apart from that tree its fruit, ate it and gave it to Adam to also eat, creation lost its glue, it lost its connection and from that moment to now countless people are longing to belong. This effect is causing so many people to be a part of things they shouldn't but there is a solution to this problem. Many years ago there was a man named Jesus who was truly God and truly man who came into our realm to let us know that the God-head hasn't forgotten about them. To let us know that we can now be a part of God's plan. See we have to understand that God as a spirit didn't know what it felt like to be cold, poor, hot, uncomfortable, or tired so he wrapped himself in flesh and came in the form of man to redeem man from their sins so that whoever would call upon his name (Jesus) will be saved from their sins, from hell and from the impending wrath of God.

Because of Jesus' sacrifice, we have the opportunity to be a part of God's family and be a part of the family business. We now can have a sense of belonging. The greatest counterpart is God's Spirit who dwells in those who believe. We now have access to the fullness of God and have no need. But when this truth and opportunity are suppressed, people will try to find God in all the wrong areas. God wants you apart of his family. He wants you to feel that you belong to him so that he can shape your beliefs and impact your behaviors.

Now let's take some time to break down this definition a little more. The definition says that a counterpart is a person or things that does one of these two things

- Hold a position
- Perform a function

Not everyone is capable of holding the positions in your life. We are not smart enough to hire the right people to hold our key positions. It is better to leave a position vacant than to hire someone that can't hold the position. God is all-encompassing He can hold every vacant position simultaneously. He is able to fill the voids of every missing position until it is His timing to release the one or people that are able to hold those key positions. Many people are not aware of all of the things they are able to do by themselves. Many people are not aware of how much of a blessing their singleness is or how much of a blessing the removal of their unnecessary friends were. God knew when it was no longer good for Adam to be alone and it was at that perfect moment where he placed him in a place of rest and removed from him his woman. See God knows where we are. He will never release key people or things to hold key positions in your life if you are stressed. Stress is a sign of a lack of trust in God or a ton of trust in oneself. Stress will wear you out and will wear out the parts of your life. In order for you to be able to hold your position in anyone's life you must avoid stress and you do so by always assessing your trust in God. God will not put more on you than you are able to bear but often times we do. We add so many parts to our lives that over time we become worn.

Everything boils down to the ingredients. We must always observe a person's ingredients or materials to see if they are able to hold a position. Those who value their position in God see value in the positions around them and will take however long to assess those that are interested. When you know you are a son or daughter of God and the precious value of your time and energy and the spiritual implication that comes with companionship, friendship partnerships etc. then you will vet everyone and everything!

Every position available in your life is too important to just let anyone hold that position. It is always worth the wait to ensure you are connected to an equal weight. The bible talks about being unequally yoked. When a person is unequally yoked with a counterfeit they find themselves stressed and broken. See the Bible was painting the picture of the importance of having two oxen of equal weight because if their weights are not equal then it will hurt or even break the neck of the stronger calf (which is worth more). That's why I always say don't ask for a better half ask or an equal whole. See when you are unequally yoked with a counterfeit you not only have to pull your weight but their lazy weight and the weight of the carriage and in doing so you break while they benefit. You only want to be connected to people where everyone is strong and everyone benefits. Many people are connected to leaches and they wonder why they always have low energy and empty wallets. Not everyone deserves the passenger or driver seat of your life. Ladies, not every man is able to lead and fellas, not every lady is able to follow. You must trust God!

What positions are vacant in your life? Do you trust God to hold that spot until the right one or group comes? See my friend positions have generational value. The wrong spouse could really tilt a home in the wrong direction. The wrong influence of a bad friend could really tilt your life in the wrong direction. You don't want to be tilted you want to be balanced. God knows how to adjust the weight in each of our lives to ensure we are balanced. You may not have everything you want right now but God has you balanced. Trust me it is better to be in an apartment driving a 12-year-old car with balance than in a mansion with a garage full of cars tilted because when things are tilted key things slide off!

It is always important to let God fill the vacancies in your life. He must be the one who does all the interviews and the hiring and firing because he knows who equal's your weight. He knows who is held up by Him while He is holding you up. For any relationship of any kind to work both parties must be held up by God. A person without a personal relationship with God will not be able to hold their part in any relationship. The only way my marriage is operating smoothly now is because my wife and I know we are incapable of doing this thing without God. He is the glue man and I am telling you, you are going to need to get to know Him now and trust Him to select because you don't want to be stuck in a relationship or partnership with someone not being held up on their end by God.

The next part of the definition is performing a function. A counterpart is a mature part; it is able to fulfill its function. Everything God has for you has a purpose; it has a particular function. For an idea, item or individual to function well it must go through test. You shouldn't trust anything or anyone that hasn't been tested. Tests prove if a thing or a person is able to function under pressure. A person or a thing is not measured by how well it function under peace but how well it functions under pressure. That's why it is not wise to partner or marry someone who hasn't been pruned or tested. All of God's parts have been tested at its peak level of functioning under pressure so that when that pressure hits it, it will continue to function without fail. Every bridge is tested against its greatest pressure to see if it's able to hold up multiple cars during traffic. These critical things must go through test to make sure no casualties occur. You don't want to be going through a storm with someone who never been through one. That's why it takes some time for counterparts to be imported because those parts are in labs being tested to ensure they are able to bare what you both will have to bear up together in the future. Only God knows what is up the road for you and He is pleading that you adhere to his warnings and trust his timing so that you won't settle for a person or a position that will not be able to bear you up. That's why you shouldn't count it strange when you go through test. You too are being tested to ensure you are a counterpart to someone else. God wants a people who can function well under persecution and under trouble. He is building a people whose knees will be too strong to bow to any other god. The Bible is very clear that in this life you will face trials and tribulations but be of good cheer He (Jesus) has overcome the world.

It takes time to build durable parts. God is wanting to make sure that your parts are able to hold your future. Do you know how heavy the future is? It doesn't matter how exciting your future is; it is heavy. It is heavy with responsibility. Blessings, promotions and responsibilities are heavy. That is why you must be careful what you are asking for. Instead of asking God for _____ ask him to make you strong enough to hold that thing or person up for its full time. Many people have a get there mentality but not a stay there mentality. They just want to be at a place so bad that they don't take the time to get rid of the bad things that will remove them from there. The goal is to function well the full time. The reason why people burn out three, five, ten years into their marriage is because they only trained for that many miles (years) or somewhere along the way they stopped training. Life is marathon not a sprint and if you train for it as a sprint you will not finish the race. You must condition yourself for your calling. So that you will be able to function long. Let's continue.

The main thing about a counterpart is that it corresponds with another person or thing. Correspond by definition is having a close similarity; match or agree almost exactly. It's hard to know what corresponds to you if you don't know you. Testing matters because purpose matters. If you are unaware of who you are how will you be able to recognize what God has for you? We were not created to just exist we were created to execute a purpose and no one not even you was created by accident. Your mom, dad, siblings, city, neighborhood, struggles were all selected for you to go through (minus abuses) they were selected for a purpose. See struggle and pain are necessary. Those who get mad at God because x, y and z happened to them are ignoring the fact that they survived it. God can use any negative and make it a positive to help shape your purpose and give you identity in Him. You must know your purpose because if not you will be selecting counterfeits trying to find your fit in this world. Right now somewhere in your city, neighborhood or across the plains are parts waiting to be shipped to you; hoping you find God and the right address for it to be shipped to you. Not all parts will be shipped at the same time; they are obedient parts; parts that will only ship out when released by God's providential hand. Not are parts were created to fit your life you must examine its ingredients and its fruit. You must get to know God and get to know yourself so that you will only select what he has for you.

VIDEO: HOW TO DISCOVER YOUR PURPOSE.

Let's briefly break down six things that clouds our judgment when it comes to counterfeits and counterparts

The six things that CLOUDS our judgment are

1. C: Comparisons
2. L: Lust
3. O: Opinions
4. U: Unrealistic expectations a lack of understanding
5. D: Doubt
6. S: Supplements

Comparison

The first thing that clouds our ability to judge well is comparisons. The Bible says that comparing ourselves amongst ourselves is not wise. It's not wise because none of us are fully aware of what is going on in another person's life. One of the worst places to eat from are social media feeds due to the temptation to compare. Many people are comparing their real life with another person's fake life. What most people post online or show offline is fabricated. When our minds are consumed with what other people have compared to what we have or don't have, it will cloud our judgment. There is a quote that says that comparison is the thief of joy, or in other words, comparison robs us of strength. The Bible says that the joy of the Lord is our strength; it also says that there is fullness of joy in the presence of God. When we compare, we leave our safety net of contentment to try and collect what others have. Only God and that individual know exactly how they got what they got. It's not wise to compare ourselves with others because we don't know exactly how they got what they got, and for many, they acquired what they have outside of God. Anything you have to obtain without God is not worth having. Comparison has a way of causing our hearts to flood with impatience leading us to burn our energy to get what others have or to have more than what they have, tempting us to compromise and cheat to eat at the same tables. One of Satan's tactics is to use the people he has caused to compromise to get you to compromise. It's no surprise that most people who compromise get their prizes early. Satan and his system delivers on-demand, not by understanding. God gives at points of understanding while Satan gives at points of demand. Satan knows the power of compromise. See compromise robs you of character. It gives out once you give in and uses what you gave into as blackmail and tools of condemnation.

The same one that tempts you into compromise is the same one that condemns you for compromising. This tactic works on many, and it's contagious. He knows that most people are not mature enough to understand contentment and its protection. So he hits people at their most immature point and gets them to compare and compromise early so that they will be surrounded by too many consequences to effectively pursue their purpose. If they try to do so, it will be challenging. The hardest people to tempt are those who are content in God. Contentment doesn't mean complacent it means commitment. You're not always going to like where you are, but you will always love the One you are there with. Most of the places we hate are hiding places designed to protect us while we are being made. They are warehouses where God is doing work on us.

When people have this perspective, they trust wherever God has them because they are committed to the overall cause. There is nothing wrong with aspirations and wanting to be somewhere better, but you must want to be with God more than the place you want to get to. Trust me where you are now with God is better than the place you aspire to be without Him. It is better to be in a shack where God is than in a mansion where He isn't!

Who are you comparing yourself to, and why? + What do they have that you want?		
People	Why	What do they have

How is comparing yourself to them affecting you mentally and emotionally?

VIDEO: HORIZONTAL COMPARISONS

Lust

The next thing that clouds many people's judgment is lust. A lot of people when they think lust they think sex but it's more than sex. Lust, by definition, is an overbearing desire for something. Love clarifies while lusting clouds. Those who know they are loved by God don't go looking for love; they are fully satisfied. With God, you have more than enough, and his love is enough to sustain, but when a person has strong desires for something, they will be susceptible to fall for Satan's counterfeits. They will try to force anything to happen to have what they want. There is nothing wrong with desires, but they must stay at their safest limits. The awareness of and the acceptance of God's love levels out desires. You go from I must have it to I want it, but I don't need it.

Lust is never satisfied. Lust will take you from desiring something small to something big. Lust starts small and builds to an uncontrollable emotion. It begins with I must have that cookie in that jar to I must have her cookies in her box. Lust will take you farther than you want to go, and you will continue to collect counterfeits and consequences that corresponds to Satan's conforming images. Those who know they are loved by God may want things but they don't need things. Those who are unaware of God's love their wants become desperate needs clouding their judgments.

What do you have a strong desire for and why? + What conceived these desires?	
What and Why	What conceived these desires?

VIDEO: DON'T TRUST LUST

Opinions

The next thing that clouds judgment are opinions. God doesn't have opinions, he has facts, and anyone's opinion that doesn't line up with God's word should be tossed. But for many, this is difficult because of how many people they have above God. Whoever has the highest seat in your life has the clearest voice in your life. It's unfortunate how many people have God either number two or not even in their top ten. Knowing God's word and knowing His character will keep your head out of the clouds of other people's opinions. Not having a clue of what His word says or who He is will lead you to accepting counterfeit opinions.

Whose opinions are affecting you now and why?		
Person	Opinions	Why?

Where do you honestly have God in your top ten? Write down the people and things that matter to you most and where they honestly fall, considering the time invested.
1
2
3
4
5
6
7
8
9
10

Unrealistic Expectations and a lack of understanding

Another thing that keeps many from spotting a counterfeit are unrealistic expectations and a lack of understanding. Unrealistic expectations are expectations that exceed the reality of a thing. It causes people to believe they are ready for something when they are not. Whenever a person has unrealistic expectations they prove they lack understanding. Full understanding helps you to see down the road; it builds patience. It helps you to see deeper into the situation and avoid unnecessary issues. Many people are not giving themselves the time they need to develop understanding and mature. Maturity is key. Many people's hearts are full of regret right now due to how they moved in immaturity. Satan loves to make people believe they are ready for a situation with no proof of maturity. He knows the power of maturity and its impact, so he ensures he sends his counterfeits into our lives through the areas we are most insecure and immature. Why do you think he is after young people? He knows their brains aren't fully developed yet, and due to a lack of development coupled with a lack of guidance, their hearts will be full of zeal. Zeal, without wisdom, leads to making and settling for bad deals. God has a season for everything, but before every moment of promotion there is a season of preparation. Trust God and take your time.

VIDEO: UNREALISTIC EXPECTATIONS

What would you like to have in life? Are you mature enough to manage it? If so, what's the proof?		
What would you like to have?	Understanding level?	Proof

Doubt

The best way to have a person accept a counterfeit is to have them doubt God and what God has put in them to do. Doubt is the fruit of deception. The first thing Satan said to Eve was, did God really say? His goal is to angle his suggestions right in the area of your greatest desire and to have you question God in that area. His goal with Eve years ago is the same with us today. He wants us to want to be a god so that there would be no need for God. So he lures us into doubting the character, integrity, and ability of God and trusting our own, or he causes us to question our abilities through Christ's Spirit. Inadequacy is another tool our enemy uses to cause us to accept counterfeit professions or careers. He will always try to make you believe that there is no money in the field of your gifting or that you are no good at it or who would want to read, listen or pay you to do x, y, or z? It happened to me for years. I used to question what God wanted me to do with the ministry I do now. I had to fight through thoughts of who is going to listen to you? You don't have a degree; no one is going to think you are credible? You should be this or that because at least you can make this amount of money. But God, who is rich in mercy, helped me to overcome those thoughts. I wouldn't be writing this sentence right now on August 7th, 2020 without the love and grace of God that inspires me to inspire you. Don't let other people's opinions, the lack of credentials or connections hinder you from pursuing what you know God wants you to do. Many people right now are in counterfeit careers sitting on their God-given ideas. Is that you? I hope not.

In what areas of your life are you doubting God and what you know He wants you to do?

Reflection: Are you in a counterfeit career? Is the career you're in really what God wants you to do?

Last but not least - **Supplements**

Many people's minds are clouded now due to the supplements they take. A supplement is something that completes or enhances something else when added to it. Many people are empty and are looking for other things to complete them or improve their performance. Christ is the only One that can complete you. If you go to another person or thing to complete you, you will end up depleted. Those who welcome the best counterpart, the Holy Spirit, and allow him to do his work in them will be clear-headed enough to see what will complement them. Every part that is for your life is an accessory to what God has already assembled. The only part you need to complete you is the Holy Spirit; everything else is an accessory that complements God's purpose for your life. When people don't understand this, they will use drugs, alcohol, relationships, food, business, money, and such things like these to try and fill that empty void. You can try and stuff everything in the world to fill that hole in your heart and you will still have a gaping hole. God is the only One that can fill the God-sized hole in your heart. Completion and wholeness in Christ are necessary for knowing what will complement or be a detriment in your life.

What are you trying to fill that hole in your heart with?

Your life as a counter.

Now let's take some time to break down the concept of our lives being a counter and how counterfeits and counterparts affect our money, diet, deeds, and work. Let's start with the definition.

A counter is a level surface (such as a table, shelf, or display case) over which transactions are conducted or food is served or on which goods are displayed, or work is conducted.

Your life is like a counter, and right now, there are deals on the table; opportunities looking for an open window to connect to your life. Not all deals; heal, and you must know that. Whatever level your mind is on right now, those are the deals you are settling for. That's why the word of God says to set your minds on things that are above. Look to the hills from which comes your help; your help comes from the Lord. He says to always look up so that you can stay up. Never make deals below God's level. Let's continue.

Counterfeits and counterparts will always affect your money, diet, deeds, and your work let's start with your money.

Money

The definition says that a counter is where transactions are made. Many people are selling their souls, exchanging them for things far below its worth. Many people at the end of their lives will regret what they sold their souls for. Your money trail will tell you a lot about what matters to you most. What do you invest your money in? What things are being sold and exchanged on the counter of your life? If you look at your bank statements, what do you see most; counterfeit purchases or counterpart purchases? Counterfeits will offer nothing useful in return. The ROI of counterfeits investments is condemnation, confusion, negative cycles, etc. Counterfeit purchases may return "good returns" early on, making you feel like it was a good investment, but in time will prove worthless. Spend with the end in mind.

What do you spend most of your money on counterfeit or counterpart purchases? →	Counterfeit purchases	Counterpart purchases?

Diet

The next thing that's impacted is your diet. The definition says that over a counter food is served. Your diet spiritually, emotionally, mentally, and physically matters. Who are the chefs in your life? What kind of food are they serving? What ingredients do they use? In this life, there are counterfeit preachers, influencers, ideologies, philosophies, meals, etc. aiming to destroy your immune systems. Like I mentioned earlier, be very careful who and what you have on your social media feeds because who you follow will try and feed you their viewpoints on life. Like I've said many times; learn how to cook for yourself because at least you will know what's in your food. Know the word of God for yourself to see the difference between a counterfeit and counterpart word. It is vitally important that you investigate what you ingest. We must eat to live, not live to eat. We must treat our entire vessel seriously and make sure that we only intake what will not take us out. We must understand that everything we ingest doesn't just impact our taste buds. The enemy wants you to focus solely on the taste while God wants you to focus on the entire digestive system. Many people are enslaved to their physical, emotional, mental, and spiritual taste buds that they have no awareness of what they are allowing into their bodies affecting their entire digestive systems. They just love sweet sermons, foods, shows, and ideologies but are not aware of how the ingredients affect their moods, family, purpose, etc. God wants us to enjoy what's organic and not what's genetically modified. He wants us to eat and enjoy in comparison to our purposes.

Questions to think on: Who are your favorite people to follow, what are your favorite foods and how are each affecting your life?

Deeds

The next thing impacted by these two are our good deeds. The definition says that over a counter goods are displayed. God doesn't care about the moves we make. He cares about the motives behind them. Real recognize real or, in other words, real recognize what's really going on. We can fool others, but we can't fool God. God wants us to do good for goodness sake. It is imperative that we genuinely do good so that our good deeds will become counterpart deeds for another person's life, inspiring them to live for God.

"Good" counterfeit deeds will always expose you later. Motives hidden in the dark areas of our hearts will always come to light. God cares about why we are doing good. When you know that God is good, you seek to do good and to do them hidden. It bothers me when I see people post a good deed that should've stayed private. The Bible talks about this behavior, where he discusses the Pharisees that pray on their porches to be seen. Jesus said that that would be their only reward. Many well-known philanthropists will be very disappointed when they reach eternity. They will find out that they did a lot of empty good deeds; good deeds that had no eternal value. Many, if not most of our good deeds shouldn't be on the counter of our lives for everyone to see.

Questions to think on: why do you do good? Do you do it to be seen or for God to be seen?

Work.

The last thing the definition says happens over counters; is work. The Bible says in Matthew 5:14-16

> 14 "You are the light of the world. A city set on a hill that cannot be hidden. 15 Nor do people light a lamp and put it under a basket, but on a stand, and it gives light to all in the house. 16 In the same way, let your light shine before others, so that they may see your good works and give glory to your Father who is in heaven.

Our work illuminates as we work unto the Lord. Just like light doesn't talk as it's working, so, shouldn't we. The text says, let your light so shine before others so that others may see your good works and give glory to your Father who is in heaven. We should just let our light do the talking. Over the counter of your life, work is being done. We were created to be doers, not advertisers. We were designed to focus on our assignments and everything connected to it. Many people live to advertise the work they've either done, plan on doing or are currently doing. Good work doesn't need commercials. The work will speak for itself. Don't allow the era of the counterfeit philosophy of post it, advertise it, promote it, have you produce half-done counterfeit work that falls apart and is no good for anyone. Do good work and let your light and work do the advertising!

Questions to think on: what quality is your work? Who are you truly working for? Are you a quiet doer or a loud advertiser?

Finally, how leveled is your surface?

What level are you on? The word repentance is important; it means to come back up. It means to confess sin and recognize where you belong. It means to change your mind and forsake sin. The level your mind is on will determine what level you are seated and what deals you make. God wants us to think above this world and really understand what is needed now. What level are you on? Is your counter underground making deals with devils and their counterfeits or raised where Christ is seated, making deals that advances the kingdom. This book was written to help you discern deeper and to think and perceive how Christ would. I love the text in John 2:23-25 which says

> 23 Now when he (Jesus) was in Jerusalem at the Passover Feast, many believed in his name when they saw the signs that he was doing. 24 But Jesus on his part did not entrust himself to them, because he knew all people 25 and needed no one to bear witness about man, for he himself knew what was in man.

This verse is powerful. Jesus had many people only believe in him due to his signs and wonders, but he on HIS PART did not entrust himself to them because he knew their hearts. The Holy Spirit in you, Christ spirit, knows the hearts of everyone. We just have to make sure that we ON OUR PART are patient enough to let the Holy Spirit reveal to us who and what is in front of us. Let's go to the next chapter.

SPIRITUAL MATHEMATICS

In this section, we are going to discuss the following;

1. What is spiritual mathematics? pg: 35
2. Who do you count on? pg: 35
3. How to do spiritual mathematics pg: 43

Let's start with what is spiritual mathematics.

Spiritual mathematics is the ability to count and perceive God's will for your life. It is the ability to walk by faith and not by sight. Many people are imprisoned by their sight. They genuinely believe that all they see is all that is, but that is far from the truth. We are spiritual beings living in a natural world. The natural world is the smallest part of the two. Believers need to walk by faith and trust in God's vantage point. The word of God is clear about how faith develops. It says that faith comes by hearing and hearing by the Word of God. God's word is the blueprint for our lives, and its scriptures are the supplements and supports that builds our faith muscle.

Believers need to know how to count what is around them and discern what God has done. If not, they will fall for Satan's counterfeits. Those who walk solely by sight are more susceptible than those who walk by faith. Those who walk by sight, see only the storm; those who walk by faith remember the words of Jesus that says you will make it to the other side. But before we get into how to do spiritual mathematics and how it helps us avoid counterfeits, let's take some time to talk about counting on God.

Who do you count on?

Contrary to popular belief, everyone has an abundance of faith. The problem is not the amount of faith, but where that faith is designated. Right now, you are sitting by faith while reading this book. Since your bed, chair, or couch has proven to you that it can hold you up, you trust it. But the moment it proves not able to hold you up you will begin to question its durability, causing your faith to shake. The sad thing is, for many people, their faith has transferred from the Creator to something, or someone created. Satan's primary goal is to have you question the faithfulness and durability of God, causing you to transfer your ultimate faith from God to your career, money, relationships, etc., setting you up to be disappointed and depressed.

Before you can accurately count what's around you, you must examine your faith in God. God can be counted on. He is the only one we should have our ultimate trust in. God is the one we should be dependent on and from that dependency told where to delegate our trust or faith. There is a difference between dependent faith and delegated faith. Dependent faith is who you have your ultimate trust in delegated faith is where God wants you to put your second level trust in. That's why it's essential to build your confidence in God so that you will know his parts for your life, durable parts that will do their jobs well because they, too, are dependent on God. That is why you must let God select your friends and spouse because he knows whether they are dependent on him or not, which causes the marriage or relationship to always find its balance. Balance is key. When both people are wholly reliant on God, their faith will be delegated onto each other appropriately. Let's continue.

Let's take some time to break down one of my favorite scriptures in the bible Proverbs 3:3-5 and the parable of the rock and the sand and learn the importance of trusting in or counting on God.

> 5 Trust in the Lord with all your heart,
>
> and do not lean on your own understanding.
>
> 6 In all your ways acknowledge him,
>
> and he will make straight your paths.

For our paths to be made straight we must do the following; we must

- Entrust our whole hearts to God
- Be little in our own eyes and
- Acknowledge God before we go down any "way."

Entrust

The verse begins with four words that are very important to understand. It says "Trust in the Lord". A Lord, by definition, is someone having power, authority, or influence; a master or ruler. We need to know Jesus as Lord. Many people are ok with Jesus being their savior but are not ok with Him being their Lord. A lot of people want to be saved from the fire of hell, but many are not wanting to be fully submitted to Jesus' lordship. The more one gets to know Jesus and understand his attributes, the more eager they will be to trust Him. One of the most vital characteristics of God is his immutability. Immutability, by definition, means unchanging. This attribute of God means that he never changes. We need to know this about God. Like the word says He is the same yesterday, today and forever. This attribute, when understood, builds trust. People change, but God doesn't. Money and things change, but God doesn't. Everything and everyone moves or changes except God. The safest place for your heart to root itself is in God. How much of your heart truly trust him? How much of your heart honestly trust his saving power and lordship? The areas of your life that do not trust God will be the very areas of your life that will cause you to fall.

How much of your heart trust God?	10%	25%	50%	75%	100%
Why the number above?					
What things in your life have you yet to entrust into Gods hands and why?					

Contrary to popular belief, everyone has a lord. Everyone has someone or something ruling over them. The only ruler that is understanding, trustworthy, and kind is Jesus. All other rulers are tyrants. My life changed when I entrusted it in the hands of God. My life used to be ruled by my insecurities and my ministry. It used to be governed by pornography and abandonment. My previous rulers were tyrants. They made me do what I didn't want to do. They led me into compromises that left me tormented by condemnation. I trusted them, but they continuously failed me. But when I gave my life over to Jesus with its insecurities and idolatries I became free and functional. I'm telling you; this place of contentment that I am in right now is so refreshing, and you can be here too, but it all begins with your heart. God knows what's best. The Master is not keeping you from fun; he just wants you to master the fundamentals. He wants you to trust that he has already worked everything out. Deep inside of our hearts are wounds. Wounds caused by those we thought we could trust. The injuries deep down in our hearts are affecting the way that we worship God. The worship I am referring to here is not referencing a Sunday service but a submitted life to Christ. It takes a lot of guts to trust God, especially when many people around you are not trustworthy. But auditing trust is our responsibility. It is our responsibility to use logic and observation to determine where we should anchor our hearts.

The next four words in the first phrase are "with all your heart", all being the keyword. For you to walk down clear paths, He must have all of your heart. A life that is not entirely founded on God will be susceptible to counterfeits. Even if your heart is 95% based on God that 5% that is left will be the angle your enemy will take against you. Every day we must assess if our hearts are fully rooted in God. Every well-built house is on one foundation. No well-built house has the garage and the main living quarters on two different foundations. No well-built house will have 95% of the house on one foundation and the other 5% on another. They will build every component of the house on one foundation. That is why many people are unstable in their ways because they are not entirely founded on God. Let's continue.

Be little in your own eyes.

The second phrase is, do not lean to your own understanding.

We shouldn't put our whole trust in others or in our own understanding or ability. We live in a society where people feel they are smart enough or at least have access to a smartphone that holds all the knowledge they need. We live in a world where people have replaced God with Google and their perceived greatness. God is greater than Google. God is greater than our most significant ability or understanding. We are limited, and He is limitless. Our understanding is a sheet of paper. His understanding is like a 5-mile thick brick wall. Leaning on our own understanding is like leaning on a sheet of paper that looks like a brick wall but can't hold us up for one second. Leaning on God is like leaning on a solid brick wall that can hold us up through this life and the one to come. We know nothing in comparison to what God knows. One of the main reasons why people fall into accepting Satan's counterparts is that they feel they know what's best for them. They think their understanding of timing is sufficient. That's why Satan wants us full of pride so that we will willingly accept his counterfeits. We must be little in our own eyes. We must know that we know nothing and that God knows everything. The word of God says in James 1:5-6

> 5 If any of you lacks wisdom, let him ask God, who gives generously to all without reproach, and it will be given him. 6 But let him ask in faith, with no doubting, for the one who doubts is like a wave of the sea that is driven and tossed by the wind.

No matter who you are or where you are right now, you lack wisdom. Wisdom, by definition, is the quality of having experience, knowledge, and good judgment; the quality of being wise. God is this definition. He is the only one fully educated on all experiences and the escapes of each. He is the one who is all-knowing and whose judgments are sound. Through the Holy Spirit, we have access to His wisdom, and all we have to do is ask. Unfortunately, though, many people don't ask God for wisdom because they don't believe he is generous or kind towards them. See, my friend God is generous with his knowledge. His ultimate desire for you is to walk in wisdom. The bible says that the fear of God is the beginning of all wisdom. To have understanding in any area of your life, you must assess the level of your reverence of God in that area. Your level of reverence will determine the length of your reach. A little reverence a lot of reaching; a lot of reverence a little reach. You can't have wisdom without reverence. God is a good God, and He, by default, deserves reverence and honor solely because of who He is. God is not evil or a tyrant, he is not greedy or wants to charge you for wisdom. He charged his Son Jesus so that you can have free access to his wisdom.

Wherever you lack wisdom, you lack awareness. Awareness leads to asking, and asking leads to acquiring and acquiring lends to applying and applying edges to advancing. That's why it's essential to know the power of adoption. If you are saved, you have been adopted. You are now a son or daughter of God. The most significant position you will hold in life is a son or daughter of God; no other position is more significant because it is from this position that you learn how to hold any other position in life. Being adopted into the family of God comes with benefits, and one of those benefits is access. Right now, you have access to God, and you can ask Him about anything, and he will answer you. God will never hold an answer back from a person who sincerely desires to be in His will. But you must be aware of the goodness of God. God is so good, and he loves you, and when you become aware of this, you won't hesitate to ask him for directions because you know that whatever he has for you is right for you. It says that he will give generously without reproach meaning with no record of wrong or disappointment. He will never hold back wisdom from those who ask in faith, trusting that He will guide.

We must always stay little in our own eyes, trusting in the leading of the Holy Spirit. Pride is one sure way to get you accepting a counterfeit.

Acknowledge

In all your ways acknowledge him,

Acknowledgment is a sign of respect! Arrogance is error-gance. You will always be in error when arrogant. Anytime we make a decision without God when it comes to the ways or paths we should walk down, we are walking in arrogance. It takes humility to slow our lives down and acknowledge God. We need to trust God's leadership. We need to be sensitive enough to hear his lead and smart enough to follow it. So many people are making significant decisions without God. They have more faith in their calculations than they do in God's omniscience. Acknowledging God is showing God the respect that he deserves. It recognizes that we know nothing, and he knows everything. In every way, we must acknowledge God.

A way, for clarity purposes, is any decision that affects purpose, people, property, power, positions and place. It's anything that alters or affects life. Life is too serious not to acknowledge the one who made it. It's not wise to marry someone you haven't talked to God about. It's not wise to move to a city you haven't spoken to God about. It's not wise to do anything that can affect many things without talking to God. A simple, "God is this right," or "should I do this, go here, entertain him, or her" could save you a lot of time and even your life. You will always regret what you failed to acknowledge God about. Many people are stuck with counterfeits wishing they would have asked God if it was in his will for them. Twenty years from now, you will be sitting on the front porch of your home, rejoicing, or regretting at the decisions you are making now. The time you use to seek God and receive confirmation from Him will keep you from wasting time later. God wants you to walk down straight paths, not crooked ones. He wants you to have a smooth journey. It is always best to take time now to check in with God than to wish you did!

Notice in verse 6, you see another three-letter word. You see the word all. God is too wise and too generous with His Wisdom to not ask him about everything. When in doubt, acknowledge him. It is better to be sure than to be sorry. You don't have to rush down the paths others are rushing down. You don't have to get married when all your friends do. You don't have to do x, y, and z as fast as everyone. Take your time. Most of the people who are rushing down the significant paths of life are rushing towards their ruin. You see, the last part says that he will make your paths straight. All of us were born onto crooked paths. We all have faced twisted and unsure scenarios or options, but those who follow this formula and count on God will see God supernaturally make their paths straight. Let God make your paths straight by trusting him with all of your heart, being little in your own eyes, and acknowledging him always.

<u>Let's take some time to break down the parable of the Rock and the sand.</u>

Build Your House on the Rock - Luke 6:47-49

> 47 Everyone who comes to me and hears my words and does them, I will show you what he is like: 48 He is like a man building a house, who dug deep and laid the foundation on the Rock. And when a flood arose, the stream broke against that house and could not shake it, because it had been well built. 49 But the one who hears and does not do them is like a man who built a house on the ground without a foundation. When the stream broke against it, immediately it fell, and the ruin of that house was great."

Jesus here was telling those within ears reach the importance of finding the Rock and not settling for sand. Let's take some time to break this powerful verse down. The first word you see is the word, everyone. This here is important because Jesus is starting off by saying that anyone is welcomed to come to Him. It doesn't matter what you have done; you can approach Him and receive salvation. Jesus' payment for sin was the full cost of everyone's sins. His atonement covers everyone's sins, even those who will not accept him. It's sad to know that everyone has an opportunity to go to heaven and be with God forever, but not everyone will take it. Let's continue. The scripture continues to break down two types of people: those who build on the Rock and those who build on sand. Let's start with those that build on the Rock.

He says those who come to me and hear my words and do them will be like a man building a house, and before he built it, he dug deep and laid the foundation on the Rock. And when the floods arose and beat on that house, the house could not be shaken because it was well built.

So many keywords in this section let's start with come, hear, and do. Many people will come to Jesus but not too many will stay. The bible says in 1 John 2:19

> They went out from us, but they were not of us; for if they had been of us, they would have continued with us. But they went out, that it might become plain that they all are not of us.

Many will start off with us and look like they are Christians, but over time, when they fade away, it will be plain they were never with us. Jesus knows the hearts of everyone and knows who is counting on Him for salvation and sanctification. And this is happening right now. So many people are walking with us right now but will fall away soon. But those who endure and count on Jesus will endure to the end. Like I said, many will come to Jesus and hear what he has to say but will not do it. Those though, that go to him, listen and apply will bear fruit. The word is very clear for us to be doers of the word, not hearers only deceiving ourselves. Those who have this formula operating in their lives will dig deep before they build-out. The word says that this man building a house... before I continue, you see it says building a house, meaning he already has the plans. Those who are wise seek God about the plans. Your house is your life. This parable is telling us that before you build, kneel. Before you build; yield. Many people are building without his plans and in doing so rush, but before I get to that point, let's continue to break this down. The text says that he dug deep through the sand to lay his foundation on the Rock. Before you build up or build-out, you must dig deep.

A wise person always looks for what is reliable. You noticed in this text it didn't say that he dug deep to lay his foundation on a rock it says he dug deep to build his house on THE Rock. Jesus is the only Rock sturdy and strong enough to build on. Those who care to last dig deep. It takes time to dig through lies to find the truth, but it is worth it. It's our responsibility to find the truth. Everything around us is pointing to the truth. Unfortunately, though, many people are either too lazy or too in love with this world to dig deep to find the Rock. The wise builder takes his or her time to dig deep beyond the deceptions of the world. He or she takes the time to see Jesus in every situation. If Jesus is not at the bottom of this, I will not start this marriage. If Jesus is not at the bottom of this career, I will not build my house here. Jesus must be at the bottom before you build an extension on to your house. See, your life exclusively should be built on the Rock, and when its time to add an extension to your home (life), you will look to see if Jesus is at the bottom of it. That's why it's so essential to go to him and hear what he has to say and do it. It's important to be disciplined and unbothered when it comes to digging deep to find the truth. Many people will ridicule you like they did Noah until the raindrops fall. Who cares what they think about how long it takes you to dig, lay the foundation, and build your house well. The goal is not to construct fast but to build to last. The goal is not to be the first one there but the last one standing.

This text begins to say that when the floods rise and beat on that house, it will not shake because it was well built. Jesus is letting us know that there will be trials and storms that will cause floods to beat against our homes, but he comforts us by saying that if you build your house on Him, you will not be shaken. Many people's homes or lives are not ready for the floods. Many will suffer a lot of damage, like the second builder who built his house or living on the sand. Sand represents the foundations of the world. It represents the top things people desire to build their lives on. Things like money, relationships, people, assets, careers, self, etc. can only hold you during the sunny days but not during the stormy nights. All of the items listed above and more are all shakable. It's only a matter of time before they are tested. Jesus has already been tested and proven able to hold up over and above time. Zealous eyes lie. They only see what they want to see. Satan will always try and tempt you to build quickly with no caution to audit what you are building on. He wants you to build high with no foundation, that's why everything is so fast now. He has accelerated everything beyond God's set speed limits. Every way of life has a speed limit that God sets to ensure safety when pursuing x, y, and z. Satan wants us to speed down these roads knowing that we will crash or end up running out of gas. He wants us to build our lives for here and not for eternity. Let's continue.

It says, but the one who hears and does not do will be like a man who built his house on the ground or sand without a foundation, and when the stream broke against it, it immediately failed, and the ruin of that house was great. SMH.

This builder wanted to build fast. It says he heard but was too lazy to do so and decided not to take his time to dig deep to find Jesus but chose to build on the sand or ground. Not only did he rely on the ground, but he laid no foundation. His house was not only missing Jesus but foundational principles of success and sanctification. Many people grew up in homes that neither taught them the Founder or the foundational principles of life. Jesus showed us how to find our life in Him. His spirit is here to help us with the nuances of our lives to help us do so, but we cannot be so zealous that we start building things without the Founder of life and his foundational principles. This foolish builder built with neither, and it continues to read that when the stream broke against it, it immediately fell, and the ruin of that house was great. It is always wise to take your time and to dig deep. It is better to be single three more years, but in those years, you're digging deep to find Jesus and the truth in every area of your life than to waste those years dating and being entangled with the wrong person building a relationship that won't last. What four-letter word do you want, fast or last? Do you want it fast or do you want it to last? It is pivotal to trust God and to be led by him. Before you can count and do spiritual mathematics, you must check to see if you're counting on God. He is reliable, immutable, trustworthy, faithful, and generous. He loves you and wants to give you his best. It is better to build a house that's built well than one that looks well. Everything looks good until the floods come. Time will prove those that count on Christ. Who are you building your life on?

How to do spiritual mathematics

Like I said before, spiritual mathematics is the ability to perceive and pursue God's will for your life. What God wants for us can be clearly seen, but for many people, their lives are too cluttered to see the obvious. God wants us to understand how to count spiritually. He wants us to understand the basic and the advanced forms of spiritual mathematics.

Count, by definition, is the ability to determine the total number of a collection of items. Right in front of you are parts that need you to count them, but before you can adequately count them, you must have the proper temperament. Let's break down another favorite scripture of mines James 1:2-4

> 2 Count it all joy, my brothers, when you meet trials of various kinds, 3 for you know that the testing of your faith produces steadfastness. 4 And let steadfastness have its full effect, that you may be perfect and complete, lacking in nothing.

Counting how things connect in the spirit realm is critical. The text above reveals another formula that shows us how we can count and connect the dots spiritually. This verse aims to show us how we can be perfect or whole, complete and lacking in nothing. Those who are whole, complete, and know they lack nothing in Christ are the only ones that can truly discern the differences between a counterfeit and a counterpart.

Before we breakdown these three critical dispositions, let's reveal the formula. The formula in this text is:

Counting it all joy + knowing the purposes of tested faith + letting patience have its full effect = wholeness, completeness, and lack of nothing.

Let's start with the first phase of this formula, counting it all joy.

To truly see what's in front of us, we must first count it all joy. Notice again we see the word all. It says for us to count it all joy. Joy is an indestructible disposition when obtained. See, joy and happiness are not the same. Happiness is based on how many conditions one has or doesn't have, while joy is based on one condition being present, and that is Christ. Joy is a way of thinking and living. The word of God says that the joy of the Lord is our strength and that there is a fullness of joy in God's presence. Joy must be our default setting when it comes to making decisions. If we are on the roller-coaster of happiness, then we will select based on desired conditions, but when you are content in Christ, and your soul has been satisfied, you will take however long you need to make a decision. Satan wants us to compare our lives to others stealing our joy. Comparison is the thief of joy like I've mentioned before. The moment you compare your conditions with the conditions of others, you lose perspective. No one fully knows the condition of a person's heart. At a first glance, we can all be fooled. A person can appear to be happy but inwardly be sad. It happens all the time. No matter how low or high you are on the economic chain, if you are not content in Christ and set on heaven, you will never be happy with what you have. You have to be clear-headed and content in your heart to truly count what's in front of you. If your mind is cluttered and your heart is impulsive, you will rush through your calculations to have certain conditions in place.

It takes strength and faith to not follow the trends. When you are aware that you are just a pilgrim passing through and your mission is to advance the kingdom of God through family and service, then you will take the items presented in front of you very seriously. See you + what's not in God's will for you will = a loss but you + the will of God will always = a gain. The enemy wants your attention on any and everything except the will of God for your life. The Bible says in Ephesians 5:15-16

> to look carefully then how you walk not as unwise but as wise, making the best use of the time for the days are evil. Therefore do not be foolish but understand what the will of the Lord is.

This scripture definitely has weight today. If there has ever been a time you should sit and count the cost and see if it's God's will for you; is now! Foolish people compare and compromise while wise people consider and carefully commit. These days are evil, and you must seek to understand what the will of the Lord is. It takes time to truly consider how you are walking and carrying yourself. It takes wisdom to really see if your life lines up with the character of God. It's a joy to be in the will of God. There is no better place on earth for you than in his will. Knowing his will is vitally important. Let's continue.

The text continues to read to count it all joy when you meet trials of various kinds. Knowing the will of God will help you understand and cope with what comes with his will.

For you to reach the next level of God, you must be readied by God. No believer escapes His pruning. The only time prosperity comes before pruning is in the dictionary. Trails are a part of the process. Let's define a trial. A trial is a period of testing. To be proven, you must be tested. Those who are content in Christ and committed to his purpose will understand and embrace their testing season. How well do you fair under testing? Your answer to this question will reveal your understanding of testing. Purpose minded people embrace tests because it's an opportunity for them to grow and mature. Complacent people don't want to grow, but committed people do. How bad do you want what you want? See, various trials make you versatile, and when you know this, you will embrace them. It's unfortunate how many people miscount. Many people see obstacles as enemies. Obstacles are opportunities. No matter where you were brought up or what you went through, it is being used to level you up. That's why it's important not to despise the days of your small or humble beginnings.

Obstacles are opportunities, but if your mind cannot understand this, your spiritual mathematics will be off. You must be tested to be approved. No test, no best. If you are unwilling to count your trials as opportunities, you will not be prepared to receive God's best! Every counterpart God has for you, you must equal in management ability, and a season of testing ensures this. Mature believers can recognize these opportunities and receive them with joy because they know that God is preparing them for something specific. What are you doing during your trial period? I'm sure you are familiar with trial periods when it comes to Netflix, Hulu, YouTube TV, etc. these companies give you a trial period to test their product before you purchase it. They give you a limited time with their product, risk-free so that you can see what comes with it and how to navigate it if you choose to commit. God does the same. Every trial period we face gives us a taste of what it will be like once we are a committed member. God does this so that when you officially get married or level up in ministry or your career, you will already be familiar with the full product because you have already experienced the trial. When you meet trials, rejoice, and count correctly because God is preparing you for something bigger.

Nothing in this life worth having comes easy. We must go through trials so that when we level up, we can stay and manage that level. So many people have plateaued because they don't like to be challenged. So they take the easy road. Nothing in life worth having comes easy. If you want to have a God-honoring marriage, ministry, career, etc., you must go through various trials to make you a versatile soldier. God wants us multifaceted. He wants us to be a Swiss army knife, not a butter knife. He wants us to be able to cut and maneuver in many ways. He wants us to be wise as a serpent and gentle like a dove. He wants us to become all things to all men that we might win some. He wants us to be salt and light. It's going to be challenging to be these things if we don't meet trials with Joy. You don't grow in comfort zones you grow in challenge zones!

I know going through trials are tough, but they are necessary for the next level. Our hearts should always desire to go from glory to glory. But for us to go from glory to glory, we must go from grind to grind. Everything in the will of God should give us Joy. It all boils down to your perspective. It is better to meet the trial with joy than to try and find it in the middle of it. Let's move to the next phase of the formula.

<u>Knowing the purpose of tested faith.</u>

The next part of the scripture says,

For you know that the testing of your faith produces steadfastness or patience. Let's break this down.

Knowledge is power. When you know the meaning of a season or the purpose of the process, you will embrace it. Knowledge increases joy. The more you know about God's will for your life, the more you can recognize what He has for you, including trials. Satan will always aim to throw higher than your knowledge of God. A verse that helps makes sense of this is 2 Corinthians 10:4-5 it says

> 4 For the weapons of our warfare are not of the flesh but have divine power to destroy strongholds. 5 We destroy arguments and every lofty opinion raised against the knowledge of God, and take every thought captive to obey Christ,

Right now, in Christ, if you are saved, you have weapons that have divine power, and one of those weapons we have access to is The Christ Mindset. We cannot defeat a spiritual enemy with natural means we need divine weapons to do so. The mindset of Christ enables us to destroy arguments, and every lofty opinion, raised against the knowledge of God. It helps us take every thought captive to obey Christ. The more we know about God and his purposes for life, the less mental resistance we will have. But if you barely know God or how he desires for things to be done, you will fall prey like Eve, and Adam did. But when you know and love Christ and desire to be in his will, you will do as he did in the wilderness and use God's word to defuse the lofty opinions of Satan. Knowing God and his word is vital in overcoming Satan's strategies and forfeiting his counterfeits. Do you know five scriptures for every challenge you are facing or will face? If not you will be vulnerable in battle. Satan loves to fight soldiers who don't have any bullets. Let's continue.

What challenges are you facing right now and what 5 scriptures could you use to combat them?				
Challenge #1: →					
Scriptures ↓				
S#1	S#2	S#3	S#4	S#5
Challenge #2: →					
Scriptures ↓				
S#1	S#2	S#3	S#4	S#5

Challenge #3: →	
Scriptures ↓	

S#1	S#2	S#3	S#4	S#5

Various trials will build your faith muscle. The higher you go in the things of God, the stronger your faith must be. New levels mean new devils. The strength of the devil on the next level is stronger than the devil on your current level. I can attest, the devils against marriage is stronger than the devils against singleness. The devil against ministry leaders is stronger than the devil against laymen. The higher you go in God, the more testing and learning you must go through. This life is not about us just living it to live it but to live it for a purpose. The Bible says in 2 Timothy 2:4

> 4 No soldier gets entangled in civilian pursuits since his or her aim is to please the one who enlisted them.

Whether you believe it or not, you are in a war, and every act you commit is an act of war. Every act you do for God is an act of war against Satan, and every act of sin is an act of war against God. The Bible says that friendship with the world is enmity with God. Or in other words, friendship with the world makes you an enemy of God. This life is nothing to just coast through; you must every day welcome the training and testing of the Holy Spirit to prepare you for the next level. A wise person can count the strength they will need for the next level. Only a person of purpose understands levels. A person of purpose knows that plateauing is not an option. They know that they must always elevate and grow. God wants our faith to be in Him so that he can develop its strength and help us to remain steadfast. Tested faith produces steadfastness. The Bible says blessed is the man or woman that remains steadfast under trial for when he or she has stood the test they will receive the crown of life that God has promised to those who love him. Your life right now is one BIG test, filled with trials of testing which aim to help you level up and produce the poise needed to see and select God's counterparts so that you can continue to play your part in God's overall plan for humanity. Let's take some time to break down steadfastness or patience.

Let, is a little but strong word. Let is another word of trust. In order to get, you must let. To get anything worth having in life, you must let God. Steadfastness, by definition, is the quality of being resolutely or loyally firm and unwavering. God wants unmovable people. He wants people that are fully committed and unable to waver. To win in life, you can't be moved or easily swayed. Its crazy how many people are being influenced off of the truth with lies. We as believers, must have a steadfast mentality. We must be steadfast knowing that God's formulas for life works and works well. We must understand the power joy gives and how various trials build our faith. The Bible says in 1 Corinthians 15:58

Therefore, my beloved brothers, be steadfast, immovable, always abounding in the work of the Lord, knowing that in the Lord, your labor is not in vain.

We must allow the immutability of God to keep us from being moved. People will try and move you, trust me. They will try to move you with their accomplishments, relationships, ideologies, insecurities, etc. into seasons prematurely. Still, you must not be moved, you must every day seek to know the will of God so that you can continue to abound in his work, knowing that your labor is not in vain. Only the work you do for God here will not be in vain. The worst thing that can happen to you as a believer is to work your whole life doing the wrong thing. There is a scripture that talks about this.

1 Corinthians 3:7-15 says

> 7 So neither he who plants nor he who waters is anything, but only God who gives the growth. 8 He who plants and he who waters are one, and each will receive his wages according to his labor. 9 For we are God's fellow workers. You are God's field, God's building.
>
> 10 According to the grace of God given to me, like a skilled master builder I laid a foundation, and someone else is building upon it. Let each one take care how he builds upon it. 11 For no one can lay a foundation other than that which is laid, which is Jesus Christ. 12 Now if anyone builds on the foundation with gold, silver, precious stones, wood, hay, straw— 13 each one's work will become manifest, for the day will disclose it, because it will be revealed by fire, and the fire will test what sort of work each one has done. 14 If the work that anyone has built on the foundation survives, he will receive a

reward. 15 If anyone's work is burned up, he will suffer loss, though he himself will be saved, but only as through fire.

This text is very clear that our work down here matters and will be tested with fire. This text shares that there are two types of materials one can use to build on Christ. It says that one group will build with gold, silver, and precious stones while the other group will build with wood, hay, and straw, but each one's work will be clearly seen on the Day of Judgement. That's why you can't compare your work with another person's work because you don't know what materials they are using. It may look well-built and indestructible now, but Jesus on the Day of Judgment will reveal what materials they really used. Many people are building with the wrong motives. Their ministry, marriage, management positions look pleasant to the naked eye, but to the discerning eye, not so good. Real recognizes real. Don't rush to build anything. Be very careful about how you build on the name of Jesus. The text continues to read that each one's work will be tried with fire, and the fire will test what sort of work was done. Man sees actions God sees attitudes. Man sees moves God sees motives. The text, next reveals the outcome. It says that those who built well and the fire proves it will receive a reward, but those who didn't build well will suffer loss though their souls are saved. It is better to go through the fire down here and build what we build to be fireproof rather than to rush and do things, losing it all in eternity. What we do down here on earth will echo in eternity. That is why we must be focused on and be faithful to the work He has called us to. Let's continue.

On our end, we must be patient and let patience have its full effect on us so that we can be whole, completed and lacking in nothing. You've seen during many updates on devices the warnings to not cut it off until the update has finished and that if you do, it could cause unwarranted damage to the device or program. The same is with us. We must let the updates at every stage finish updating. Many people are surrounded by consequences due to them either not wanting the update (salvation) or stalling or stopping the updates (sanctification). God gave us his Spirit that in His timing plans to update and upgrade us. Those who are discerning let those updates finish because they know who they need to be to have what they desire to have. Our goal is to be whole so that we can hold. Many people want to hold things, but they are not strong enough to hold it for its set duration. You have to become a certain level of whole to hold marriage well. Not to hold it for a couple of years but for God's predestined time frame.

Spiritual mathematics is having the ability to count backwards. It's having the ability to assess what one desires and determine from the assessment what manner of person they must be to hold that. What do you wish to hold? Do you have the strength to hold it? What trial period are you in right now, and what test are you facing? How could these tests strengthen your faith? How do you welcome these trials? Are you living life pursuing conditions or are you content with where God has you? No matter what you want to hold or enjoy, you need to be whole, complete, and aware that you lack nothing in Christ. You must be a person that is whole enough to hold what God wants you to hold. You must be completed in Christ with no desire to be completed. See, like I've said before, only Jesus can complete you. The hole in your heart is Christ sized not bite sized. No matter who or what you try to cover that hole with, you won't be able to. God is the only one that can complete you, and he must do so because when you let him complete you, you won't settle or fall for Satan's tricks. Those who are complete in Christ are the only ones able to complement another person or place in life. So many people are looking to be competed, and they wonder why they are not able to complement anything or anyone.

Next, we must be tapped into the source that gives us access to everything we need. Right now, in Christ, you lack nothing. Right now, you have everything you need that pertains to life and godliness. For every situation, you have access to the love, joy, **peace**, patience, kindness, goodness, faithfulness, gentleness, and self-control you need to operate as Christ would in that situation. Many people are spending a lot of money and time to get what Christ gives freely through His spirit. People are doing all kinds of things to get love, peace, joy, faithfulness, etc. but are coming up empty-handed. It is better to have a little and be full of all you need than to have everything but still missing everything.

Only those who are whole, complete, and know they lack nothing are able to do spiritual math and recognize the difference between a counterfeit and a counterpart.

Spiritual mathematics worksheet

What would you like to hold?		
Are you whole enough to hold these items or individuals?	Yes	No
Are you meeting a trial or in the middle of one? →	Meeting	Middle
What are the trials?		

What level is your joy right now?

1	2	3	4	5	6	7	8	9	10

How could this trial be testing and building your faith? How will your tested faith help you to hold the items above?

How patient are you overall?

1	2	3	4	5	6	7	8	9	10

If applicable, why are you impatient?

Are you truly ready for what you are desiring? (whole)
What are you pursuing to complete you? What do you not trust Jesus to complete in you and why? (complete)
What do you feel you lack? (lacking nothing)

Spiritual mathematical equation

- I desire to hold
- What trials am I facing or may have to face to be whole, complete and full enough to hold what I desire?
- How content in God must I be to meet and endure the trials that will help me hold what I desire?

Trial										
Was this trial self-inflicted or God sent?									Self-inflicted	God sent
If self-inflicted what adjustments do you need to make and how could God use this for your good?										
How could this trial help me hold _____										
What level was your joy when you met this trial?					What level is your joy in the middle of this trial?					
1	2	3	4	5	1	2	3	4	5	
Support scriptures										
Trial										
Was this trial self-inflicted or God sent?									Self-inflicted	God sent
If self-inflicted what adjustments do you need to make and how could God use this for your good?										
How could this trial help me hold _____										

What level was your joy when you met this trial?					What level is your joy in the middle of this trial?				
1	2	3	4	5	1	2	3	4	5
Support scriptures									

HOW TO DISCERN AND HOW GOD CONFIRMS

HOW TO DISCERN AND HOW GOD CONFIRMS

In this section we are going to talk about the following things

1. What is discernment pg: 57
2. How to increase your discernment pg: 59
3. What is confirmation pg: 61
4. Why we need confirmation pg: 63
5. How God confirms pg:69
6. Why people settle and how not to settle pg: 71
7. Good vs. God pg: 87

Let's start with what is discernment.

Discernment, by definition, is the ability to judge well. It is the ability to see beyond what's present. We've discussed briefly in the spiritual mathematics portion of the book and previous chapters the concept of discernment, but in this section, we are going to dig deeper for your understanding. Our goal with discernment should be for it to be automatic. It should be our goal to be so close to God that we can automatically discern a counterfeit or a counterpart at any moment. It is possible to be able to know always. The level of your fellowship and focus will determine if your discernment flourishes. Like the definition says discernment is an ability, an ability that is the fruit of availability. The more we are available to God, the more this ability grows in our lives. We must train our eyes to always see beyond what's present. In this world, you cannot just rely on your natural eyes; you must rely on your spiritual ones. We are to learn how to engage in this world gently and kindly while at the same time reading everything in front of us. Let's take some time to break down a formula for discernment. There are three phases I want to cover, and they are

1. Wellspring
2. wellness and
3. judge well

For you to judge well, you must be connected to the wellspring. A wellspring is an original and bountiful source of something. God's Spirit is our wellspring. He is a unique and beautiful source. The Bible says in Jeremiah 17:7-8

> 7 "Blessed is the man who trusts in the Lord,
>
> whose trust is the Lord.
>
> 8 He is like a tree planted by water,
>
> that sends out its roots by the stream,
>
> and does not fear when heat comes,
>
> for its leaves remain green,
>
> and is not anxious in the year of drought,
>
> for it does not cease to bear fruit."

This verse is so powerful it says the one who trust in the Lord is blessed and is like a tree planted by water who sends its roots by the stream. Let's break this down. Blessings come from resting. Like I said before, it's important for our full trust to be in God and for us to send all of our roots to him. Your roots will determine your fruits. One root in the wrong stream will affect your fruit. To experience true blessings, your whole life must find the stream. Is your mind in the stream? Is your heart in the stream? Is your singleness in the stream? Is your marriage in the stream? Are your finances in the stream? Are your children in the stream? Are all of you in the stream?

God is our original source. Satan wants God to be perceived as an outdated or old source, not the original. He wants your roots in contaminated streams. He wants your fruit to be genetically modified, not organic. He wants you through your own free will to send your roots into his streams, contaminating you, causing you to be unclear and not able to discern. You must UNPLUG today and find your original stream. Let's keep going. It then says that this person or tree does not fear when heat comes for its leaves remain green and is not anxious in the year of drought, for it does not cease to bear fruit. Wow, this is so powerful. Basically, when you find God as your source inside of you and trust in him, you will not be moved or affected by what happens above or around you. Climates in this world will change, but one thing won't change, and that's the Holy Spirit in you who is a never-ending stream. It doesn't matter if there is famine, drought, or heat; your countenance won't change, and you will have fruit in every season. You must know God as your source if you want to accurately discern.

Once your roots find this well, you will begin to get well. Wellness is vital when it comes to discernment. Unhealed wounds will affect how well you judge. Unforgiveness, resentment, anger, envy, jealousy, pride, and the like will affect how well you can judge a counterfeit or a counterpart. These internal traits come from contaminated wells. You must always audit what you allow to influence you. That's why it's essential to live as simple and as disconnected as possible so that there won't be any loud opinions. What on the inside of you is affecting how you see what's on the outside? God wants you well, and being rooted in His well will ensure you will be.

Once your roots have found the wellspring and you have allowed God's power to heal your internal wounds producing contentment, you will then know how to judge well. Judging well comes from knowing the judge well and letting Him make you well. This will position you in a place of peace and poise needed to see what's really in front of you. Like I said before, we must simplify our lives so that we can be still more often increasing our sensitivity. When your life is continuously being bombarded with unnecessary things, you will always find yourself busy doing the wrong stuff clouding your ability to judge.

Activity

- What are your roots?
- What are they rooted in?
- What wounds are affecting your wellness?
- Why are you not ok?

How to increase your discernment.

Now let's talk about how you can develop better discernment. For one, let's make it clear that you and I have on the inside of us the knowledge of right and wrong. Each of us can discern what is right and wrong whether saved or not saved. The problem lies in what we lie in. The more we lay in God, the clearer our ability to judge becomes, but the more we lay in the things of the world, the more clouded our ability to judge becomes. With that being said, let's go over these points below.

Be **Anchored** in God's love.

To develop discernment, you must first anchor yourself in God's love. The word of God says perfect love cast out all fear. In God's love, there is no need to be afraid. Fear is the root of many people's impulsiveness. They are worried they will miss out, so they rush. But when you know that you are adopted and are a son or daughter of the most high God, you don't let anything rush you. See, God's love builds self-love, and self-love limits the distribution of love. Those who are loved by God limit what comes close to that love. They know the difference between love and heart. There are levels to love. Like I've mentioned before, everyone deserves some access to your love, whether it be a wave or kind gesture, but not everyone deserves access to your heart. Those whose fears have not been perfected by God's love will give counterfeits access to their hearts. You must be anchored in God's love to truly discern well.

Understand that there are **absolute truths**.

To develop your ability to discern, you must be a pursuer of Truth, the bible says that the Truth sets us free. How can we fully embrace the power of choice if we don't know the power of Truth? So many people are reckless in their decision making because they have no desire to follow the Truth. Truth is a person. Jesus said I am the way the Truth and the life and no man can come to the Father except through me. God will never give us a faith that cannot be fact-checked. Right now you can fact check your faith to see if it's real. It all starts with the process of elimination. Anyone with common sense can tell that we live in an intelligently designed world and that they too are an intelligent design. Just like a painting proves a painter and a building proves a builder, so does creation prove there is a Creator. A wise person seeks the Truth before they build. If your mind is not trained to pursue Truth, you will believe any lie. You just can't accept what people say; you must discipline yourself to seek the Truth behind every matter. It is lazy and irresponsible to just take another person's word for it or to just believe anything. You must desire to know Truth and train your mind to eliminate options so that you can truly discern what's in front of you.

Questions to think on: Why do you believe what you believe? What proves what you believe is true?

Take time to **access**.

Time is always on the side of those who respect it. Those who respect themselves respect their time and will take their time to make sure they are in God's will. Your discernment increases the more you take your time to count the cost. No matter what you do in life, it will cost you a piece of your life. Your time = your life. Like I've said in many videos, you spell time, L I F E. When God, you, family, and purpose matter, your time increases in value. Those who discern are quick to learn, not quick to earn. People who are quick to earn quickly spend their time, but those who are quick to learn spend their time wisely. Since your time equals your life, spend it wisely. VIDEOS!

Make **acknowledging** God and **asking** for help a habit.

To discern the will of God, He must be number one in your life. Wise people talk to God and acknowledge Him before doing anything. God wants to help us, but we must acknowledge the help and acknowledge that we always need help. The more you acknowledge Him for who is, the holder of all Truth, you will always find your paths straight.

Accept what he accepts and **abhor** what he abhors.

To accurately discern a counterfeit from a counterpart, you must deeply love what God loves and sincerely hate what God hates. When you love what he loves, you will always find yourself connected with the right things. When you hate what he hates, you will never find yourself entangled in sin or anything that will affect your relationship with God and your focus. When you deeply feel these two things, you will immediately spot a counterfeit or a counterpart.

Apply the word of God in your life

You have to know the word of God to see God's will, and you have to apply the word to advance in the will of God. The more you know the word of God, the more you will see the difference.

Determine **access** points and levels

Like I said earlier, not everyone deserves access to your heart. To develop your discernment, you must limit access. You must be very aware of people and at what level they deserve access to your presence

Learn from your **accidents**

Last but not least, to develop your discernment, you must learn from your accidents. Its ok to make mistakes if you plan to learn from them.

When we focus and remain faithful to doing these things we begin to see our discernment increase. Before we move to confirmation

What is Confirmation?

God is not the author of confusion; he is the author of clarity. God wants his people clear and confident, not confused, and uncertain. Satan's system thrives in the lives of those who are confused and unsure. He knows he has a better chance of affecting a confused person than a clear and active person. God holds all wisdom. He holds the answer to every decision and is willing and ready to give us as much understanding as we are prepared for. Keywords "ready for." The issue for us when it comes to what God has told us is not if but when. The distance between the moment we hear and the moment we receive is a long-distance at times, and for many, they break away due to the time-frame more so than the warfare. But God along the path between the two destinations have laid on them markers of confirmation designed to keep you firmly connected to his word.

The definition of the word confirm is in the word; con-firm or firm connection. A firm connection is the goal of a confirmation. When we are reminded of what God wants us to do, it tightens our relationship to God and his word. On the other hand, the enemy seeks to con-fuse or, in other words, fuse within our minds suggestions that will weaken our connection to God and what he has told us, causing us to question and doubt God. The greatest weapon the enemy has against us, and God is doubt. The moment you walk in doubt against God is the moment you choose to be dependent on something other than him. God is not slack concerning His promises he will come when it's time, but his time is what we frequently have a problem with. We spend a lot of time focusing on the timeframe instead of utilizing that time to renew our frame of mind. God acts based on two things: His will and His timing, both of which are perfect. There is nothing we can do that can make him work sooner or later. He has been resting since the 7th day. Everything from day 7th has been done, and there is nothing earth can do about it. The bible even says that Jesus was slain before the foundations of the earth, meaning the work was already done. The moment we realize just how perfect His timing is, the more firm our connections will be with whatever we are waiting for.

See, instead of waiting for God, we should be waiting on God. I love the scripture that says they that wait on the Lord shall renew their strength that word wait I like to mean wait as in serve. No one's strength is renewed, sitting looking at the clock. It is restored by using that time serving. Many people are waiting for God for this big moment but are not serving him moment by moment. When your mind trusts that God will fulfill his promises, it opens up your mind to be creative and intentional in serving Him until it comes. Whiners, complainers, and those who watch the clock are no use to God. Things we asked God for should catch us by surprise when they come because we forgot that we even asked for them. God knows what we need, and he knows how long it will take to get to us, and with that, he sets markers of confirmation along your path to keep you firmly connected to his promises.

Before we go forward, let's break down the definition of confirmation. Confirmation means to give new assurance of the validity of, remove doubt about by authoritative act, or indisputable fact. It also means to make firm or firmer.

God knows how difficult life is and how much gets in the way of us hearing him and us receiving what was requested or made known. But he gives with this journey confirmation or the new assurance of His validity and the removal of all doubt through His authoritative act or indisputable facts. Off of his authority alone, we should believe, but life is full of moments where doubt takes a seat next to us, making its case. The definition also says to make firm or firmer. See confirmation is not just about the moment before or the moment of receiving but also the moments after receiving. Like for my wife and me, God confirmed she was the one for me before we were married, he confirmed it many times before the marriage, and he utilized the wedding in and of itself as confirmation. He is now still confirming his hand on our marriage, making our grip on each other firmer.

Confirmation is not just to alleviate doubt but deepen bonds. Only God knows the weight of your blessing, and he knows that all blessings are burdens. Marriage is a blessing, but it is also a burden. Having children is a blessing, but they are a burden. The burden in the right context doesn't mean an unnecessary burden; it means its original weight.

All good things have weight, and we have to be able to uphold that weight. Before a beam is placed to hold a bridge or a building in place, it is first tested with immense pressure to find its breaking point so that the scientist or engineers can know the peak amount of weight this beam can hold. They do these tests before to ensure no catastrophic events will occur in the future. The beams are tested by pressure and winds to make sure nothing can move it. Just like those beams, we, too, go through tests to see our breaking points. God wants to make sure you can handle the weight of marriage before you are married so that your family won't fall apart. God will not put more on you than you can bear. How much can you carry? Many people want the moment of promotion but are ill-equipped and unknowledgeable about managing and sustaining the promotion. Just as quickly as you get it, can be as quick as you can lose it. If you get it quickly, you lose it easily. Nonetheless, God confirms his written and whispered word to us to give us a new assurance and to make us firmer.

Why do we need confirmation?

1. So that we won't connect or be committed to the wrong things
2. So that we can navigate calmly
3. So that we can conserve our energy
4. So that we can create freely
5. So that we can see clearly

Let's break down each briefly. We need confirmation so that we won't connect or be committed to the wrong things. God knows that along the path of your life are bad things that will tempt you, attack you, and test you. He knows how luring Satan's offers are, but He gives us his word as a testament to his name, letting us know not to compromise because He will act. Satan wants us to operate from his suggestion that God is delaying. God never delays because everything with Him is in the done category, not the doing category. See, God is above time. Anything above time is set, and eternal everything within time is moving. Everything in eternity is done. Everything within time is doing what has already been done. Satan knows this and wants the bulk of people to either doubt the existence of God or doubt that God exists for their unique situation. God exists not just globally but uniquely for you. If he has told you something or has promised something to you through His written or whispered word, you have no need to doubt him and connect or become committed to the wrong things. All you need to do is trust him!

What are you currently connected to? (People, places, positions etc.)	What evidence from God proves you should be connected to it?

We need confirmation so that we can navigate calmly. With God, there is no need to worry about if or when all we have to do is rest in the fact that He spoke. See, life is best when you live it in his flow. You don't have to walk critically or cranky you can walk calmly knowing that God will do what he said he was going to do. When our minds are renewed and understand God's character and timing, then when it seems like everyone is getting what you desire before you, you still walk calmly, knowing that when it's your turn, no one will be able to take it away. I have a secret; most of the people getting what you want seemingly ahead of you are, in most cases, settling. People settle when they seek their own way. Most people end up losing their firm grip when they begin to compare their lives with those who've settled. The experience of those who are settled in God is higher than the life of those who are settling. Those that are settling are restless people looking for rest outside of God, and His will. Those who are settled are not moved by what they see because their hope is settled in God.

What is causing you to be anxious?

Who are you comparing yourself to, why and how is it affecting your calmness?

Why is it important to be settled?

We need confirmation so that we can conserve our energy. God sends a confirmation to let us know to pace ourselves. Many people lose a lot of energy seeking and settling. They forget that whatever you do on your own accord without God, you are responsible for sustaining it. A lot of unnecessary energy is wasted in many people's lives due to them tending what they've settled outside of God's timing and will for. I've learned recently how to pace myself. I use to be the guy who would overwork, thinking that the more I put out, the more I can bring in. This is true in a sense but not necessary. We are in this world not of this world, meaning we don't have to rush and be overly productive. God is a God of balance. He said in Ecclesiastes that there is a time for everything. There is a time to work, and there is a time to rest. I've learned to capitalize on resting seasons because when it's time to work, I will have the energy. God can't build through a person who is always burned out. God sends a confirmation to conserve our energy.

On a typical day where does your energy go?	
Hours	Wasted or invested wisely
6am -12pm	
1pm-6pm	
7pm-12am	
1am -5am	

In what ways are you spending unnecessary energy?

Are you in a resting season if so what is tempting you not to rest?

What could be up the road that God is confirming to you, you should rest up for or conserve your energy?

We need confirmation so that we can create freely. Often we find ourselves distracted from the assignment of the hour focusing on an assignment that isn't even on the books for us this year. God sends us confirmation so that we won't waste time worrying about when the next phase is coming neglecting the step we currently are on. God knew not to tell Adam about Eve because if he did, Adam would rush naming the animals so that he can have Eve. He kept that info away from him until the right moment. Sometimes it seems like God is not clear or quiet about a matter, but He is this way because if He told you who your spouse was or the day and the hour you were going to get x, y or z, then you would not only ruin what you are working on but you would also destroy what's next. He wants us to enjoy Him now. He reassures us that He's got us so that we can focus on the task at hand.

What should you be working on now?	
What are you anticipating and Is it aiding or affecting your assignment now?	
Anticipating	Aiding or affecting

We need confirmation so that we can see clearly. Perspective is everything. For many of us, nothing is wrong with our eyes. The issue is what is behind our eyes. The problem is not in our ability to see but how we perceive what we see. God sends a confirmation to refocus and retrain our eyes and keep our eyes on the higher mark. He assures us and firms us up so that we won't be distracted by what we see. We, as believers, are supposed to walk by faith, not by sight. In many instances, these two will conflict and contradict each other in our lives, but when our faith is secure, we can faithfully navigate the brief moments of sight. Just because it is before your eyes doesn't mean God is not a God of His word. He says, let God be true and every man a liar. When in a season of testing, God will confirm His word and prepare a table in the presence of your enemies. Right as you read this sentence, God has made your table. It doesn't matter who or what is against you, soon, you will eat well in their midst if you faint not.

What challenges or opportunities are you facing right now and how do you see them?		
Challenges/opportunities	By faith or by sight	← Why this answer?

How God Confirms

Now let's talk about how God confirms. God confirms;

Confidentially: He keeps it between you and Him and desires for you to keep it between the two of you. He does this so that confusion can't come in between what He told you. Unfortunately, though many people like Joseph tell their dreams to people who cannot handle or interpret their dreams, leading them down 18 years of unnecessary pits and prisons. Whatever God tells you, keep it between you and Him unless otherwise directed.

Clearly: God is a God of details. He doesn't stutter; He doesn't have a hard to interpret accent. He is clear. The problem lies in our clutter. God speaks to us clearly, but our cluttered minds interfere with His words. Declutter your life so that you can hear from God.

Concretely: 90% of what we need to know about this Christian life can be found in the Bible. The other 10% is nuanced based, and He sent His Holy Spirit to help us make sense of those things. When we find it hard to understand the Bible or see what we need, all we have to do is ask the author, The Holy Spirit, and He will help us with tough decisions day in and day out. When in doubt, check His word and ask His Spirit.

Creatively: He is creative in sending confirmation. Not all of his confirmations are dispatched the same way. He's original in the fact that he knows exactly how to reassure Himself or His word to us that will connect to us deeply. God is not going to waste his time or yours sending confirmation that will not have an astounding effect on your faith, increasing it. He will creatively send it through a coworker, a person at the grocery store, a car sticker, a billboard, a random commercial. God knows how to get your attention, letting you know He's got you.

Calmly: God is never rattled and neither should you. You know the speaker of the words in your heart by the presence that comes with. God's words come with peace Satan words come with pressure. God will never ruffle the lake of your soul; He gently confirms his word to it.

Communally: God confirms through community. God uses his hand-selected community for you like friends, family, and those a part of your church fellowship to verify His word for you, whether through correction or encouragement. Remember, these people are hand-selected by God and will, in a biblical way, help reassure God's word.

Causally: God confirms causally sometimes for no apparent reason, just to let you know you're on the right path and to keep going.

Continuously: God's confirmation never stops as I said about my marriage. To this day, God is confirming that we are for each other to let us know not to lose grip on Him or each other. God does this so that we can maintain the main things.

Confirmation tracker

#1 What has God spoken to you about you or your life?							
Around what day and time? →							
Through which method did He speak to you? Person, post etc. →							
How did He or is He confirming this to you?							
Confidentially	Clearly	Concretely	Creatively	Calmly	Communally	Casually	Continuously
Follow up confirmations							
Describe confirmation + Scriptural Support							Date and time
1							
2							
3							
#2 What has God spoken to you about you or your life?							
Around what day and time? →							
Through which method did He speak to you? Person, post etc. →							

How did He or is He confirming this to you?							
Confidentially	Clearly	Concretely	Creatively	Calmly	Communally	Casually	Continuously
Follow up confirmations								
Describe confirmation + Scriptural Support							Date and time
1							
2							
3							

Let's transition to why people settle and how not to settle.

Why do people settle for counterfeits?

Many people are settling for things significantly less than they should. They are settling for items that are outside of God's purpose and plans for them. God never intended for us to settle for anything that was not sent by him but before we continue let's see why people settle using the word SETTLE;

People settle

S:

Because they are afraid to start over. Many people settle because they feel why start over and do it the right way when they are already shoulders deep in the wrong way. Some think that it is better to have someone than to have no one and instead go through unnecessary pain and drama to have someone. No one or no item is worth unnecessary drama. It is better to swim to shore and get on the right relation-ship than to be stranded on a broken one with the wrong one no matter how long it's been.

Check if this applies to you →	

If applicable, why:

Because of their need for security. People settle to feel secured. No place or person outside of the will of God can secure you. Through insecurities, many people settle for a relationship, a job, etc. to receive an immediate sense of security. Still, they will find out over time that those things will only make them more vulnerable. Only Jesus can secure your insecurities. Never let desperation lead you into false security.

Check if this applies to you →	

If applicable, why:

Because they have a savior's complex, some people stay in a bad relationship or situation because they think they are Jesus. They believe they can save a person or a situation exclusively. If they want to be saved, they will go to Jesus, not you. Anyone or anything you try to save outside of God, you will be responsible for sustaining it. Give them and your situation to God and let him save the complex.

Check if this applies to you →	
If applicable, why:	

Because they have Low Self-esteem, some people settle due to them not seeing themselves as high as they should. They see themselves as not worthy of anything good from God, so why ask or wait for Him? It doesn't matter your past; you don't have to settle. God renews, redeems, replenishes, and restores. But it's going to be hard for you to receive and enjoy it if you are unable to see yourself correctly.

Check if this applies to you →	
If applicable, why:	

E:

<u>Emotional Ease</u>. Some people settle for fleeting moments of emotional ease. I use to do this all the time with honey buns, and Bo jangles. Instead of waiting to get home to eat something healthy, I would rush to a 7/11 or a Bo jangles just to grab me something to eat to alleviate a bad day. What I came to learn over time was that these brief snacks might have given me emotional ease, but they led to complications in my body over time. The items and people we use for emotional comfort are not beneficial to settle for because that two to twenty-five minutes of sex may make you feel emotionally at ease but, in return, may give you a lifetime of consequences.

Check if this applies to you →	

If applicable, why:

T:

<u>God is taking too long</u>. Many people settle for counterfeits because God is just taking too long. They have allowed the pace of the world to cause them to become impatient. God drives the speed limits He set and will never drive faster. If you trust him and let him drive, you will get to your destination safe and sound. God is always late on our terms because if he always comes when we want him, mentally, we will treat him as a Jeanie or a slave. He arrives late for us and on time for Him to build our faith. A faith not tested is a faith that cannot be trusted.

Check if this applies to you →	

If applicable, why:

<u>Trust Issues with God</u>. A lot of people settle for counterfeits due to them not trusting God. The enemy works overtime to make sure we don't believe in God. So why wait for the one when there is one right in front of you? Why wait on God; will he come through? He hasn't yet! It's funny we always blame God for where we are but never look in the mirror. Why will God give you what you want if you are not ready for what you want from Him? The problem is not should we trust God; it should be, should God trust us?

Check if this applies to you →	

If applicable, why:

T:

<u>Tension or pressure</u>. Many people settle for counterfeits due to internal and external stresses. They have such strong desires in them or strong opinions around them that they consume them. Many people are unwilling to wait for Patience to have her perfect work on them, so they instead let impatience work to get them the "perfect" thing. Or they have such strong connections to a person or a group that they allow them to pressure them into a relationship or a situation that they will soon have regrets for.

Check if this applies to you →	

If applicable, why:

L:

<u>Loneliness. Falling for what looks the part</u>. Loneliness is one of the top reasons why people settle for counterfeits. Most people are not comfortable with being alone with themselves. They always feel that they need to have someone to occupy their time, keeping them from addressing their deep dark issues. Being alone is the prerequisite to being alongside someone. If you are not willing to be alone with God, how will you be able to be alongside a significant other and God? Loneliness is a mindset. It's being overly consumed with the idea of being alone. It blinds you from the benefits of being alone and developing.

Check if this applies to you →	
If applicable, why:	

E:

It's Easy or more comfortable to stay. Some people settle for counterfeits because it is more comfortable or more convenient to stay. Walking with God is not easy. It can be hard at times. I believe it's hard at times because of how hard our hearts are at times. Pruning is a necessity; without it, maturity is never achieved. Many people do not want to do it God's way, so they settle for the easy way out, but they fail to realize that what comes easy goes easy and what you work hard to acquire rarely expires.

Check if this applies to you →	
If applicable, why:	

Let's transition and talk about how to know if you've settled or are on the path to settling also using the word SETTLE.

You've settled or are settling when;

S: You've either sought for it or are seeking for it. To find everything that God has for you, you must seek Him first. The Bible says to seek the kingdom of God first, and His righteousness and all these things will be added unto you. For items to be added, we must find the kingdom of God and all of His righteousness. Now, what does this mean? When God's kingdom and your position in it are what you seek first every day, all the things that will assist you in managing that position will be added. A spouse will be added, children will be added, and money and resources will be added to help your place in His kingdom.

You must also seek all His righteousness, meaning you must endeavor to seek and engage the right way for every situation. How can we be a righteous living spouse if we're not a righteous living person? Now don't get me wrong, we are the righteousness of God in Christ Jesus, but for things to be added for us to steward our position must match our patterns. I can be righteous positionally, but for God to relinquish stuff within my care, I must have righteous living that comes from my mind being renewed. Anything you seek for without acknowledging God, you are settling for it. Everything we need for our lives down here is in God. When you seek Him, you find you and everything that he has for you.

Check if this applies to you →	
If applicable, why:	

E: You are either emotionally indecisive or emotionally unstable. You know you've settled or are on the path to settling for a counterfeit when you are emotionally indecisive and changeable. Those who have settled will always find themselves halt between two opinions meaning they will not be happy with what they have. One minute they are, and the next minute they are not, they will begin to see the imbalance of their relationship. They will start to see that this thing doesn't fit, but they are too involved to leave and too frustrated to stay. Those who are seeking and will end up settling for a counterfeit are those who are right now emotionally unstable. They want what they want so bad that they are now bypassing God, and seeking a man or a woman or a job without Him and time will prove they should have waited on Him.

Check if this applies to you →	
If applicable, why:	

T: You either didn't take the time to thoroughly examine or you are currently not taking the time to investigate thoroughly. Those who've settled for a counterfeit and know they did can see that they didn't do their due diligence. They jumped in without discerning. They ignored the warnings of the Holy Spirit and only checked the tires but not the transmission. They didn't take the time to examine themselves, the other person, or the other thing, and now they are stuck with a consequence.

Those who are on the path to settling for a counterfeit are involved with someone or something and have the opportunity to escape. Their infatuation is hindering them from seeing the obvious red flags and the glaring red exit sign and time will again prove that they wished they would have taken their time. Time is one of your greatest assets. And when you value yourself and time, you will take however long to make sure what you have is from God. Never let impatience or infatuation lure you into doing something without consulting God. Cast down those vain imaginations, flood out those futile emotions, and use Christ's mind to discern what's in front of you. Satan knows that most people are too emotionally wounded to take the necessary time to examine his offers. Some offers of his are so evident that he uses them just to make a mockery of our emotional dysfunctions.

Check if this applies to you →	
If applicable, why:	

T: You either didn't trust God with it or are currently not trusting God with it. Those who've settled for a counterfeit know that they didn't trust God with their singleness, frustrations, and worries and now have to deal with the consequences of not trusting Him. Those who are about to settle for a counterfeit trust themselves more than they do God and are on a pursuit without him. When they come back home with what they thought was great for them, they will overtime wish they would have trusted God.

| Check if this applies to you → | |
|---|---|//
| If applicable, why: | |

L: Your love is either confused, not there, or you're pursuing love, not knowing who love is. You know you've settled for a counterfeit when your love is confused. See confirmation must be the foundation of our marriages or career path because we can always go back to the day, the hour, and even to the color carpet, you were standing on when God confirmed it to you. Most people have no reference point of God saying anything about who they are with or what they have. Confirmation brings peace during tough times in a marriage or career because you know that God's will, will not lead you where His grace won't keep you. But those who've settled have no reference point. Those who are on the path of settling are looking for love in all the wrong places. They are looking to be healed by everyone else but God, who is Love.

Check if this applies to you →	
If applicable, why:	

E: It either came too easy, or you are pursuing the easy way out. Don't trust anything that comes easy because easy comes easy goes. Those who've settled for counterfeits felt no resistance in getting it. What was given was given smoothly. Anything that comes into your life, and you know you are not prepared for it is not for you. Satan loves to send us things when we are not ready for them because he knows an immature believer will believe it's God's timing for them to have it. God moves based on his will, schedule, and maturity; if he sees you are not ready for it, he will not send it.

Those who are setting themselves up to settle are always looking for the easy way out. They are looking for the easy way out of their singleness, marriage, and struggle. Not all struggles mean God is not in it, most struggles He is in because he uses them to strengthen you. Don't allow tough times to get you looking around for the easy way out. God will never bring you around, under or over tough times; he will always bring you through them.

Check if this applies to you →	
If applicable, why:	

Now let's talk about how to not settle!

<u>How to not settle.</u>

S: Seek and stay in the will of God. Be settled, but don't settle. Those that are settled in who they are in Christ understand value. They will never settle for anything that can be used to separate them from God regarding his endorsement. To not settle for anything outside of Gods will you have to seek and stay in his will. The safest place on earth is in the will of God. Those who cherish this mindset refuse to settle because they are settled in God, and they trust him. Our trust for God rust when we either think he is taking too long or when we don't profoundly believe that he exist for our unique situations. Don't let your trust in God rust away due to idolatrous desires. His will is for your safety. Now, what is the will of God? God's will is your salvation, sanctification, proper stewardship, self-control, and all of these items are evident in His script, His word. God wants you to be saved. His will is to sanctify you into a place of maturity that leads to the proper stewardships of the main things in life with self-control. He has a specific purpose for you, and it will be hard to know what that is and function in it if you are not willing to seek salvation and sanctification. Sometimes we focus so much on our purpose capital P instead of the daily purposes required of us in his word. If you take care of what is written, you will begin to clearly see your overall purpose.

What is God's will or purpose for your life?

E: Always vent emotionally to God and educate yourself on the differences between what's vain and what's valid. Trust me, it is not easy navigating this life as a Christian. It is painful at times, and it's hard to get our minds and emotions on the same pages within the word of God. But what helps me not settle is to know that I can go to God and vent emotionally and go to his word and his Spirit to determine what's vain and valid in my mind. People settle when they have no guards at the doors of their thoughts and heart. You are responsible for what comes in and out of your mind and heart. God is the only one able to handle the hottest and the darkest matters of your heart. He wants you to go to him and vent about why you hate being single and why you want to have this or that. He wants you to go to him first so that he can wrap you with his peace and change the way you see what you see. Unfortunately, though many of us rather go vent to people we know will lean towards what we really want to do so that we can receive "validation" to do what we want to do instead of desiring God's will. God knows it's challenging to do this thing, but he says he is near the brokenhearted in his word. Not only should we vent to God, we should also be sound mentally to intellectually know the differences between what's vain and valid. Not everything that makes sense is sensible for you. Not all valid things are valid. The Bible talks about that there are things that are permissible and lawful, but they are not beneficial, meaning you're free to do it, but in doing those things, you will lose your freedom. Vent and think before you accept or pursue anything.

What do you need to emotionally vent to God about?	
Vent #1	Vent #2

What are the main thoughts you're struggling with now? Are they vain or valid? What scriptures support them			
Thoughts			
Vain or valid? →		Vain	Valid
Scriptural supports			
S#1	S#2	S#3	

T: Take your time and let time prove to you what you need to know. One of your greatest assets is time. Those who respect their time use their time for their advantage. Patience and impatience are fruits that reveals a person's respect for time. People who are patient understand the purpose of time and allow time to do a lot of the work for them. They know time heals and time reveals, but those who are impatient have no respect for time. They care more about their immediate needs than they do about what's truly beneficial.

Those who take their time make their time useful and utilize their time to make the best decisions and see the obvious.

> Do you use your time wisely? If not how could you employ your time to work for you and not against you?

T: Trust God with everything you can't and shouldn't control. There are things that we can't and shouldn't control. To not settle, we must understand this principle. See, if you try to control what you can't control, you will lose control and create chaos. We were not designed to carry and control everything. God created us to have a dependency on him and to have a partnership with him. There are certain cares we cannot carry due to how we are built. Anything that causes unnecessary stress is something we weren't supposed to carry. The problem lies though in our pride. See, we think we are smart enough and strong enough to do what only God can do. God created marriage for mature audiences only. God is the only one that can adequately control a marriage. There may be parts for us to carry within it, but outside of Him, we crumble under marriages weight. Like I always say, people don't break a marriage, the standards of marriage break people! There are just certain things we can't do without God. The moment we realize this is the moment, items become lighter and doable.

> What are the things in your life you are trying to control but you know only God can control? + Why are you trying to control it?

What in your life should be under your control and what should be under God's control?		
Your control	God's control	Why?

L: Never forget that you are never a-lone or in desperate need. With God, you are never alone and shouldn't be desperate. He says He is near us and that he doesn't forsake the righteous. Loneliness is a state of mind. It's the overindulgence in the idea of being alone like I said before. Those who know they are loved by God don't need anybody because need leads to perversion. Too many of us are in deep need, and it's causing us to settle for counterfeits. The only person you need is God; everything else is a want. Trust me, you don't want anyone around you who needs you, you want to be surrounded by people who want you. Need is dangerous. When someone needs something badly, they will do bad things to have it. In God, you have everything you need; He is your source and is full of all of your resources. The problem though lies in us wanting what we want, how we want it, and when we want it. These wants stem from our desperate need to be seen, heard, felt, known, etc. Those who are loved by God are ok with being alone because they know they are never alone or in desperate need.

If applicable, why do you feel lonely?

In what ways has God shown you that He is there?

What do you desperately need and how could that desperate need set you up to settle or be in danger?

E: Stay away from easy. Last but not least, stay away from easy. Embrace difficulty and learn from your painful experiences. The goal is to conquer tough times, not create them. Those that create tough times create unnecessary struggles for themselves, but the struggle that comes from just simply living and following God don't run from them run through them and let them shape you. Everything worth having is on the opposite side of fear and struggle. Avoid the easy and embrace the hard.

In what ways do you always seek the easy way out and why?	How could this behavior affect you down the road?

What difficulty are you facing now and how should you navigate through it?

As time pass how did you fare during that difficult time

Good vs. God

When it comes to making decisions, it's not always the difference between what's good and bad, but what's good and God. What's good for you is not always God's fit for you. Let's break it down.

Good vs. God

1. Good parts could help you, but God's parts will help you
2. Good parts could be good for you, but God's parts are surely good for you
3. Good parts may work for you, but God's parts will work for you always
4. Good parts may have worked for others, but God's parts will surely and exclusively work for you
5. Good parts may make you cents, but God's parts will make your money make sense
6. Good parts may look good, but God's parts are good
7. Good parts may work online, but God's parts work on and offline

The Bible says in 1 Corinthians 10:23

23 "All things are lawful," but not all things are helpful. "All things are lawful," but not all things build up.

In this life, you will be faced with many good parts, parts that will look like they will benefit you or may even be lawful to do, but we mustn't be deceived. The more you become familiar with God, the more you will be able to recognize the differences.

Let's break down each:

<u>Good parts could help you, but God's parts will help you</u>

Not all help is the same. Could in this sentence is key. It could help you, but will it? See, God's parts written in his word and expressed in action will supernaturally help. The goal is not to receive just natural help but a natural help backed by spiritual support. Satan will send a plethora of good parts your way with great reviews, but those parts will only hold up or help the flesh. The only parts we should want in our lives are the ones God is in because if he is in it, you will win at it!

<u>Good parts could be good for you, but God's parts are surely good for you</u>

There are a lot of good options for you, but not too many God options for you. There are many men and women that could make good husbands and wives, but one slightness in their goals and aspirations could drive you away from your calling. God has undoubtedly good things for you, individuals, and item's that, too, are backed and infused by Him, helping you fulfill your goodness in the world. To audit good things, you must know God's goodness because the embraced goodness of God will limit what you reach out for? You must always be willing to tell a good thing, no. Those who know God's yes are willing to tell anything no.

Good parts may work for you, but God's parts will work for you always

I only want workers that are hired by God for me. You either get the work you've paid for or the work Jesus has paid for. Good parts are limited parts; they are only skilled at a certain level. They may work well in your life now, but as you mature, they will expire. Most people are plateaued at the level of their workers. They have the mentality of this will work for me versus God; what do you want to work on me? We must be worked out to work out God's will for us, and we must welcome God's workers that will ensure we are in shape and sustained for the next level. Patience will always be your trainer. Let her and her associate's Love, Pruning, and Discipline help work you out.

Good parts may have worked for others, but God's parts will surely and exclusively work for you.

This goes with the section above, but not everything that worked for others will work for you. God is doing a unique work in all of us. He doesn't always do everything the same. His efforts towards us are modified to his specific will for us. Don't envy what may have happened in another person's life that you overlook how God is working on you. All of us were saved the same, but not all of us are being sanctified the same. Each of our sanctification processes is different due to our different upbringings, fears, mistakes, etc.

Good parts may make you cents, but God's parts will make your money make sense

There are many opportunities out there that can make you rich but cannot make you wealthy. There is a set limit God has for us financially based on his will and our stewardship ability. He knows what amount of money you are indeed able to manage without compromise. There is a scripture that says in Proverbs 30:8-9

> 8 Remove far from me falsehood and lying;
>
> give me neither poverty nor riches;
>
> feed me with the food that is needful for me,
>
> 9 lest I be full and deny you
>
> and say, "Who is the Lord?"
>
> or lest I be poor and steal
>
> and profane the name of my God.

God has a central place for each of us, and this should be our heart. We should not want one cent more or one cent less than what God sees fit for us. God will birth and bring out of you if you allow him, a level of stewardship that will aid his kingdom and your family. You can't have a sustained surplus without stewardship. Are you in the right career? Are you pursuing and establishing the business' God wants you, or are you chasing after money and a way of living? Don't lose your heart and your family looking for more money. Wealth is holistic, not specific!

<u>Good parts may look good, but God's parts are good</u>

Looks can be deceiving. How you look out will determine what you look at. Having the right perspective is key between deciding between good and God. There are many shiny and attractive parts out there that may be good, but given by the wrong hands with the improper motive will cause damaging effects. Never accept things at face value; always aim to see the value behind the face because many things presented to us have on a mask!

<u>Good parts may work online, but God's parts work on and offline</u>

Many people are treating their social media pages as their front porches to practice their righteousness. It looks good online, but there is no fruit of it offline. Not everyone online is your friend or cares to know everything about you. There are a lot of Christendom trends in our world, and a lot of people are using social media as a way to grow, show, know, and go, but we must be wise online. Not everything offline should go online. Make sure your offline is more valuable and fruitful than your online.

HOW TO PROPERLY TEST EVERYTHING

In this chapter we are going to cover how to properly test the many things you will face in your life. We are going to cover the following points

1. Why we should test pg: 91

2. What to test pg: 97

3. What is required to properly test pg: 99

4. The following parts to test pg: 103

*Each of the first three points will spell the word TEST.

Why should you test?

You should test because

1. T: Your <u>time</u> is valuable

2. E: Your <u>energy</u> is limited

3. S: Of <u>self-care</u> and <u>stewardship</u>

4. T: You need to reach your <u>targets</u>

<u>Your time is valuable.</u>

Like I've said before, you spell time L.I.F.E. Your time equals your life. You must test what's in front of you because you do not have much time here on this earth. The Bible says that your life is just a vapor. You we're sent here for a specific purpose with a certain amount of time to fulfill it. You do not have time to entertain anything that is not a part of God's plan for you. It's crazy how many minutes we spend on things that have nothing to do with our purpose. Everything we do must support our reason for living. Everything from recreation to entertainment must support our sanctification and our assignment. Many things will come and present themselves to you, but you must always ask, is my time with them, or it worth my investment? What kind of return will I get on this investment?

On average how do you spend your time?	Wisely	Not so wisely

On average by the day how do you spend your time and what return are you making on each investment?		
Time	Spent doing	Return on investment
6am-12pm		
1pm-6pm		
7pm-12am		
1am-5am		

Your energy is limited

Each day based on your daily routines, you have a certain amount of energy you can pull from. It's unfortunate though how many people are operating from burnout. It's hard to truly earn-out when you're burned out. The enemy wants his counterfeits to burn your premium energy. He wants these leaches to drain you of your time and life. Those who honor their time and their energy become very selective about how they spend them. What is impacting your energy daily? What are your routines? Are you operating from full or from empty?

What in your life right now is giving you energy and how?
1
2
3
4
5

6	
7	

What in your life right now is grabbing your energy with no return and how?

1	
2	
3	
4	
5	
6	
7	

What routines should you implement to increase your energy?

1	
2	
3	
4	
5	

Where should you invest your energy?

1	
2	
3	
4	
5	

Self-care and stewardship

You must test because of self-care. If it doesn't care for you, then you shouldn't care for it. The formula to love is

God's accepted perfect love produces self-love, and self-love distributes love proportionately.

You should have boundaries. Not everyone deserves access to you. There is a difference between you and your love. Like I've said before, everyone deserves some access to your love, but not everyone deserves access to your heart. Meaning that everyone should at least get a hello or some kindness and respect from you, but not everyone deserves access to your heart. The Holy Spirit knows the motives of everyone, and you must trust his leading. Self-care is the fruit of contentment. Those that are content in God are not easily impressed or pressed to have something because they have everything in God.

Questions to think on: How well are you? Are you taking care of yourself?

Secondly, you must test to steward what you have. Some people only want to be around you because of what's around you. You must test to protect what you've built, acquired, tended produced, etc. So many people have lost so much because of perceived loyalty. My pastor, Pastor Gool, said something very valuable he said there is a big difference between loyalty and faithfulness. Many will be faithful to you, but not many will be loyal to you. People will be faithful to you if you keep what they want around you, but the moment those things are gone, they cease to be faithful. But those that are loyal will stick around no matter what's there or not there. You must test to protect your best.

What is within your care right now, who all has access to it, should they and how well are you stewarding it?			
Questions → Items/individuals under your care ↓	Who all has access to it?	Should they? Why or why not?	How well are you stewarding it or them? + what adjustments do you need to make?

To reach your targets

You must test because you have targets and goals to achieve. All counterfeits either distract you from your goals or keep you from developing them. Those who have a strong why will always take their time to examine what's in front of them. They don't have time to waste on things that do not support their goals and dreams. For years I turned down fun to work on my fundamentals and my funds, and today I am thankful that I did. Even in writing this book, I had to say no to a lot of things because of my goals. Not too many people have goals and will feel a certain way when you don't have spare time to devote to their nothingness. We're too old to be always going here and there and hanging out and whatnot. Its focus time. You must test so that you can become your best.

What are your goals? What do you want to accomplish in life?

What is distracting you from these goals?

What to test?

In this section I am going to show you what to observe when you're presented with options that are after your time, energy, care, stewardships, and targets.

Before you serve observe its

- T: Temperament
- E: End Result
- S: Scriptural Supports
- T: Timing

The bible says you will know a tree by its fruit and below I will show you the obvious fruit that is mostly evident when dealing with counterfeits and counterparts.

Let's start with temperament.

Temperament is a person's or things character, nature, deposition, etc. Everyone has tendencies that are hard to hide. A person's temperament is a person's temperature. That is why it is essential to always be set on joy and set on contentment, so it becomes easy to spots one's temperament. Those who put themselves on depression, sadness, envy, lust, and things like these will not recognize the counterfeits around them. When you are set on God and set on the right things, you will find it easy to identify a person's tendencies or temperament. How a person reacts under pressure or being denied what they truly want from you will reveal a lot to you about who sent them. How it's sent will tell you a lot about who sent them. Satan pressures and everything sent by him will do so also. Everything from God comes with peace and assurance, and everything from Him will embody his character. How is he approaching you? How is she approaching you? How are they approaching you? Are they peaceful, gentle, understanding, kind, patient, etc.? or are they pressuring, pulling, impulsive, impatient, etc.?

End result

Next, you must examine the end result. What will happen if you do or accept x, y, or z? What are the corresponding outcomes? It is always important to count the cost and think three moves ahead. When you give yourself time to consider what's in front of you through, you will see its holes or its ability to hold. That's why it's critical to be content and not eager to have anything. Satan's system feeds off the eager and impulsive because he knows they will not take their time to count the cost or examine the immediate or inevitable consequences. Before you begin, think about its end.

Scriptural Supports

Next, you must examine if it's supported by scripture. If it's not supported by scripture, then it will not support you. It is God's promises that ultimately support us, not the false promises of people. If it contradicts scripture, it will bring conflict into your life. What does the word of God say about the fruit of the people in your life? What does it say about the patterns or practices you are tempted to engage in?

Timing

Is it the right time? God will not send anything into your life that you are not mature enough to hold. If it's in your life a week after a wound was created then it is not for you. If it comes and you are too eager about it, then it's not for you. If it's in front of you and you know you are not mature enough to manage it, it was not sent by God. God will never send anything or anyone into your life that will be in direct conflict against His Spirits work in you. God's timing is perfect, and you must trust it. God loves you too much to give you everything you desire prematurely. He is too good to provide you with anything that he knows you want more than Him or will put before Him. Counterfeits will always try to fit itself into your time prematurely, while counterparts will always be a part of the times for you. Want it when God wants you to have it.

Next, we are going to talk about what is required to test properly. The traits below are traits you must aim to grow in, to test what's in front of you properly. A lacking in any of these areas could create vulnerabilities or angles for the enemy to cause you to fall for one of his counterfeits.

The following are required in order to properly test

1. T: Full Trust in God
2. E: Emotional Intelligence
3. S: Scriptural Soundness and Sanctification
4. T: Thoroughness and Passed Test

Full trust in God

Throughout this book, we talked about the importance of fully trusting God and making Jesus the rock you build on. To properly test, you must fully not partially trust God. You must be anchored in Him. You must be fully persuaded on who He is. You must be a friend of His and familiar with His faithfulness. Anywhere you have a partial or no trust in God will be the areas you welcome and accept Satan's counterfeits. If you do not trust God to get you through the season you are in or match you with your mate; you will be susceptible to flirt with Satan's alternatives.

Emotional Intelligence

To indeed be able to discern and test what is in front of you, you must have a strong EQ or, in other words, emotional intelligence. By definition, emotional intelligence is the capacity to be aware of, control, and express one's emotions and handle interpersonal relationships judiciously and empathetically. We need to know how to interact with ourselves and others. It is crucial that we are constantly aware of our emotional state and how to engage others with empathy and understanding. You must know how to read yourself and others. You must always be mindful of your heart in conjunction with what is presented in front of you. You must be aware of all potential or present idolatries and hidden agendas and be honest with yourself, knowing your abilities and capabilities. You must also know how to read people and know your capabilities in serving them or helping them. Sometimes we make ourselves counterfeit saviors in others' lives rather than pointing and sending them to the One who can heal. You must not be so focused on the physical look of a thing that you don't take the time to examine its and your emotional maturity.

Scriptural soundness and Sanctification

Earlier in the book, we talked about how Satan aims to throw things higher than your knowledge of God and his word. Jesus showed us how we are to respond to Satan, and that is with the word. The bible even mentions how our only weapon against the enemy is the word of God. Knowing who God is, who you are in Him, and your weaponry, which is God's word, is vital in understanding the difference between a counterfeit and a counterpart. Soundness means accuracy; it means knowing how to divide rightly. The word of God says in 2 Timothy 2:15 King James Version

> 15 Study to show yourself approved unto God, a workman that needs not to be ashamed, rightly dividing the word of truth.

Every believer is called to be a theologian. We were not called to be ignorant. You must know the word for yourself. What are the five scriptures that can solve and aid in your current situation? What are 5 scriptures you use to combat _____? Satan loves a solider with no bullets. What do you have in the chamber?

To properly test, you must be deep in the sanctification process of the spirit, meaning allowing him to mature you and produce fruit in you. Babes cannot recognize the difference between a counterfeit or a counterpart due to their lack of understanding. That is why we must allow the Holy Spirit to prune and groom us so that we are mature enough to recognize a counterfeit or a counterpart.

Thoroughness and Passed Test

To properly test what is in front of you, you must be thorough, dotting every i and crossing every t. You must be detailed and diligent. You must also have some passed tests or victories under your belt. The taste of success will keep you from wanting to taste defeat. When you have experienced God's goodness and the favor that comes through faithfulness, you will not want to taste anything contrary. Tasting and experiencing one counterpart will make you not want to taste a counterfeit.

Nest, Rest, Test, Best

Before we get into the different areas that require testing lets break down the process of testing well and selecting God's best. The formula is

1. Nest
2. Rest
3. Test
4. Best

To select God's best, you must first build a nest in his presence. You must decide to settle down and trust him. Many people are building a nest in resources and not in God, who is their source. Everything worth enjoying is on the rest side, not the stress side of life. You set yourself up to either not get to enjoy or not able to thoroughly enjoy when you are stressed. The word of God says In Philippians 4:6-8

> 6 do not be anxious about anything, but in everything by prayer and supplication with thanksgiving let your requests be made known to God. 7 And the peace of God, which surpasses all understanding, will guard your hearts and your minds in Christ Jesus.
>
> 8 Finally, brothers, whatever is true, whatever is honorable, whatever is just, whatever is pure, whatever is lovely, whatever is commendable, if there is any excellence, if there is anything worthy of praise, think about these things.

Peace is pivotal. Life is not going to be easy, and there will be times you will be tempted to worry and be anxious about marriage, money, management opportunities ministry, etc. but you must stay settled in God's presence and trust that in His time he will come through for you. The first part of this text is a command that says, do not be anxious. Anxiety and worry are offensive to a God that can do anything. God is telling us not to worry because he is able. Worry creeps in when we either don't believe God is able or we assume his ability. Many people assume against God's attributes. They think he is one way when he isn't. They will begin to believe he will do one thing, and when he doesn't in light of his character and our maturity, we worry and abort trusting in Him and try to work it out ourselves. Worry will always lead you to become worn. God wants us to rest in him and to trust His timing. It continues to say, do not worry about anything, keyword anything. There is not one thing on this planet we should worry about. God built our bodies not to worry; that's why stress and worry have adverse effects on us because we weren't made to do so.

We were built to have fellowship with God, a balanced relationship that leads to us sharing responsibilities. We were built to rest, not stress. Did you know that stress is the root cause of all diseases? Satan knows this and wants us to be mentally consumed with the next chapter of our lives before the current one is written. He knows that those who worry are more susceptible to accept his counterfeits. Anything that causes you to worry, you should either alter your outlook or remove that thing or person out of your life altogether. A cluttered mind leads to a messy life; a clear mind leads to a more straightforward life. The best life is the simple life a life lived for a purpose.

The verse adds that with everything by prayer and thanksgiving, make our request known to God; this is pivotal. God wants us to bring everything to Him first. Whoever you bring your problems to first, you trust most. Everything burdensome must be channeled through him first. Many people bring their issues to people and their posts online before they carry them within God's presence. God wants you to bring everything, not burry everything. Many people are burying their issues, setting themselves up to blow up down the road. God must be the first person we vent to because he will help us one, get it off of our chest and secondly see the issue in light of His ability and word. Those who do not take this opportunity set themselves up to making emotional decisions that produce real consequences. We must bring our request to him because he will reveal our responsibility level towards the request, or become aware of it. I love it when it says with thanksgiving. IF all you do is bring a request to him and never couple it with thanksgiving, then your relationship with God is one-sided. Thanksgiving reveals trust. It says I trust you, God, with my cares, with my worries, and with my request, and I trust you know what's best for me. Gratitude is the best attitude, and God loves an atmosphere of gratitude.

Verse 7 lets us know our confirmation. God may not always send you the package you desire when you desire it, but he will send you His confirmation number with tracking number #PEACEPIL47. His peace is more important than the desired package, promotion, person, etc. His peace is proof that He heard and that the best thing for you has already been settled. God has already chosen the next best outcome for you. Many of the requests we had were immature, and God, like a good father, hears but only gives what's best. That's why many people leave God because they hate that he doesn't produce when they want him to, and they either remove their nest in him or never create one and find themselves stressed out. Do you not know that there are stressed and burned out millionaires and billionaires? Many of these people have the money to purchase protection but none to buy peace. True peace is from God. The word says the peace of God, not the peace of this world. The peace of this world is partial and temporary. Just like a spider can find itself in a mansion, so can a demon. Tormentors don't need any clearance. You can go to any island in the world and stay in any 7-star hotel and live in the most fortified gated communities but still be tormented. It is better to be in a shack where God's peace is than in a fortified mansion where his peace is not.

It continues to read that His peace will do two things it will surpass your understanding, and it will guard your heart and mind through Christ. Notice through whom? It's hard to have peace when you are doing things outside of what the Prince of Peace wants you to do. There's peace in the purposes of God. If you're going to prevail, stay in the purpose of God. The word of God says that many are the plans in a person's heart, but it will be the lord's purpose that prevails. His peace, which is in his presence and his goal for you, will surpass your understanding. That's why it is important to adhere to the formula in the text, which is to couple with your prayers and supplication; thanksgiving. Thanksgiving is what unlocks God's peace because it will cause you to receive and trust His timing and plan. It will settle you despite what your mind, friend, spouse, parent is saying. No man's understating can fully grasp the ways of God. He says my ways are your ways, and my thoughts are not your thoughts. God is not like us. He sees and moves differently than us. That's why He only send us his peace because that's all we need. As believers, we should remain settled on the fact that he heard and that he sent us his peace and leave it at that. We waste precious time trying to peek into the plans of God. Once we receive our peace, we should continue to work. His peace is designed to get us back into production mode, not reduction mode. It was designed for us to keep moving. God's peace is so vital to our mental, emotional, and physical health. The text says that his peace will keep or guard our hearts and minds. The bible talks about how many people's hearts will fail them in the last days because of fear. Whatever has your heart will determine if it will prevail or fail in times of trouble. There is coming a time where everyone's idols will fail them, and those who built their lives on the rock will find themselves still standing amid chaos. It is vitally important that you are nested and rested in his presence because it will keep your hearts from failing and your minds from becoming ill.

Only those who have built their nest in God's presence and have chosen to rest in it continuously will test well and have God's best.

Now let's take some time to examine 13 potential counterfeits and counterparts and learn how to test each.

<u>We must discern/ test the following parts</u>

- Parents and Family pg: 105
- Friendships pg: 113
- Companionships pg: 138
- Influencers, Mentors, Counsel pg: 119
- Teachings pg: 147
- Habits pg: 131
- Opportunities and ambitions pg: 153
- Resources and tools pg: 161
- Words pg: 165
- Thoughts pg: 165
- Emotions pg: 179
- Choices pg: 169
- Locations pg: 175

PARENTS

Parents and or family

Let's start with your parents. The only thing on this list you didn't have a choice in the matter is your parents. They are who they are. The comforting thing about this, whether good or bad, is that God chose them. Nothing happens without God knowing. No matter how functional or dysfunctional they were or are, they have a part to play. No one can play it perfectly, but God has a way of, if you choose, to have it perfectly play out for your good. Some of us grew up in either the far from perfect or the far beyond perfect homes, meaning some of our upbringings were either horrible or overly helpful. The house is the devil's playground. He loves dysfunction. He loves to use the dysfunction in both parents to warp the mind of their child. He knows that any home that is not fully submitted to God or endeavoring to do so is vulnerable. Joshua said it best in the bible; he said as far as me and my house, we will serve the Lord, the critical phrase is; as far as me. If both parents do not share these sentiments, then the house is vulnerable. How can children learn how to serve the lord if the parents aren't? The demons assigned to your family tree work day in and day out to ensure the generational curses of your great grands are passed down to and through you. Demons are territorial, and they work from generation to generation of families working to keep their agendas passing down. The best passage to do so is through parents.

The good news is, your life is your life, and you can stop all generational cures and start generational blessings. Not all the parts that were handed down to you through your parents are useful now. Many kids are mentally tied to the opinions of their parents, and it's unfortunate. At some point, you will have to serve God for yourself and learn how to be your own person. Some parents are trying to live vicariously through their children to somehow pay themselves back for what they didn't accomplish. You owe nobody nothing but love. There are so many people out here now still tormented by what their parents did or didn't do. Yes, you had to answer to them growing up, but now that you are older, you have to answer to God, and God warned that he didn't come to bring peace but a sword to cut, turning father against son mother against daughter. I rather please God and offend everyone than to offend God trying to please everyone. In many homes, there are some good parts that should be passed down through you, but make sure they are parts God wants to add.

Honor your father and mother.

I've gotten many questions recently about how one should interact and engage a disrespectful parent who screams they should still be honored as a mother or father. Here is some advice if you are struggling with this. First off, the word says to honor your father and mother. Those two titles have definitions. A father is one who instructs a mother is one who nurtures. There are levels of honor. Honoring another person should never surpass your honoring of God and yourself. The moment someone demands you to honor them, but they are not honoring you, then it's time to modify your display of honor. There is a difference between a disposition of honor and the delegation of honor. Just like levels of love must be earned, so are levels of honor. Your heart honors them, but you don't have to honor them with your time, energy, or efforts. Many parents are deeply wounded and are through their wounds, hurting their children. There is a difference between being here for them vs. being there for them. You're here for them through prayer or encouragement, but you can't be there for them and be abused. Many people's parents are just sperm donors and a doorway that brought them into this world. The more they become like fathers and mothers, the more you can delegate your time, etc.

So how do you do this? You one establish your honor for God and reestablish your commitment to Him no matter your friend, family, foe, or feelings. Secondly, you show honor of self. You assess your self-worth and self-love and attach it to God's love of you and determine what you will and will not tolerate from anyone. Once those two things are done, I want you to write out both parents' names on a sheet of paper and write down their issues; this will help you build empathy and not have you develop resentment. After you have done this, I want you to under that, write down how they are treating you and how it makes you feel. Once you have written that out, I want you to first vent and commit those feelings to God and then write out how you plan to engage them going forward. If or when they make mention of your change of behavior that is when you have a conversation with them and let them know that you love them but you can't be mistreated (voice out mistreatments) I honor you as my mom or dad, but I will not be honoring you with x, y, and z until you treat me better. Now be prepared for the demon to come out and call you names and try to hit below your belt. Be prepared for this because in certain situations, depending on the parent's issue, it could get ugly. But never forget what the word of God says, it says that we wrestle not against flesh and blood but demons and principalities, etc. That is why I mentioned assessing their mental and emotional health to build empathy. Learn now how to process offense through empathy because if not, what they may say may hurt you.

QUESTIONS

1. Trust in God
2. Emotional Intelligence
3. Soundness in scripture + sanctification
4. Thoroughness and passed test

Where is your trust level with God in this areas?										
1	2	3	4	5	6	7	8	9	10

Why the # above?	How can you increase your trust in Him in this area?

Where's your EQ levels? →	Clueless	Cloudy	Somewhat clear	Confidently clear

Why did you select the option above?	What are you discerning is going on with your parents?

How sound are you scripturally in this area? →	Sound	Not as sound as I should be

If applicable, what scriptures should you meditate on to increase your soundness?

S1	S2	S3	S4	S5

How thorough are you with matters like these? What supports systems do you need to help you pass this test?

How close are you with your mom?					How close are you with your dad?				
1	2	3	4	5	1	2	3	4	5

Why the # above	Why the # above

What were the good parts of your upbringing?	What were the bad parts of your upbringing?

What from your upbringing is still affecting you negatively now?	What from your upbringing is still affecting you positively now?

What have your parents done to you that you have yet to forgive them for?

1. Time
2. Energy
3. Self-care + stewardship
4. Targets

How is this matter affecting your time?	How is this matter affecting your energy?
How is this matter affecting your self-care and stewardships?	How is this matter affecting you hitting your targets?

Advice + Guidance Checklist

1. Temperament
2. End result
3. Scriptural support
4. Timing

What is their advice?

What is their temperament when giving this advice?

What would be the end result if you listened?

Does scripture support what they are doing or saying for you to do? What do the scriptures say about this?

Is it the right time to do what they are saying?

FRIENDS

Friendships

Fri-ends are those who will be there for you till the end. Notice you can't spell friend without end. Everything you do must be with the end in mind, and the only one that has all ends in mind is God, so it will be wise for us to let him select our friends. Social media has warped and diluted the definition of friends or followers. Not everyone who is a friend is one, and not everyone following you is following you for good reasons. It will be rare to have more than three reliable friends in life because being friends is a responsibility. A person with many friends is tired and confused. They are tired due to helping all their friends and are confused by listening to their opinions. Who are your friends right now, and how well are they functioning as such? The enemy loves to slip within the vulnerable moments of our lives, people with a common interest but with an immature intelligence to feed our minds with loose interest. How many people made dumb decisions from the advice of "friends" whether to have sex with their boyfriend or girlfriend, go to parties or waste their time? Both you and I have, and what did it get us at the end; nothing. It is best to be alone and productive then around a bunch of friends going nowhere.

The number one friendship you should cultivate first is God because that friendship will be the foundation of all friendships. Building a strong bond with God keeps you productive and content. It will keep you from "needing" friends. Every piece, including friendship, are specific and selected for a particular purpose. I don't have many friends, and I'm content with that, and I am not a friend to everyone, and I am satisfied with that. Being a friend and being friendly are two different things. I am friendly with everyone but not a friend to everyone because being a friend is a free job. You don't get paid monetarily to be a friend. There are going to be seasons where you will have to work overtime and other seasons where you are off. Imagine having to be a friend to seven people who are all leaning on you to be there for them. It may be time for you to make some cuts and to cut away from some of your friendships.

How to know if your FRIENDS are solid

- F: They are following God to. If they are not following God, then their thoughts and advice aren't either. Examine their fruit to see if they are sincerely following Jesus.

- R: They are ready and eager to help. Real friends are committed and support at the level of their ability.

- I: They help with and celebrate your ideas. Reliable friends support your dreams and not with just words but with action and money. Any friend that asks for a discount is not a real friend. A real friend buys two or three of everything you offer if they are able, and when you win, they celebrate, and when you fail in the development of your idea, they help elevate you to get back to it.

- E: They are not envious or jealous of your growth. Your growth inspires them not expires them. Real friends grow with you fake friends slow with you, meaning they don't want you to become too much because they feel they will lose you. If you lose them while you're growing, then it proves they were never your friends.

- N: They respect your no and help you say no. No is a complete sentence, and real friends recognize it. A person who loves your yes more than they understand your no is not a real friend. Also, real friends help you say no. They help you say no to anything that doesn't line up with God's character or word.

- D: real friends are disciplined and are developing personally. Real friends are too productive, working on their lives to be consumed with yours. Real friends are disciplined, meaning they are not going to be all over the place around you, having you do the same.

I hope this checklist helps you select or cut off some friends.

Where is your trust level with God in this areas?									
1	2	3	4	5	6	7	8	9	10
Why the # above?					How can you increase your trust in Him in this area?				
Where's your EQ levels? →		Clueless	Cloudy	Somewhat clear				Confidently clear	
Why did you select the option above?					What are you discerning is going on with your parents?				

How sound are you scripturally in this area? →	Sound	Not as sound as I should be
If applicable, what scriptures should you meditate on to increase your soundness?		
How thorough are you with matters like these? What supports systems do you need to help you pass this test?		

Friends → Questions ↓	
Are they following God? What fruit are they bearing as proof? What are their habits?	
How eager are they to help?	
How do they support your ideas?	

How do they respond to your growth and focus?	
Do they respect your no and hold you accountable? How?	
Are they disciplined and developing? How so?	
Is this the right time to be their friend? Is your friendship mutual or mismanaged?	
How is their friendship affecting your time, energy, self-care/stewardship and you reaching your targets?	
Are they a counterfeit or counterpart friend?	

Friend's advice

Friend → Questions ↓	
What is their temperament?	
What will be the end result of their advice?	
What does the word of God say about their advice?	
Is it the right time to do what they are advising?	
Friend → Questions ↓	
What is their temperament?	
What will be the end result of their advice?	
What does the word of God say about their advice?	
Is it the right time to do what they are advising?	

COUNSEL

Mentors, counsel and influencers

Not all "mentors" were meant to be in your life. Throughout life, you will encounter men or women who will either desire to help you or want to help you but know that God must select these individuals. Those who were meant to mentor you will be people God picks to help mold you into the person ready to steward a particular place in His kingdom. A mentor is a person who is already managing the position you desire to have, exceptionally well. They are people who have walked down the path you are currently walking down. It's important to let God select this person because not everyone took the straight path to where they are; some took the crooked route and may suggest you take those routes. There is only one right way to the right place, and that's through Integrity Blvd.

Where is your trust level with God in this areas?									
1	2	3	4	5	6	7	8	9	10
Why the # above?					How can you increase your trust in Him in this area?				

Where's your EQ levels? →	Clueless	Cloudy	Somewhat clear	Confidently clear
Why did you select the option above?		What are you discerning is going on with your parents?		

How sound are you scripturally in this area? →	Sound	Not as sound as I should be

If applicable, what scriptures should you meditate on to increase your soundness?
How thorough are you with matters like these? What supports systems do you need to help you pass this test?

Who are your mentors or who do you desire to be your mentors?	
Mentors/desired → Questions ↓	
How did they become your mentor or why do you want them to be your mentor?	

How's is their integrity what fruit are they bearing?	
What are their ambitions?	
What is the state of his or her family? Are their priorities in order?	
Are you desiring their mentorship more than you desire mentorship from the Holy Spirit?	

Are they a counterfeit or counterpart mentor?	

Mentors advice and name → Questions ↓	
What is the temperament of their advice?	
What would be the end result of their advice if you pursue it?	
What does the scriptures say about their advice?	
Is it the right time to pursue this advice?	
How would pursuing this advice affect your time, energy, self-care/stewardships and targeting your goals?	

Counsel

Not all counsel is wise counsel. Some people are eating the fruits of someone else's lousy counsel. The enemy loves counterfeit counsel, counsel that sounds good but is not sound. All counsel must be rooted in God's word and must be confirmed through the Holy Spirits leading. God will not lead someone into your life to counsel you against the leading of His Spirit and His word. The enemy loves when we consult groups and Google before we consult God. Before we seek external counsel, we should always seek our internal counsel. He gave us His Spirit, who is twenty billion times more powerful than Google, to assist us. Google can search a lot of things, but one thing it cannot search is God. The Bible says the spirit of God knows God's deep things, and everything that pertains to you is in God, and the fullness of God is in you right now through His Spirit on standby to console and counsel you. This doesn't mean God doesn't use people to console or counsel us, but we must discipline ourselves to trust our first counselor and allow God to use others for confirmation.

Never listen to a person whose life doesn't match their advice

Where is your trust level with God in this areas?									
1	2	3	4	5	6	7	8	9	10

Why the # above?	How can you increase your trust in Him in this area?

Where's your EQ levels? →	Clueless	Cloudy	Somewhat clear	Confidently clear

Why did you select the option above?	What are you discerning is going on in this area?

How sound are you scripturally in understanding this matter?	Sound	Not as sound as I should be
If applicable, what scriptures should you meditate on to increase your soundness?			

What counsel have you recently received or are receiving now and from whom? → Questions ↓	
What is the temperament of the counsel and the one giving it?	
What would be the end result of this counsel if you pursue it?	
What does the scriptures say about this counsel?	
Is it the right time to pursue this counsel?	

How would this counsel affect your time, energy, self-care/ stewardships, and targeting your goals?	
Is this a counterfeit or counterpart counsel?	

Influencers.

Be very leery who you allow to influence you because whoever you allow influencing you could be causing you to get the flu. Not everyone is a good influence. Many people have flown off their peaks of promise to problematic pastures due to bad influences. It would be best if you always protected your external and internal environment. Influences are subtle; they prey on ill-informed and insecure individuals, luring their minds to mold an image contrary to the one God wants them to bear.

Where is your trust level with God in this areas?									
1	2	3	4	5	6	7	8	9	10
Why the # above?						How can you increase your trust in Him in this area?			

Where's your EQ levels? →	Clueless	Cloudy	Somewhat clear	Confidently clear
Why did you select the option above?		What are you discerning is going on in this area?		
How sound are you scripturally in understanding this matter?			Sound	Not as sound as I should be
If applicable, what scriptures should you meditate on to increase your soundness?				

Who are your top influencers online and offline? → Questions ↓	
What do you admire most about them?	

What fruit are they bearing?	
What traits of theirs are rubbing off on you?	
Do their actions, post etc. line up with the character and word of God?	
Should they be an influencer in your life? Why and why not?	

How is their influence affecting your time, energy, self-care, and you targeting your goals?	
Are they a counterfeit or counterpart influence?	

HABITS

Habits

Not all habits should be a part of our lives. The clearer we are about our purpose, the sharper our habits will be. We, by default, are creatures of habit, and we eat the fruits of those habits. What do you -habitually do? What are you usually making happen? See, your ha-bits are little bits that make things ha-ppen. What are those little things you do over and over that are contributing to your success or failures?

Your habits should help you, not hinder you. Many habits may feel like they are helping you initially, but they will prove not so helpful over time. Paul said when he was a child, he spoke and thought like one, but he put those childish ways or habits away when he became a man. Your habits now should match your age and the stage you desire to stand on. If not, you will be just a boy or a girl in the audience watching someone else perform on your stage. See repetition is the mother of learning, and you are the result of what you repeatedly do. If you want to change what is happening in your life, change your habits. Satan wants you to have counterfeit habits, habits that contradict, and conflict with your purpose. How can you fulfill your purpose if you practice habits that go against your health and your wealth? See, healing happens when habits change. Many people are sick right now because of what they eat, enjoy, and the environments they CHOOSE to be in. You must be purpose minded and select private habits that will help your purpose.

Where is your trust level with God in this areas?									
1	2	3	4	5	6	7	8	9	10
Why the # above?					How can you increase your trust in Him in this area?					
Where's your EQ levels? →				Clueless	Cloudy	Somewhat clear			Confidently clear	

Why did you select the option above?	What are you discerning is going on in this area?
How sound are you scripturally in understanding this matter?	Sound	Not as sound as I should be
If applicable, what scriptures should you meditate on to increase your soundness?			

What's happening in your life and what ha-bits are contributing to it?	
Happenings	Contributing habits

What would you like to happen in your life and what ha-bits would help make it happen?	
Happenings	Contributing habits

What are your predominant habits? →	
Are they helpful or hurtful and how so?	

What conceived these habits?	
What does the word of God say about these habits?	
How are these habits affecting your time, energy, self-care/stewardships and you targeting your goals?	
Is this a counterfeit or counterpart habit?	

COMPANION

Companion

Millions of people either have a deep desire for a companion or are deeply disgruntled with the one they have. Many people are looking to be completed by someone so bad that they never become entirely completed by Jesus. God has two companions for us; the Holy Spirit and our spouse. God has someone for you that is fit for you and your purpose. The problem lies in impatience. The enemy wants a counterfeit in the passenger seat or your life's driver seat, affecting your purpose. See purpose means a lot to God, and each piece, especially your spouse, is hand-selected because he knows that if one can put a thousand to flight, two can put ten thousand to flight. It's sad, though, that many relationships are doing nothing to help the kingdom of God. You need to understand God's timing. God's timing is perfect for everything, including marriage.

Right now, God is preparing you and your significant other and has a moment in time for you both to meet. It is better to be single than sorry. So many married people right now are full of regrets due to them rushing into a relationship. It takes a particular renewed mind to manage marriage, and without a renewed sense, it will be hard to maintain one. Do you idolize love? Do you want a significant other more than God? Idolatry has a way of making marriage bigger than it needs to be. It will have people who want the idea of love, but won't be the individual they need to be to be in love. Many people have an idea of what they want in a spouse, but their expectations will crush them when they meet an individual. Satan loves when people idolize the concept of love. He wants them to daydream about love and envy others' love taking their time away from God and development. It takes a long time to build a man and woman of God. It takes time to heal each person's wounds and shape their perspectives to see life how it was designed to be seen. You have to be ok with time. Time always moves slower when you look at it, but time will seem to move quickly when you have a purpose for that time. You must be mission-minded as a single person to be groomed for the missions of marriage. Do you have a mission statement for your life? Do you know why God sent you here? If not, then you have no time to think about marriage. Those who think about marriage more than their current assignment will set themselves up to fall for Satan's counterfeit. Most bad marriages and relationships started off with desperation, idolatry, impatience, manipulation, fear, emotions, and dispositions. Contentment is the safest place to decide from because contentment always leans us to consult God. Like I said before, it is better to be single than sorry.

For those that are dating, God's grace is sufficient for you. It can help you get out of a relationship that is not for you. If you know deep down on the inside that the person you are with is not for you, let them go, and if it is hard for you to let them go, ask yourself why is it so hard? It is better to be single than with someone who is not for you. Your time is too valuable to have it occupied with someone God doesn't have for you. Satan's systems are designed to steal your time, kill your energy, and destroy your purpose, and the best way to do that is to pair you up with a counterfeit husband or wife. He knows emotions are like super glue, and when pressed with the soul of another will cause connections. That's why it is crucial not to awaken love before its time because its emotions will glue itself with whom it believes is its lover. Without God, your soul will never be satisfied, and it will spend its time seeking love. I have some great resources on my website iamunplugged.com that will help you process your singleness and prepare you for marriage. Those resources are

- The Purpose of Singleness (book and course)
- The Purpose of Freedom (book on soul ties and strongholds)
- Dating Prep (book and card game)
- Available at IAMUNPLUGGED.COM

Where is your trust level with God in this areas?									
1	2	3	4	5	6	7	8	9	10
Why the # above?					How can you increase your trust in Him in this area?			

Where's your EQ levels? →		Clueless	Cloudy	Somewhat clear	Confidently clear
Why did you select the option above?			What are you discerning is going on in this area?		
How sound are you scripturally in understanding this matter?				Sound	Not as sound as I should be
If applicable, what scriptures should you meditate on to increase your soundness?					

Singles

How content are you with your singleness or what's your temperament about singleness and marriage?										
1	2	3	4	5	6	7	8	9	10

Why the number above?

Why do you want to be married?

What should you be focusing on?

If you were married now with the character, you have now, what would be the end result of your marriage?

What does the word of God say about the emotions you are feeling now?

Why is this the right or not the right timing to pursue a relationship?

Do you match what you are asking for?		
What do you want in a companion, spouse etc.?	In what way do you compliment them in this area?	In what ways do you not compliment them in this area and in what areas do you need to improve?

Those who are dating:

Who are you dating or courting at the moment → Questions ↓	
How did the relationship begin?	
How long have you all been dating or in a relationship?	
What is his or her temperament?	
If you married this person right now, what would be the end result of your marriage?	
Does he or she compromise scripture or suggest you to do so?	

Is it the right time for this relationship?	
Why should you leave or stay in this relationship?	
If applicable: Why is it hard to leave this relationship?	
Is he or she a counterfcit or a counterpart + proof	

TEACHINGS

Teachings

The bible talks about that in the last day's people will not be able to endure sound doctrine, and my friend it is happening now. Not all teachings are inspired by the Holy Ghost. We live in a time where people want quick and gentle lessons to help motivate them to pursue the life they want, not the life to come. They don't have time to endure sound doctrine because their lives are full of extracurricular actives. See the things that matter; take time to learn, and there are no quick ways or cliff notes to these matters. The devil has removed and modified some fundamental teachings to deceive the masses into believing that his idea of doctrine is true. The Bible says that people will be seduced by doctrines of devils, doctrines that will lead to death and the decay of the soul and spirit. God wants us to know how to rightly divide the Word of truth and be willing to let it cut us into the men and women we need to be to manage key areas of his Kingdom. What are you being taught? Do you know how to compare it to the Word? If the only time you read your Bible or hear the Word is on Sunday mornings or through a screen, you will be vulnerable to deception. The best meals are meals that are cooked at home. The best cookbook for your spiritual meals is the Bible. It is best to know the organic ingredients of God's Word for yourself so that you won't consume the GMO versions of it. Know the Word for yourself so that when you do eat out (go to church), you will know what to eat and what to pass on.

Take some time to watch the videos below to learn how to spot a false teacher and their false teachings as well as how to study your Bible.

Videos

- How to read your Bible
- Signs of a false teacher.

Marks of a false teacher or a teacher that is preaching falsely

1. Their messages are more about you and them than they are about Jesus
2. They rarely talk about sin, repentance, or they mention there is no need to repent.
3. They seem too much into themselves or their brand.
4. The circle, they role with, is questionable
5. They say or allude to Jesus not being the only way
6. They twist scripture or find a way to put you and themselves into the text, making it again all about you and them.

Where is your trust level with God in this areas?				
Why the # above?	How can you increase your trust in Him in this area?			
Where's your EQ levels? →	Clueless	Cloudy	Somewhat clear	Confidently clear
Why did you select the option above?	What are you discerning is going on in this area?			
How sound are you scripturally in understanding this matter?	Sound	Not as sound as I should be		
If applicable, what scriptures should you meditate on to increase your soundness?				

Who are your favorite preachers or teachers? →	
Why are they your favorite?	
What do they predominately teach?	
Are their messages more about Jesus or you and them?	
Do they mention in healthy way sin, repentance and dying to self or do you rarely hear them mentioned	
Does their platform point to Jesus or do they point to them?	

Who are their friends and what fruit do they bear? (check their social media accounts)	
When they preach from a text do they twist it or do they speak truth from it? (Read 10 versus above and below the text to see if it's in context.	
What is their temperament?	
What would be the effects of listening to their messages?	
What does the word of God say about them?	
Do you idolize them?	

How are they affecting your time, energy, self-care, stewardships and targeting your goals?	
Are they a counterfeit or counterpart teacher?	

OPPORTUNITIES

Opportunities and Ambitions

Not all open doors are held open by God. The problem is not always the closed doors but the ones that open for us. We confuse all open doors as a sign that this is the way God wants us to walk through. You will come across a lot of opportunities in your life, but you must know the difference. Our lives should be on pace with God. We should develop a relationship with the Holy Ghost that is so deep that we, at a moment's notice, know what window of opportunity to climb through. See, life is full of possibilities. Right now, you have the chance to do a lot of things, but it's within the patterns of your obedience to the Holy Spirit that will determine if you capitalize on all the ones that are for you. We miss tailored opportunities due to poor patterns. There is a saying that says success happens when opportunity meets preparation. No preparation, no capitalized opportunities. But beware, there are counterfeit opportunities that aim to capitalize on your preparation as well. The devil is a gentleman too at opening doors he will open doors quick to gain ownership or control of your development. How many musicians, artists, singers, preachers, talented and gifted people have prepared themselves their whole lives for a moment but through impulsiveness, walked through the devil's door?

Some people right now are trapped in contracts and situation-ships begging to get out. See, the blessings of God adds no sorrow. It may add struggle, but never sorrow; there is a difference. No matter what you do for God, there will be a struggle, but there will never be sorrow. Sorrow means resentment; it means regret. It means you wish you never done it or accepted it. Satan's deals will always be good initially; how else will he get you to buy-in. He knows that once you taste and like what he has to offer, he can use that addiction to access your gifts and talents. He wants your gifts and talents to build his Kingdom, not God's. Do you have sorrow with your blessings?

You must also understand that your most significant opportunities are oftentimes masked in obstacles. Many people have walked away from significant opportunities due to them thinking it was an obstacle. Obstacles make us. Often we will feel considerable opposition in the areas of our greatest opportunity to grow and mature. Many people have left God's job, church, plan, etc. due to either opposition, laziness, or not wanting to be stretched. Don't run from obstacles or be influenced to walk away from the opposition—those who run or are influenced away typically climb through Satan's window of opportunity. What open doors are you facing?

Where is your trust level with God in this areas?										
1	2	3	4	5		6	7	8	9	10
Why the # above?						How can you increase your trust in Him in this area?				
Where's your EQ levels? →		Clueless	Cloudy		Somewhat clear			Confidently clear	
Why did you select the option above?						What are you discerning is going on in this area?				
How sound are you scripturally in understanding this matter?						Sound	Not as sound as I should be			
If applicable, what scriptures should you meditate on to increase your soundness?										

What opportunities or masked obstacles do you have in front of you? → Questions ↓	
How prepared are you for them?	
What is the temperament of the opportunity?	
What would be the end result if you pursued this opportunity?	
What are you discerning God is saying to you about this opportunity?	

What does the word of God say about this opportunity?	
Is it the right time to pursue this opportunity?	
How could this opportunity affect your time, energy, self-care/stewardship and you targeting your goals?	

Ambition

Luke 9:25

For what does it profit a man if he gains the whole world and loses or forfeits himself?

It is pointless to gain without God. Many people are pursuing counterfeit ambitions leading them into counterfeit careers. They are lured by their desire to be kings and queens with no need for a God. Better is a little where the fear of the lord is than with much without it. It is better to be content with what you have than to strive to have everything. God is your provider, and those who know this slow their lives down and enjoy each day God has made for them. Trust me; I know the lures of ambition and how it will motivate you to move outside God's pace. I know how it is to have an aim to build an empire here to make my name great. But that's all vain and fleeting. Our ambition should be to honor God with and in everything, to be family men and women, raising Godly seed, advancing his Kingdom, and loving our neighbors. We should be about our father's business. It's unfortunate how many people are miles away from where they need to be? It's crazy how many people's ambitions have them blinded from the obvious, blinded from their sons, daughters, wives, and husbands' needs. The Bible says to love not the world, nor the things in the world; if any man loves the world, the father's love is not in him. For all that is in the world are the lust of the flesh, the lust of the eye, and the pride of life that is passing away with this world. It is not wise to fall in love with something that is passing away. Why do you want to be successful? Is it to prove to your family, friends, or foes that you are somebody? Your somebodieness comes from God. Those who know they are accepted and loved by God do not need to rush or prove anything because they are fully content in the one that chose them. You don't have to prove anything to anyone. It is better to go at God's pace and get to where you got to go unscathed than to have to repeat multiple steps or be surrounded by regrets and consequences. Anything gathered quickly leaves quickly. Slow money stays around longer than quick money.

Where is your trust level with God in this areas?										
1	2	3	4	5	6	7	8	9	10	
Why the # above?						How can you increase your trust in Him in this area?				

Where's your EQ levels? →	Clueless	Cloudy	Somewhat clear	Confidently clear
Why did you select the option above?		What are you discerning is going on in this area?		
How sound are you scripturally in understanding this matter?			Sound	Not as sound as I should be
If applicable, what scriptures should you meditate on to increase your soundness?				

What are you ambitious about? What drives you, and why? →	
What is your temperament now in pursuing your aspirations? (hot, cold or indifferent)	

What is the end goal of your aspirations? Who benefits and doesn't benefit?	
What would be the end result if you had what you are ambitious about right now?	
What does the Word of God say about your kind of ambition?	
Is this the right time to pursue these aspirations?	

TOOLS

Tools

Tools should aid a work not to take away from it. There are specific tools for a specific task. Not all tools are needed at every moment. You can't build a house with just a wrench; you may need it periodically, but you can't solely complete a house with one. You need all kinds of tools. Not all tools need to be used. Sexual tools were only meant to build up a marriage, not a boyfriend and girlfriend relationship. Tools outside of the right timing can be destructive. Whether body part, money, car or house, each tool is a tool to solve a problem. As believers, we are to use these parts properly and through the help of the Holy Spirit. A tool not used according to its purpose can be a weapon. Are the tools in your toolbox hurting or helping you? Are they hurting or helping someone else? The Bible says it is better to cut an arm or pull an eye out (metaphorically) if it causes you to stumble than to have all your members or parts and hit hell wide open. It is better to cut people, ideas, thoughts, friends, shows, songs, etc. and live life how God wants you to live rather than have these things and become earthly and ineffective for the Kingdom of God. We are holy tools, tools that should only have God's fingerprints on them, and everything we touch or use should be used for His glory.

Where is your trust level with God in this areas?									
1	2	3	4	5	6	7	8	9	10
Why the # above?					How can you increase your trust in Him in this area?					
Where's your EQ levels? →				Clueless	Cloudy	Somewhat clear			Confidently clear	
Why did you select the option above?					What are you discerning is going on in this area?					

How sound are you scripturally in understanding this matter?	Sound	Not as sound as I should be
If applicable, what scriptures should you meditate on to increase your soundness?		

Tools → Questions ↓			
How are you using them?			
What is your temperament in using them?			
What will be the end result of using them right now the way you are using them?			

What does the scripture say about the tools you're using and how you are using them?			
Is it the right time to use this tool?			

THOUGHTS

Thoughts and Words.

Your words are the fruit of your thoughts, and your thoughts are the fruit of your influences. How you think, how you speak, and the environments you allow to influences you matters. Thoughts and words were designed to help carve a path for you. They were your tools to mold ideas, manage your place of dominion, and build up those around you. One of the top bad habits we have as people is flawed thinking and speaking habits. For some people, it's too late. Their flawed thinking and speaking patterns have already created a world they are forced to live in. Your world today is a reflection of yesterday's words. Words and thoughts have extreme power, and Satan knows it. If he can have us think poorly, then we will live poorly. There is a proper way to think and speak, and our worlds won't turn out properly until our words do. The Bible says that as a person thinks in their heart, so are they it also says that the tongue is a rudder guiding the ship. The good thing about it all is that your words and your thoughts are yours. You have the power to bite your lip and to nip your heart. You can think above your circumstances and speak according to God's Word for you. If you want to change the world, you are living in change your thoughts and your words.

God cares about how we think and talk because he gave the thoughts and the words of a person, power. Demons listen carefully. They know the power of your thoughts and words; they know the legal clearances they give them. Suppose Satan can infuse your environment with demonic influences, shaping the way you think. In that case, he can have you speak in alliance to it, opening the door for his demons to occupy what your words legally allow. He doesn't want you to communicate with clarity and authority. He doesn't want you tearing his Kingdom down with your comments. He wants your faith-filled words to give him rights into your life, not them rightly destroying his Kingdom. Whose world is crumbling down around your words yours or the devils?

Where is your trust level with God in this areas?									
1	2	3	4	5	6	7	8	9	10
Why the # above?					How can you increase your trust in Him in this area?					

Where's your EQ levels? →	Clueless	Cloudy	Somewhat clear	Confidently clear
Why did you select the option above?		What are you discerning is going on in this area?		
How sound are you scripturally in understanding this matter?			Sound	Not as sound as I should be
If applicable, what scriptures should you meditate on to increase your soundness?				

What category represents your words overall? →		Poor	Proper
What category represents your thoughts? →		Poor	Proper
Where did this kind of thinking and talking stem from?			
Thinking	Talking		
What is the temperament behind your words and thinking and why?			
Words	Thinking		
What is the end result of this way of thinking and talking?			

What does the Word of God say about this way of thinking and speaking?

Processing your thoughts
What thought are you struggling with?
Where did this thought come from?
What does the word of God say about the gist of your thought?

S1	S2	S3	S4

What makes this thought vain or valid?
What new thought should you put in its place?

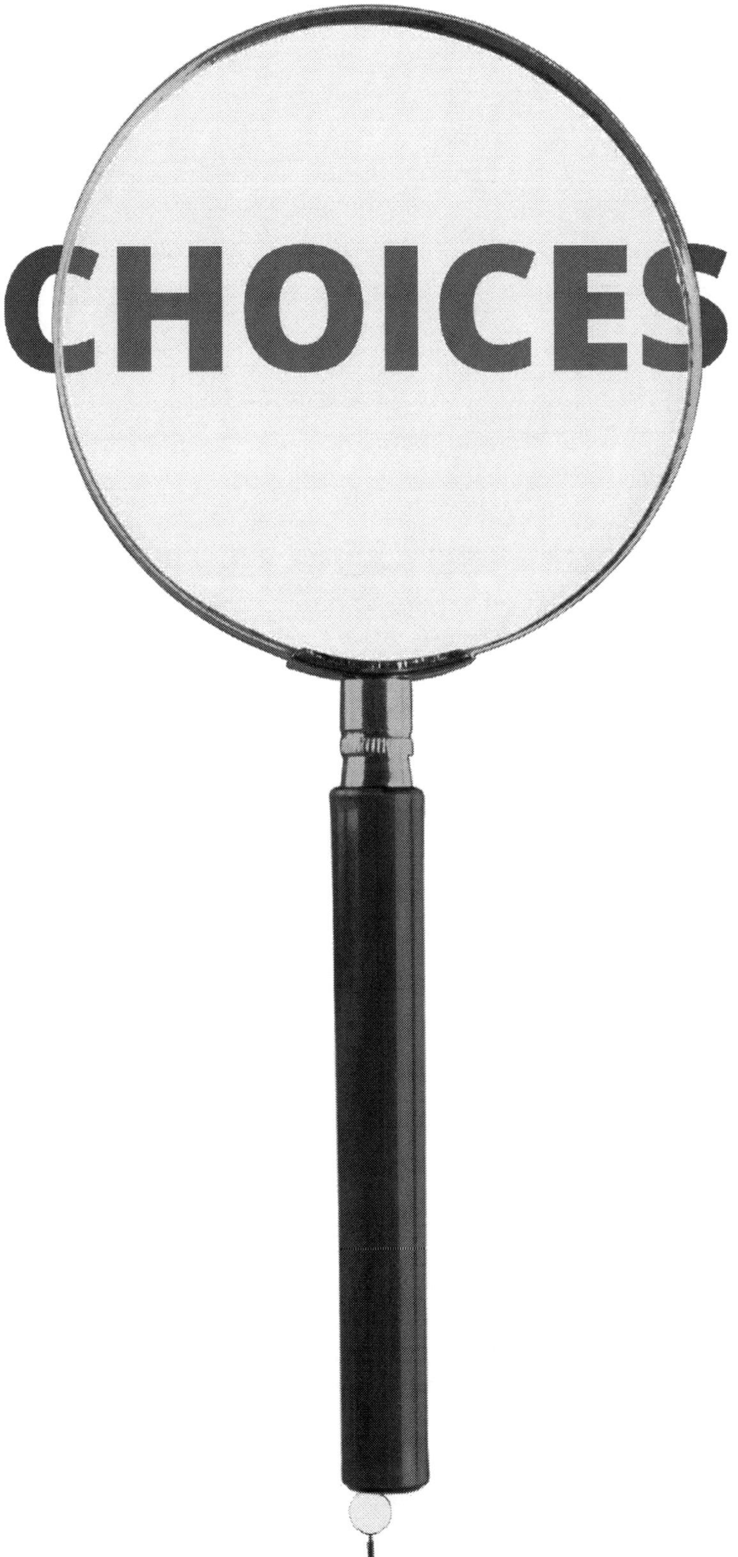
CHOICES

Choices

There are counterfeit and counterpart choices. Choices like your words are powerful. All choices, no matter what, have consequences, whether good or bad or immediate or eventually. Significant decisions must be audited first. We are to use our renewed minds to make the right choices. God has given us the gift of free will, and we can get out of life as much as is allocated to us, but to do so, we have to walk wisely. So many people are choosing the wrong things to be a part of their lives. Not everything has a receipt for you to take back or a lifetime warranty to get a new one or refurbish the one you have. Some consequences are lifelong. God can save you from your sins, but He doesn't always save you from its consequences. Demons prey on people who don't know how to count. He preys on them because those who can't do basic spiritual math will always draft the wrong conclusions. Demons want to fill your life full of consequences to make it extremely difficult for you to dedicate your time, energy, and resources to fulfilling your purpose. Your purpose deserves fresh energy renewed daily through eating right, rest, sleep, and joy, but if those energies are taken up tending to negative consequences, you will never fulfill your purpose. It is always vital to think three moves ahead because not all consequences are set within the first move. This system wants us to be impulsive and impatient, leading us to make quick decisions without thinking about them. He knows that if he can cause you to see what you desire to do more significant than it should be seen, he can get you to latch on to his bait. They put the sweetest part of their trap behind the initial decision hoping to create an addiction, and once they got you, the second move or season is designed to get you comfortable. Once they have you satisfied, then you are hit with the consequence. But when you can think three moves ahead, you will be able to spot the enemy's apparent tricks.

Where is your trust level with God in this areas?											
1	2	3	4	5	6	7	8	9	10
Why the # above?						How can you increase your trust in Him in this area?			

Where's your EQ levels? →	Clueless	Cloudy	Somewhat clear	Confidently clear
Why did you select the option above?		What are you discerning is going on in this area?		
How sound are you scripturally in understanding this matter?			Sound	Not as sound as I should be
If applicable, what scriptures should you meditate on to increase your soundness?				
S1	S2	S3	S4	S5

What category best describes the type of choices you make? →	Good	Bad
Why are you making these kinds of decisions?		
What is your temperament when making these choices, and why?		

What would be your end result if you continuously make these kinds of choices?
What does the Word of God say about these kind of choices?
Is this the right timing to make these decisions?
How are your choices affecting your time, energy, self-care/stewardship and you targeting your goals?

Before you make a decision – Think 3 moves ahead.

What choice are you about to make?				
Is it a good or bad decision? →			Good	Bad
Why the answer above?				
Consequence of the 1st move	Consequence of the 2nd move	Consequence of the 3rd move		
How will this choice affect your time, energy, self-care/stewardships and you targeting your goals?				

PLACES

Locations and Places

Locations are tools. They are designed to house and provide resources for our purpose. It's astounding how many people move without God. Pursue and quit jobs without consulting him. Not all locations are a part of God's will for your life. Locations have above them governing bodies. Cities, towns, key facilities, and homes have over them territorial flags. Spiritual flags that mark territories for either God or Satan. A believer who doesn't know who they are or their authority will walk behind enemy lines with no way or knowledge to defend themselves. Discernment must guide us because if God moves you into a city or gives you a job or place to stay, then wherever you are will be respected. The will of God will never lead you, where His grace won't keep you. There is safety in the will of God and danger outside of it. Never long to lodge somewhere more than you long to lodge in the presence of God. Blossom, where God has placed you, don't bail from it.

Also, don't be discouraged when it's time to move. Sometimes God ruffles the nest to get you to fly to a safer tree. Never love a place so much that you are not able to leave it. Many people have lost their lives, resources, etc. due to staying at a place God was trying to get them to leave. No matter where you desire to be, where God wants you will always be safer and better.

Where is your trust level with God in this areas?									
1	2	3	4	5	6	7	8	9	10
Why the # above?					How can you increase your trust in Him in this area?				
Where's your EQ levels? →					Clueless	Cloudy	Somewhat clear		Confidently clear

Why did you select the option above?	What are you discerning is going on in this area?		
How sound are you scripturally in understanding this matter?		Sound	Not as sound as I should be
If applicable, what scriptures should you meditate on to increase your soundness?			
S1	S2	S3	S4	S5

Where do you live, work, and or frequent the most? → Questions ↓	Live	Work	Frequent
Are these places where God has placed you?			
What are you influenced to do there?			
Did you consult God about this place? If so/ if not, why?			

Where does God want you at the moment?			
What could be God's reason to have you where you are?			
Why don't you like where you are? Is it a valid reason to leave?			
How are these places affecting your time, energy, self-care/ stewardship and you targeting your goals?			

EMOTIONS

Emotions

Emotional intelligence is key to winning in life. Knowing your emotions and recognizing others' emotions will help you navigate life with little to no issues. Many people have no control over their emotions, and their demons love it. People who act before they think are not safe to be around because you don't know what their triggers are, and even if you do, other people who invade may not. Do you have emotions, or do your emotions have you? Why do your emotions have you? What triggers certain emotions, and in what ways can you tame them? The answer to these questions is vital.

Emotions are just indicators of how you feel but are not always factual. So many people have become emotionally attached to the wrong things due to them ignoring the red flags. You must always seek the facts behind your feelings. Your emotions should not always dictate your motions. We must train our brains to look through our emotions to make sure they are truly warranted. There is nothing wrong with feeling sad, but it is incredibly wrong and a sin to be depressed. Most people are not at the level they need to be to nip sadness. Sadness should always be channeled to God and not left unattended. Sadness left to itself with no investigation of God's Word to stabilize it will turn to depression, and this is true with every emotion. Emotions left unattended or not sifted by God's Word will decay and turn to ravenous emotions; emotions that rule us. This world system is designed to make people emotional and easily triggered. It is designed to think for people.

Whoever controls how a person thinks can control the way they feel and whoever controls the way a person feels can control their actions. We were given emotions to help us feel the world and feel it the right way. To weep with those that weep and rejoice with those that rejoice. To find our joy in God and to enjoy him. Joy is the best emotion to have. It is the one emotion that regulates all other emotions. Joy is a perspective that settles our souls, keeping it from becoming too emotional about things God has already settled. Those who love and trust God and can predict how things will turn out for their good will know how to process their emotions. Now don't get me wrong; you will face some tough times, and this is in no way to skip over the fact that life sucks, but no matter what we are facing or will meet, God is there and has it already worked out in your favor. What you should always do in the meantime is to process what you are feeling? What caused this feeling? How is or could God be using this for my good? Are these feeling's valid or vain? How can I channel these feelings to God? Where must I go to vent these feelings? How can I channel these emotions to something productive? You must always give yourself time to vent and vet your feelings so that you will lean more to the side of victor and not a victim.

Where is your trust level with God in this areas?										
1	2	3	4	5	6	7	8	9	10	

Why the # above?	How can you increase your trust in Him in this area?

Where's your EQ levels? →	Clueless	Cloudy	Somewhat clear	Confidently clear

Why did you select the option above?	What are you discerning is going on in this area?

How sound are you scripturally in understanding this matter?	Sound	Not as sound as I should be

If applicable, what scriptures should you meditate on to increase your soundness?

What are your dominant emotions and what conceived them or what event sparked these emotions?	
Who or what triggers these emotions and how did they become triggers?	
What does the word of God say about these emotions?	
What are the facts behind these feelings?	
What feelings could you exchange with these negative feelings? And what thoughts could you think on to dilute these feelings?	

Feeling processor	
What are you feeling right now? →	
Who or what triggered this feeling?	
What were you feeling before this feeling was triggered was it positive or negative?	
Could this feeling be due to digestion?	
What does the word of God say about this feeling?	
What actions should you do now to reverse this feeling?	
If you continue with this feeling what consequences could occur?	

Why should you overcome this feeling?	
What are the facts behind this feeling?	
What did you do with the feeling and what did you learn or what adjustments do you need to make for the next time?	

SCRIPTURAL SUPPORT

Table of Contents

Accountability – Page 190

A Parent's Duty – Page 191

Appearance – Page 193

Anger/Rage – Page 194

Arguments – Page 196

Attitude – Page 198

Bad Habits – Page 201

Baptism – Page 202

Beauty – Page 205

Belief – Page 206

Blessing – Page 207

Your Body – Page 209

Boldness – Page 212

Children – Page 213

Comfort – Page 216

Community and Church – Page 217

Communication – Page 220

Conceit/Pride – Page 222

Confidence – Page 223

Confusion – Page 225

Contentment – Page 226

Correction – Page 227

Courage – Page 231

Dating – Page 232

Death – Page 234

Depression - Page 238

Emotions – Page 240

Enemies – Page 235

Envy – Page 242

Eternal Life – Page 244

Faith – Page 247

Fasting – Page 249

Fear/Worry – Page 251

Food & Clothes – Page 254

Forgiveness – Page 255

Friends – Page 259

Fruitfulness – Page 257

Giving – Page 260

God's Correction – Page 263

God's Protection – Page 264

Gossip/Rumors – Page 267

Grace – Page 268

Guidance – Page 270

Healing – Page 289

Heart – Page 273

Help In Troubles – Page 277

Holy Spirit – Page 280

Honesty – Page 282

Hope – Page 285

Humiliation – Page 286

Humility – Page 287

Husbands – Page 288

Impatience – Page 292

Increased Life – Page 293

Integrity – Page 294

Joy/Happiness – Page 297

Kindness – Page 299

Laziness – Page 300

Loneliness – Page 302

Love – Page 303

Loving God – Page 306

Lust – Page 308

Lying – Page 310

Marriage – Page 312

Meekness – Page 313

Money – Page 315

Obedience – Page 318

Patience – Page 321

Peace – Page 322

Persecution – Page 323

Prayer – Page 326

Prosperity – Page 329

Purpose – Page 331

Repentance – Page 333

Rest and Sleep – Page 336

Reputation – Page 338

Revenge – Page 340

Salvation – Page 342

Satan – Page 344

Seeking God – Page 346

Self-Denial – Page 348

Selfishness – Page 349

Sexual Sins – Page 351

Shame – Page 353

Sickness/Disease – Page 354

Sin – Page 355

Slander – Page 358

Stillness – Page 359

Submission – Page 361

Temptations – Page 362

The Love of God – Page 363

Time – Page 367

Thoughts and The Mind – Page 369

Trials – Page 371

Trust – Page 372

Wisdom – Page 373

Work – Page 376

Youth – 380

Scriptures on Accountability

2 Corinthians 5:10

"For we must all appear before the judgment seat of Christ, so that each one may receive what is due for what he has done in the body, whether good or evil.

Romans 14:12

"So then each of us will give an account of himself to God."

Proverbs 27:17

"As iron sharpens iron, So a man sharpens the countenance of his friend."

Matthew 12:36-37

"I tell you, on the Day of Judgment people will give account for every careless word they speak, 37 for by your words you will be justified, and by your words you will be condemned."

Galatians 6:1-5

"Brothers, if anyone is caught in any transgression, you who are spiritual should restore him in a spirit of gentleness. Keep watch on yourself, lest you too be tempted. Bear one another's burdens, and so fulfill the law of Christ. For if anyone thinks he is something, when he is nothing, he deceives himself. But let each one test his own work, and then his reason to boast will be in himself alone and not in his neighbor. For each will have to bear his own load."

James 5:16

"Therefore, confess your sins to one another and pray for one another, that you may be healed. The prayer of a righteous person has great power as it is working."

1 Thessalonians 5:11

"Therefore encourage one another and build one another up, just as you are doing."

Hebrews 4:13

"And no creature is hidden from his sight, but all are naked and exposed to the eyes of him to whom we must give account."

Ecclesiastes 4:9-12

"Two are better than one, because they have a good reward for their toil. For if they fall, one will lift up his fellow. But woe to him who is alone when he falls and has not another to lift him up! Again, if two lie together, they keep warm, but how can one keep warm alone? And though a man might prevail against one who is alone, two will withstand him—a threefold cord is not quickly broken."

Jeremiah 17:10

"I the Lord search the heart and test the mind, to give every man according to his ways, according to the fruit of his deeds."

Matthew 7:3-5

"Why do you see the speck that is in your brother's eye, but do not notice the log that is in your own eye? Or how can you say to your brother, 'Let me take the speck out of your eye,' when there is the log in your own eye? You hypocrite, first take the log out of your own eye, and then you will see clearly to take the speck out of your brother's eye."

Luke 16:10-12

"One who is faithful in a very little is also faithful in much, and one who is dishonest in a very little is also dishonest in much. If then you have not been faithful in the unrighteous wealth, who will entrust to you the true riches? And if you have not been faithful in that which is another's, who will give you that which is your own?"

James 3:1

"Not many of you should become teachers, my brothers, for you know that we who teach will be judged with greater strictness."

Children

Scriptures for Parents

Proverbs 22:6

"Train up a child in the way he should go, and when he is old he will not depart from it."

Colossians 3:21

"Fathers, do not provoke your children, lest they become discouraged."

Proverbs 29:17

"Correct your son, and he will give you rest; Yes, he will give delight to your soul."

Deuteronomy 11:19

"You shall teach them to your children, speaking of them when you sit in your house, when you walk by the way, when you lie down, and when you rise up."

Psalms 78:4-7

"Telling to the generation to come the praises of the Lord, and His strength and His wonderful works that He has done. For He established a testimony in Jacob, and appointed a law in Israel, which He commanded our fathers, that they should make them known to their children; That the generation to come might know them, the children who would be born, that they may arise and declare them to their children, that they may set their hope in God, and not forget the works of God, but keep His commandments..."

Genesis 18:19

"For I have known him, in order that he may command his children and his household after him, that they keep the way of the Lord, to do righteousness and justice, that the Lord may bring to Abraham what He has spoken to him."

Exodus 13:8

"And you shall tell your son in that day, saying, 'This is done because of what the Lord did for me when I came up from Egypt"

Deuteronomy 4:9,10

"Only take heed to yourself, and diligently keep yourself, lest you forget the things your eyes have seen, and lest they depart from your heart all the days of your life. And teach them to your children and your grandchildren, especially concerning the day you stood before the Lord your God in Horeb, when the Lord said to me, 'Gather the people to Me, and I will let them hear My words, that they may learn to fear Me all the days they live on the earth, and that they may teach their children"

Ephesians 6:4

"And you, fathers, do not provoke your children to wrath, but bring them up in the training and admonition of the Lord."

Scriptures on Appearance

Genesis 1:27

"So God created man in his own image, in the image of God he created him; male and female he created them."

John 7:24

"Do not judge according to appearance, but judge with righteous judgment."

1 Samuel 16:7

"But the Lord said to Samuel, "Do not look on his appearance or on the height of his stature, because I have rejected him. For the Lord sees not as man sees: man looks on the outward appearance, but the Lord looks on the heart."

2 Corinthians 5:12

"For we do not commend ourselves again to you, but give you opportunity to boast on our behalf, that you may have an answer for those who boast in appearance and not in heart."

1 Corinthians 6:19-20

"Or do you not know that your body is a temple of the Holy Spirit within you, whom you have from God? You are not your own, for you were bought with a price. So glorify God in your body."

1 Peter 3: 3-4

"Do not let your adornment be merely outward - arranging the hair, wearing gold, or putting on fine apparel - rather let it be the hidden person of the heart, with the incorruptible beauty of a gentle and quiet spirit, which is very precious in the sight of God."

Matthew 6:16

"Moreover, when you fast, do not be like the hypocrites, with a sad countenance. For they disfigure their faces that they may appear to men to be fasting. Assuredly, I say to you, they have their reward."

1 Thessalonians 5:22

"Abstain from every form (appearance reads the KJV) of evil

Proverbs 31:30

"Charm is deceitful, and beauty is vain, but a woman who fears the Lord is to be praised."

Psalm 139:14

"I praise you, for I am fearfully and wonderfully made. Wonderful are your works; my soul knows it very well."

Matthew 23:28

"So you also outwardly appear righteous to others, but within you are full of hypocrisy and lawlessness."

Colossians 3:17

"And whatever you do, in word or deed, do everything in the name of the Lord Jesus, giving thanks to God the Father through him."

1 Peter 3:3-4

"Do not let your adorning be external—the braiding of hair and the putting on of gold jewelry, or the clothing you wear— but let your adorning be the hidden person of the heart with the imperishable beauty of a gentle and quiet spirit, which in God's sight is very precious."

John 4:24

God is spirit, and those who worship him must worship in spirit and truth."

Scriptures on Anger

James 1:19, 20

"So then, my beloved brethren, let every man be swift to hear, slow to speak, slow to wrath; for the wrath of man does not produce the righteousness of God."

Ephesians 4:31, 32

"Let all bitterness, wrath, anger, clamor, and evil speaking be put away from you, with all malice. And be kind to one another, tenderhearted, forgiving one another, even as God in Christ forgave you."

Psalms 145:8

"The Lord is gracious and full of compassion, slow to anger and great in mercy."

Nehemiah 9:17

"You are God, Ready to pardon, and Gracious and merciful, Slow to anger, Abundant in kindness..."

Psalms 30:5

"For His anger is but for a moment, His favor is for life; Weeping may endure for a night, But joy comes in the morning.

Ecclesiastes 7:9

"Do not hasten in your spirit to be angry, for anger rests in the bosom of fools."

Proverbs 16:32

"He who is slow to anger is better than the mighty, and he who rules his spirit than he who takes a city."

Proverbs 15:18

"A wrathful man stirs up strife, but he who is slow to anger calms contention."

Proverbs 29:22

"An angry man stirs up strife, and a furious man abounds in transgression."

Psalms 37:8

"Cease from anger, and forsake wrath; do not fret - it only causes harm."

Proverbs 22:24, 25

"Make no friendship with an angry man, and with a furious man do not go, lest you learn his ways and set a snare for your soul. "

Proverbs 15:1

"A soft answer turns away wrath, but a harsh word stirs up anger."

Colossians 3:21

"Fathers, do not provoke your children, lest they become discouraged."

Proverbs 19:11

"The discretion of a man makes him slow to anger, and his glory is to overlook a transgression."

Proverbs 21:19

"Better to dwell in the wilderness, than with a contentious and angry woman."

Matthew 5:22

"But I say to you that whoever is angry with his brother without a cause shall be in danger of the judgment..."

Romans 12:19, 21

"Beloved, do not avenge yourselves, but rather give place to wrath; for it is written, "Vengeance is Mine, I will repay," says the Lord. Therefore 'If your enemy is hungry, feed him; If he is thirsty, give him a drink; For in so doing you will heap coals of fire on his head.' Do not be overcome by evil, but overcome evil with good."

Proverbs 25:21, 22

"If your enemy is hungry, give him bread to eat; and if he is thirsty, give him water to drink; for so you will heap coals of fire on his head, and the Lord will reward you."

Colossians 3:8

"But now you yourselves are to put off all these: anger, wrath, malice, blasphemy, filthy language out of your mouth."

Proverbs 14:17

"A quick-tempered man acts foolishly, and a man of wicked intentions is hated."

Scriptures on Arguments

2 Timothy 2:23-25

Have nothing to do with foolish, ignorant controversies; you know that they breed quarrels. And the Lord's servant must not be quarrelsome but kind to everyone, able to teach, patiently enduring evil, correcting his opponents with gentleness. God may perhaps grant them repentance leading to a knowledge of the truth,

2 Timothy 2:14

Remind them of these things, and charge them before God not to quarrel about words, which does no good, but only ruins the hearers.

James 4:1-3

What causes quarrels and what causes fights among you? Is it not this, that your passions are at war within you? You desire and do not have, so you murder. You covet and cannot obtain, so you fight and quarrel. You do not have, because you do not ask. You ask and do not receive, because you ask wrongly, to spend it on your passions.

2 Timothy 2:16

But avoid irreverent babble, for it will lead people into more and more ungodliness,

Proverbs 21:9

It is better to live in a corner of the housetop than in a house shared with a quarrelsome wife.

Proverbs 15:1

A soft answer turns away wrath, but a harsh word stirs up anger.

2 Corinthians 10:5

We destroy arguments and every lofty opinion raised against the knowledge of God, and take every thought captive to obey Christ,

1 Timothy 6:4

He is puffed up with conceit and understands nothing. He has an unhealthy craving for controversy and for quarrels about words, which produce envy, dissension, slander, evil suspicions,

Romans 12:2

Do not be conformed to this world, but be transformed by the renewal of your mind, that by testing you may discern what is the will of God, what is good and acceptable and perfect.

Matthew 7:3

Why do you see the speck that is in your brother's eye, but do not notice the log that is in your own eye?

James 1:19

Know this, my beloved brothers: let every person be quick to hear, slow to speak, slow to anger;

Proverbs 18:2

A fool takes no pleasure in understanding, but only in expressing his opinion.

Titus 3:9

But avoid foolish controversies, genealogies, dissensions, and quarrels about the law, for they are unprofitable and worthless.

Philippians 2:14-16

Do all things without grumbling or questioning, that you may be blameless and innocent, children of God without blemish in the midst of a crooked and twisted generation, among whom you shine as lights in the world, holding fast to the word of life, so that in the day of Christ I may be proud that I did not run in vain or labor in vain.

Romans 14:1

As for the one who is weak in faith, welcome him, but not to quarrel over opinions.

Proverbs 21:23

Whoever keeps his mouth and his tongue keeps himself out of trouble.

Scriptures on Attitude

Philippians 2:14-15

Do all things without grumbling or questioning, that you may be blameless and innocent, children of God without blemish in the midst of a crooked and twisted generation, among whom you shine as lights in the world,

Proverbs 17:22

A joyful heart is good medicine, but a crushed spirit dries up the bones.

Philippians 4:8

Finally, brothers, whatever is true, whatever is honorable, whatever is just, whatever is pure, whatever is lovely, whatever is commendable, if there is any excellence, if there is anything worthy of praise, think about these things.

Philippians 2:5

Have this mind among yourselves, which is yours in Christ Jesus,

Romans 12:2

Do not be conformed to this world, but be transformed by the renewal of your mind, that by testing you may discern what is the will of God, what is good and acceptable and perfect.

Philippians 4:8-9

Finally, brothers, whatever is true, whatever is honorable, whatever is just, whatever is pure, whatever is lovely, whatever is commendable, if there is any excellence, if there is anything worthy of praise, think about these things. What you have learned and received and heard and seen in me—practice these things, and the God of peace will be with you.

Colossians 3:23

Whatever you do, work heartily, as for the Lord and not for men,

Philippians 2:14

Do all things without grumbling or questioning,

Ephesians 4:23

And to be renewed in the spirit of your minds,

1 John 1:9

If we confess our sins, he is faithful and just to forgive us our sins and to cleanse us from all unrighteousness.

1 Peter 4:1

Since therefore Christ suffered in the flesh, arm yourselves with the same way of thinking, for whoever has suffered in the flesh has ceased from sin,

James 4:10

Humble yourselves before the Lord, and he will exalt you.

2 Peter 3:9

The Lord is not slow to fulfill his promise as some count slowness, but is patient toward you, not wishing that any should perish, but that all should reach repentance.

Colossians 3:17

And whatever you do, in word or deed, do everything in the name of the Lord Jesus, giving thanks to God the Father through him.

Matthew 6:33

But seek first the kingdom of God and his righteousness, and all these things will be added to you.

Ephesians 6:4

Fathers, do not provoke your children to anger, but bring them up in the discipline and instruction of the Lord.

Ephesians 4:31-32

Let all bitterness and wrath and anger and clamor and slander be put away from you, along with all malice. Be kind to one another, tenderhearted, forgiving one another, as God in Christ forgave you.

Galatians 5:22-23

But the fruit of the Spirit is love, joy, peace, patience, kindness, goodness, faithfulness, gentleness, self-control; against such things there is no law.

Colossians 3:10

And have put on the new self, which is being renewed in knowledge after the image of its creator.

Hebrews 13:15

Through him then let us continually offer up a sacrifice of praise to God, that is, the fruit of lips that acknowledge his name.

Philippians 2:3-5

Do nothing from rivalry or conceit, but in humility count others more significant than yourselves. Let each of you look not only to his own interests, but also to the interests of others. Have this mind among yourselves, which is yours in Christ Jesus,

1 Thessalonians 5:16-18

Rejoice always, pray without ceasing, give thanks in all circumstances; for this is the will of God in Christ Jesus for you.

Romans 15:5 May the God of endurance and encouragement grant you to live in such harmony with one another, in accord with Christ Jesus,

Philippians 4:6

Do not be anxious about anything, but in everything by prayer and supplication with thanksgiving let your requests be made known to God.

Matthew 5:22

But I say to you that everyone who is angry with his brother will be liable to judgment; whoever insults his brother will be liable to the council; and whoever says, 'You fool!' will be liable to the hell of fire.

Philippians 1:27

Only let your manner of life be worthy of the gospel of Christ, so that whether I come and see you or am absent, I may hear of you that you are standing firm in one spirit, with one mind striving side by side for the faith of the gospel,

Colossians 3:16

Let the word of Christ dwell in you richly, teaching and admonishing one another in all wisdom, singing psalms and hymns and spiritual songs, with thankfulness in your hearts to God.

Colossians 3:15

And let the peace of Christ rule in your hearts, to which indeed you were called in one body. And be thankful.

Romans 12:10

Love one another with brotherly affection. Outdo one another in showing honor.

Scriptures on Bad Habits

1 Corinthians 6:12

"All things are lawful for me," but not all things are helpful. "All things are lawful for me," but I will not be enslaved by anything.

2 Timothy 2:16

"But shun profane and idle babblings, for they will increase to more ungodliness."

Galatians 5:19-21

"Now the works of the flesh are evident, which are: adultery, fornication, uncleanness, lewdness, idolatry, sorcery, hatred, contentions, jealousies, outbursts of wrath, selfish ambitions, dissensions, heresies, envy, murders, drunkenness, revelries, and the like; of which I tell you beforehand, just as I also told you in time past, that those who practice such things will not inherit the kingdom of God."

Proverbs 17:20

"He who has a deceitful heart finds no good, and he who has a perverse tongue falls into evil."

Proverbs 12:19-22

The truthful lip shall be established forever, but a lying tongue is but for a moment. Deceit is in the heart of those who devise evil, but counselors of peace have joy. No grave trouble will overtake the righteous, but the wicked shall be filled with evil. Lying lips are an abomination to the Lord, but those who deal truthfully are His delight.

Mark 7:20-23

"And he said, "What comes out of a person is what defiles him. For from within, out of the heart of man, come evil thoughts, sexual immorality, theft, murder, adultery, coveting, wickedness, deceit, sensuality, envy, slander, pride, foolishness. All these evil things come from within, and they defile a person."

Scriptures on Baptism

Acts 2:38

And Peter said to them, "Repent and be baptized every one of you in the name of Jesus Christ for the forgiveness of your sins, and you will receive the gift of the Holy Spirit.

Acts 22:16

And now why do you wait? Rise and be baptized and wash away your sins, calling on his name.'

1 Peter 3:21

Baptism, which corresponds to this, now saves you, not as a removal of dirt from the body but as an appeal to God for a good conscience, through the resurrection of Jesus Christ,

Mark 16:16

Whoever believes and is baptized will be saved, but whoever does not believe will be condemned.

John 3:5

Jesus answered, "Truly, truly, I say to you, unless one is born of water and the Spirit, he cannot enter the kingdom of God.

Matthew 28:19

Go therefore and make disciples of all nations, baptizing them in the name of the Father and of the Son and of the Holy Spirit,

Romans 6:4

We were buried therefore with him by baptism into death, in order that, just as Christ was raised from the dead by the glory of the Father, we too might walk in newness of life.

1 Corinthians 12:13

For in one Spirit we were all baptized into one body—Jews or Greeks, slaves or free—and all were made to drink of one Spirit.

Ephesians 4:5

One Lord, one faith, one baptism,

Galatians 3:27

For as many of you as were baptized into Christ have put on Christ.

Romans 6:3-4

Do you not know that all of us who have been baptized into Christ Jesus were baptized into his death? We were buried therefore with him by baptism into death, in order that, just as Christ was raised from the dead by the glory of the Father, we too might walk in newness of life.

Acts 2:41

So those who received his word were baptized, and there were added that day about three thousand souls.

Matthew 3:11

"I baptize you with water for repentance, but he who is coming after me is mightier than I, whose sandals I am not worthy to carry. He will baptize you with the Holy Spirit and fire.

Romans 6:3

Do you not know that all of us who have been baptized into Christ Jesus were baptized into his death?

Matthew 3:16

And when Jesus was baptized, immediately he went up from the water, and behold, the heavens were opened to him, and he saw the Spirit of God descending like a dove and coming to rest on him;

Colossians 2:12

Having been buried with him in baptism, in which you were also raised with him through faith in the powerful working of God, who raised him from the dead.

Colossians 2:12-13

Having been buried with him in baptism, in which you were also raised with him through faith in the powerful working of God, who raised him from the dead. And you, who were dead in your trespasses and the uncircumcision of your flesh, God made alive together with him, having forgiven us all our trespasses,

Matthew 28:19-20

Go therefore and make disciples of all nations, baptizing them in the name of the Father and of the Son and of the Holy Spirit, teaching them to observe all that I have commanded you. And behold, I am with you always, to the end of the age."

Acts 8:38

And he commanded the chariot to stop, and they both went down into the water, Philip and the eunuch, and he baptized him.

John 1:33

I myself did not know him, but he who sent me to baptize with water said to me, 'He on whom you see the Spirit descend and remain, this is he who baptizes with the Holy Spirit.'

Acts 8:12

But when they believed Philip as he preached good news about the kingdom of God and the name of Jesus Christ, they were baptized, both men and women.

Acts 10:48

And he commanded them to be baptized in the name of Jesus Christ. Then they asked him to remain for some days.

Acts 10:47

"Can anyone withhold water for baptizing these people, who have received the Holy Spirit just as we have?"

Mark 1:4

John appeared, baptizing in the wilderness and proclaiming a baptism of repentance for the forgiveness of sins.

Titus 3:5

He saved us, not because of works done by us in righteousness, but according to his own mercy, by the washing of regeneration and renewal of the Holy Spirit,

Scriptures on Beauty

Ecclesiastes 3:11

"He has made everything beautiful in its time..."

Psalm 139:14

I praise you, for I am fearfully and wonderfully made. Wonderful are your works; my soul knows it very well.

Proverbs 31:30

"Charm is deceitful and beauty is passing, but a woman who fears the Lord, she shall be praised."

Proverbs 11:22

"As a ring of gold in a swine's snout, so is a lovely woman who lacks discretion."

1 Peter 3:3-4

"Do not let your adornment be merely outward - arranging the hair, wearing gold, or putting on fine apparel - rather let it be the hidden person of the heart, with the incorruptible beauty of a gentle and quiet spirit, which is very precious in the sight of God."

Matthew 23:27,28

"Woe to you, scribes and Pharisees, hypocrites! For you are like whitewashed tombs which indeed appear beautiful outwardly, but inside are full of dead men's bones and all uncleanness. Even so you also outwardly appear righteous to men, but inside you are full of hypocrisy and lawlessness."

Proverbs 20:29

"The glory of young men is their strength, and the splendor of old men is their gray head."

Philippians 4:8

"Finally, brethren, whatever things are true, whatever things are noble, whatever things are just, whatever things are pure, whatever things are lovely, whatever things are of good report, if there is any virtue and if there is anything praiseworthy—meditate on these things

Proverbs 6:25-29

25 Do not desire her beauty in your heart,

and do not let her capture you with her eyelashes;

26 for the price of a prostitute is only a loaf of bread,[a]

but a married woman[b] hunts down a precious life.

27 Can a man carry fire next to his chest

and his clothes not be burned?

28 Or can one walk on hot coals

and his feet not be scorched?

29 So is he who goes in to his neighbor's wife;

none who touches her will go unpunished.

Scriptures on Belief:

John 3:16

"For God so loved the world that He gave His only begotten Son, that whoever believes in Him should not perish but have everlasting life."

Acts 10:43

"To Him all the prophets witness that, through His name, whoever believes in Him will receive remission of sins."

John 1:12

"But as many as received Him, to them He gave the right to become children of God, to those who believe in His name:"

John 3:18

"He who believes in Him is not condemned; but he who does not believe is condemned already, because he has not believed in the name of the only begotten Son of God."

John 3:36

"He who believes in the Son has everlasting life; and he who does not believe the Son shall not see life, but the wrath of God abides on him."

Acts 16:31

"So they said, "Believe on the Lord Jesus Christ, and you will be saved, you and your household."

John 12:46

"I have come as a light into the world, that whoever believes in Me should not abide in darkness."

John 6:35

"And Jesus said to them, 'I am the bread of life. He who comes to Me shall never hunger, and he who believes in Me shall never thirst.' "

Mark 9:23

"Jesus said to him, 'If you can believe, all things are possible to him who believes.' "Immediately the father of the child cried out and said, "I believe; help my unbelief!"

John 20:29

"Jesus said to him, 'Thomas, because you have seen Me, you have believed. Blessed are those who have not seen and yet have believed' "

John 6:47

"Most assuredly, I say to you, he who believes in Me has everlasting life."

Scriptures on Blessing

Proverbs 10: 6

"Blessings are on the head of the righteous, but violence covers the mouth of the wicked."

Philippians 4:19

And my God will supply every need of yours according to his riches in glory in Christ Jesus.

Luke 6:38

Give, and it will be given to you. Good measure, pressed down, shaken together, running over, will be put into your lap. For with the measure you use it will be measured back to you."

Numbers 6:24-26

The Lord bless you and keep you; the Lord make his face to shine upon you and be gracious to you; the Lord lift up his countenance upon you and give you peace.

John 1:16

And from his fullness we have all received, grace upon grace.

2 Corinthians 9:8

And God is able to make all grace abound to you, so that having all sufficiency in all things at all times, you may abound in every good work.

James 1:17

Every good gift and every perfect gift is from above, coming down from the Father of lights with whom there is no variation or shadow due to change.

Psalm 21: 6

"For You have made him most blessed forever; You have made him exceedingly glad with Your presence."

James 3:10

"Out of the same mouth proceed blessing and cursing. My brethren, these things ought not to be so."

Psalm 21: 3

"For You meet him with the blessings of goodness; You set a crown of pure gold upon his head."

Zechariah 8: 13

"And it shall come to pass that just as you were a curse among the nations, O house of Judah and house of Israel, so I will save you, and you shall be a blessing. Do not fear, let your hands be strong."

Galatians 3: 14

"that the blessing of Abraham might come upon the Gentiles in Christ Jesus, that we might receive the promise of the Spirit through faith."

Ephesians 1: 3

"Blessed be the God and Father of our Lord Jesus Christ, who has blessed us with every spiritual blessing in the heavenly places in Christ"

Proverbs 10: 7

"The memory of the righteous is blessed, but the name of the wicked will rot."

Psalm 41: 1

"For You, O LORD, will bless the righteous; with favor You will surround him as with a shield."

Psalm 106: 3

"Blessed are those who keep justice, and he who does righteousness at all times!"

Revelation 5: 12

"...Worthy is the Lamb who was slain To receive power and riches and wisdom, And strength and honor and glory and blessing!"

Scriptures on Your Body

Genesis 1:26-27

Then God said, "Let us make man in our image, after our likeness. And let them have dominion over the fish of the sea and over the birds of the heavens and over the livestock and over all the earth and over every creeping thing that creeps on the earth." So God created man in his own image, in the image of God he created him; male and female he created them.

Corinthians 6:19-20

Or do you not know that your body is a temple of the Holy Spirit within you, whom you have from God? You are not your own, for you were bought with a price. So glorify God in your body.

Leviticus 19:28

You shall not make any cuts on your body for the dead or tattoo yourselves: I am the Lord.

1 Corinthians 3:16-17

Do you not know that you are God's temple and that God's Spirit dwells in you? If anyone destroys God's temple, God will destroy him. For God's temple is holy, and you are that temple.

1 Corinthians 9:27

But I discipline my body and keep it under control, lest after preaching to others I myself should be disqualified.

Romans 12:1

I appeal to you therefore, brothers, by the mercies of God, to present your bodies as a living sacrifice, holy and acceptable to God, which is your spiritual worship.

1 Corinthians 6:18

Flee from sexual immorality. Every other sin a person commits is outside the body, but the sexually immoral person sins against his own body.

1 Corinthians 15:44

It is sown a natural body; it is raised a spiritual body. If there is a natural body, there is also a spiritual body.

1 Corinthians 6:19

Or do you not know that your body is a temple of the Holy Spirit within you, whom you have from God? You are not your own,

2 Corinthians 5:10

For we must all appear before the judgment seat of Christ, so that each one may receive what is due for what he has done in the body, whether good or evil.

Romans 6:13

Do not present your members to sin as instruments for unrighteousness, but present yourselves to God as those who have been brought from death to life, and your members to God as instruments for righteousness.

1 Peter 3:3-4

Do not let your adorning be external—the braiding of hair and the putting on of gold jewelry, or the clothing you wear— but let your adorning be the hidden person of the heart with the imperishable beauty of a gentle and quiet spirit, which in God's sight is very precious.

Psalm 139:14

I praise you, for I am fearfully and wonderfully made. Wonderful are your works; my soul knows it very well.

1 Samuel 16:7

But the Lord said to Samuel, "Do not look on his appearance or on the height of his stature, because I have rejected him. For the Lord sees not as man sees: man looks on the outward appearance, but the Lord looks on the heart."

2 Corinthians 5:17

Therefore, if anyone is in Christ, he is a new creation. The old has passed away; behold, the new has come.

Matthew 6:25-26

"Therefore I tell you, do not be anxious about your life, what you will eat or what you will drink, nor about your body, what you will put on. Is not life more than food, and the body more than clothing? Look at the birds of the air: they neither sow nor reap nor gather into barns, and yet your heavenly Father feeds them. Are you not of more value than they?

1 Timothy 4:8

For while bodily training is of some value, godliness is of value in every way, as it holds promise for the present life and also for the life to come.

1 Thessalonians 5:23

Now may the God of peace himself sanctify you completely, and may your whole spirit and soul and body be kept blameless at the coming of our Lord Jesus Christ.

Philippians 1:20-22

As it is my eager expectation and hope that I will not be at all ashamed, but that with full courage now as always Christ will be honored in my body, whether by life or by death. For to me to live is Christ, and to die is gain. If I am to live in the flesh, that means fruitful labor for me. Yet which I shall choose I cannot tell.

1 Corinthians 12:27

Now you are the body of Christ and individually members of it.

1 Corinthians 12:12

For just as the body is one and has many members, and all the members of the body, though many, are one body, so it is with Christ.

1 Corinthians 10:31

So, whether you eat or drink, or whatever you do, do all to the glory of God.

1 Corinthians 6:13

"Food is meant for the stomach and the stomach for food"—and God will destroy both one and the other. The body is not meant for sexual immorality, but for the Lord, and the Lord for the body.

Scriptures on Boldness

Proverbs 28:1 ESV / 284 helpful votes Helpful Not Helpful

The wicked flee when no one pursues, but the righteous are bold as a lion.

Acts 28:31

Proclaiming the kingdom of God and teaching about the Lord Jesus Christ with all boldness and without hindrance.

Ephesians 3:12

In whom we have boldness and access with confidence through our faith in him.

Acts 4:31

And when they had prayed, the place in which they were gathered together was shaken, and they were all filled with the Holy Spirit and continued to speak the word of God with boldness.

Acts 4:29

And now, Lord, look upon their threats and grant to your servants to continue to speak your word with all boldness,

2 Corinthians 3:12

Since we have such a hope, we are very bold,

Hebrews 13:6

So we can confidently say, "The Lord is my helper; I will not fear; what can man do to me?"

Acts 4:13

Now when they saw the boldness of Peter and John, and perceived that they were uneducated, common men, they were astonished. And they recognized that they had been with Jesus.

Joshua 1:9

Have I not commanded you? Be strong and courageous. Do not be frightened, and do not be dismayed, for the Lord your God is with you wherever you go."

Ephesians 6:19

And also for me, that words may be given to me in opening my mouth boldly to proclaim the mystery of the gospel,

2 Timothy 1:6-7

For this reason I remind you to fan into flame the gift of God, which is in you through the laying on of my hands, for God gave us a spirit not of fear but of power and love and self-control.

Hebrews 4:16

Let us then with confidence draw near to the throne of grace, that we may receive mercy and find grace to help in time of need.

Psalm 138:3

On the day I called, you answered me; my strength of soul you increased.

Scriptures on Children

Proverbs 17:6

"Children's children are the crown of old men, And the glory of children is their father. "

Acts 16:31

"For the promise is to you and to your children, and to all who are afar off, as many as the Lord our God will call."

Acts 16:31

"So they said, 'Believe on the Lord Jesus Christ, and you will be saved, you and your household.' "

Isaiah 54:13

"All your children shall be taught by the Lord, and great shall be the peace of your children."

Isaiah 44:3

"For I will pour water on him who is thirsty, and floods on the dry ground; I will pour My Spirit on your descendants, and My blessing on your offspring;"

Mark 10:14-16

"But when Jesus saw it, He was greatly displeased and said to them, 'Let the little children come to Me, and do not forbid them; for of such is the kingdom of God. Assuredly, I say to you, whoever does not receive the kingdom of God as a little child will by no means enter it.' And He took them up in His arms, laid His hands on them, and blessed them."

Psalms 127:3-5

"Behold, children are a heritage from the Lord, The fruit of the womb is a reward. Like arrows in the hand of a warrior, So are the children of one's youth. Happy is the man who has his quiver full of them; They shall not be ashamed, But shall speak with their enemies in the gate."

Psalms 128:3

"Your wife shall be like a fruitful vine In the very heart of your house, Your children like olive plants All around your table."

Psalms 107:41

"Yet He sets the poor on high, far from affliction, And makes their families like a flock."

Job 21:11

"They send forth their little ones like a flock, And their children dance.

Ephesians 6:1-3

"Children, obey your parents in the Lord, for this is right. "Honor your father and mother," which is the first commandment with promise: "that it may be well with you and you may live long on the earth."

Colossians 3:20

"Children, obey your parents in all things, for this is well pleasing to the Lord."

Leviticus 19:3

"Every one of you shall revere his mother and his father... I am the Lord your God."

Deuteronomy 5:16

"Honor your father and your mother, as the Lord your God has commanded you, that your days may be long, and that it may be well with you..."

Proverbs 6:20

"My son, keep your father's command, and do not forsake the law of your mother."

Proverbs 13:1

"A wise son heeds his father's instruction, but a scoffer does not listen to rebuke."

Proverbs 15:5

"A fool despises his father's instruction, but he who receives correction is prudent."

Proverbs 20:11

"Even a child is known by his deeds, whether what he does is pure and right."

Proverbs 10:1

"A wise son makes a glad father, but a foolish son is the grief of his mother."

Proverbs 28:7

"Whoever keeps the law is a discerning son, but a companion of gluttons shames his father."

Proverbs 23:15, 16

"My son, if your heart is wise, my heart will rejoice—indeed, I myself; yes, my inmost being will rejoice when your lips speak right things."

Proverbs 23:22

"Listen to your father who begot you, and do not despise your mother when she is old."

Proverbs 23:24-26

"The father of the righteous will greatly rejoice, and he who begets a wise child will delight in him. Let your father and your mother be glad, and let her who bore you rejoice. My son, give me your heart, and let your eyes observe my ways."

Ephesians 6:1-4

"Children, obey your parents in the Lord, for this is right. "Honor your father and mother" (this is the first commandment with a promise), "that it may go well with you and that you may live long in the land." Fathers, do not provoke your children to anger, but bring them up in the discipline and instruction of the Lord."

Scriptures on Comfort

Psalms 46:1- 3

"God is our refuge and strength, A very present help in trouble. Therefore we will not fear, Even though the earth be removed, And though the mountains be carried into the midst of the sea; Though its waters roar and be troubled, Though the mountains shake with its swelling."

Psalms 138:7

"Though I walk in the midst of trouble, You will revive me; You will stretch out Your hand Against the wrath of my enemies, And Your right hand will save me."

Psalms 18:2

"The Lord is my rock and my fortress and my deliverer; My God, my strength, in whom I will trust; My shield and the horn of my salvation, my stronghold."

Psalms 22:24

"For He has not despised nor abhorred the affliction of the afflicted; nor has He hidden His face from Him; But when He cried to Him, He heard."

Psalms 37:24

"Though he fall, he shall not be utterly cast down; For the Lord upholds him with His hand."

Nahum 1:7

"The Lord is good, A stronghold in the day of trouble; And He knows those who trust in Him."

Psalms 37:39

"But the salvation of the righteous is from the Lord; He is their strength in the time of trouble."

Psalms 55:22

"Cast your burden on the Lord, And He shall sustain you; He shall never permit the righteous to be moved."

John 16:33

"'These things I have spoken to you, that in Me you may have peace. In the world you will have tribulation; but be of good cheer, I have overcome the world.' "

Matthew 11:28

"Come to me, all you who labor and are heavy laden, and I will give you rest."

2 Corinthians 1:5

"For as the sufferings of Christ abound in us, so our consolation also abounds through Christ."

Psalms 9:9

"The Lord also will be a refuge for the oppressed, A refuge in times of trouble."

Lamentations 3:31- 33

"For the Lord will not cast off forever. Though He causes grief, Yet He will show compassion According to the multitude of His mercies. For He does not afflict willingly, Nor grieve the children of men. "

Psalms 27:14

"Wait on the Lord; be of good courage, And He shall strengthen your heart; Wait, I say, on the Lord!

Scriptures on Community and Church

Hebrews 10:24-25

And let us consider how to stir up one another to love and good works, not neglecting to meet together, as is the habit of some, but encouraging one another, and all the more as you see the Day drawing near.

Galatians 6:2

Bear one another's burdens, and so fulfill the law of Christ.

Ecclesiastes 4:9-12

Two are better than one, because they have a good reward for their toil. For if they fall, one will lift up his fellow. But woe to him who is alone when he falls and has not another to lift him up! Again, if two lie together, they keep warm, but how can one keep warm alone? And though a man might prevail against one who is alone, two will withstand him—a threefold cord is not quickly broken.

Acts 2:42-47

And they devoted themselves to the apostles' teaching and the fellowship, to the breaking of bread and the prayers. And awe came upon every soul, and many wonders and signs were being done through the apostles. And all who believed were together and had all things in common. And they were selling their possessions and belongings and distributing the proceeds to all, as any had need. And day by day, attending the temple together and breaking bread in their homes, they received their food with glad and generous hearts, ...

Matthew 18:20

For where two or three are gathered in my name, there am I among them."

1 Thessalonians 5:14

And we urge you, brothers, admonish the idle, encourage the fainthearted, help the weak, be patient with them all.

Matthew 22:37-40

And he said to him, "You shall love the Lord your God with all your heart and with all your soul and with all your mind. This is the great and first commandment. And a second is like it: You shall love your neighbor as yourself. On these two commandments depend all the Law and the Prophets."

Matthew 5:13-16

"You are the salt of the earth, but if salt has lost its taste, how shall its saltiness be restored? It is no longer good for anything except to be thrown out and trampled under people's feet. "You are the light of the world. A city set on a hill cannot be hidden. Nor do people light a lamp and put it under a basket, but on a stand, and it gives light to all in the house. In the same way, let your light shine before others, so that they may see your good works and give glory to your Father who is in heaven.

1 Corinthians 12:25-27

That there may be no division in the body, but that the members may have the same care for one another. If one member suffers, all suffer together; if one member is honored, all rejoice together. Now you are the body of Christ and individually members of it.

1 John 1:7

But if we walk in the light, as he is in the light, we have fellowship with one another, and the blood of Jesus his Son cleanses us from all sin.

1 Corinthians 1:10

I appeal to you, brothers, by the name of our Lord Jesus Christ, that all of you agree, and that there be no divisions among you, but that you be united in the same mind and the same judgment.

Psalm 133:1-3

A Song of Ascents. Of David. Behold, how good and pleasant it is when brothers dwell in unity! It is like the precious oil on the head, running down on the beard, on the beard of Aaron, running down on the collar of his robes! It is like the dew of Hermon, which falls on the mountains of Zion! For there the Lord has commanded the blessing, life forevermore.

Romans 12:16

Live in harmony with one another. Do not be haughty, but associate with the lowly. Never be wise in your own sight.

Colossians 3:13

Bearing with one another and, if one has a complaint against another, forgiving each other; as the Lord has forgiven you, so you also must forgive.

Romans 12:4-5

For as in one body we have many members, and the members do not all have the same function, so we, though many, are one body in Christ, and individually members one of another.

James 5:16

Therefore, confess your sins to one another and pray for one another, that you may be healed. The prayer of a righteous person has great power as it is working.

Proverbs 17:17

A friend loves at all times, and a brother is born for adversity.

Scriptures on Communication

James 1:19

Know this, my beloved brothers: let every person be quick to hear, slow to speak, slow to anger;

Ephesians 4:29

Let no corrupting talk come out of your mouths, but only such as is good for building up, as fits the occasion, that it may give grace to those who hear.

Proverbs 15:1

A soft answer turns away wrath, but a harsh word stirs up anger.

Psalm 141:3

Set a guard, O Lord, over my mouth; keep watch over the door of my lips!

Colossians 4:6

Let your speech always be gracious, seasoned with salt, so that you may know how you ought to answer each person.

Proverbs 15:2

The tongue of the wise commends knowledge, but the mouths of fools pour out folly.

Proverbs 12:18

There is one whose rash words are like sword thrusts, but the tongue of the wise brings healing.

Psalm 19:14

Let the words of my mouth and the meditation of my heart be acceptable in your sight, O Lord, my rock and my redeemer.

Proverbs 18:2

A fool takes no pleasure in understanding, but only in expressing his opinion.

2 Timothy 2:16

But avoid irreverent babble, for it will lead people into more and more ungodliness,

Proverbs 18:13

If one gives an answer before he hears, it is his folly and shame.

Proverbs 25:11

A word fitly spoken is like apples of gold in a setting of silver.

Proverbs 10:19

When words are many, transgression is not lacking, but whoever restrains his lips is prudent.

Proverbs 16:23

The heart of the wise makes his speech judicious and adds persuasiveness to his lips.

Jeremiah 1:9

Then the Lord put out his hand and touched my mouth. And the Lord said to me, "Behold, I have put my words in your mouth.

Proverbs 18:21

Death and life are in the power of the tongue, and those who love it will eat its fruits.

Proverbs 13:17

A wicked messenger falls into trouble, but a faithful envoy brings healing.

Colossians 3:8

But now you must put them all away: anger, wrath, malice, slander, and obscene talk from your mouth.

Ephesians 4:15

Rather, speaking the truth in love, we are to grow up in every way into him who is the head, into Christ,

Matthew 15:18-19

But what comes out of the mouth proceeds from the heart, and this defiles a person. For out of the heart come evil thoughts, murder, adultery, sexual immorality, theft, false witness, slander.

Scriptures on Conceit and Pride

Proverbs 16:18

Pride goes before destruction, and a haughty spirit before a fall.

Proverbs 21:4

"A haughty look, a proud heart, And the plowing of the wicked are sin."

Proverbs 14:3

"In the mouth of a fool is a rod of pride, but the lips of the wise will preserve them."

Proverbs 27:2

"Let another man praise you, and not your own mouth; A stranger, and not your own lips."

Proverbs 28:25,26

"He who is of a proud heart stirs up strife, but he who trusts in the Lord will be prospered. He who trusts in his own heart is a fool, but whoever walks wisely will be delivered."

Isaiah 5:21

"Woe to those who are wise in their own eyes, And prudent in their own sight!"

Proverbs 26:12

"Do you see a man wise in his own eyes? There is more hope for a fool than for him."

Proverbs 16:18

"Pride goes before destruction, and a haughty spirit before a fall."

Psalms 119:21

"You rebuke the proud - the cursed, who stray from Your commandments."

Luke 16:15

"And He said to them, 'You are those who justify yourselves before men, but God knows your hearts. For what is highly esteemed among men is an abomination in the sight of God.' "

Proverbs 8:13

"The fear of the Lord is to hate evil; Pride and arrogance and the evil way And the perverse mouth I hate. "

John 5:44

"How can you believe, who receive honor from one another, and do not seek the honor that comes from the only God?"

Mark 9:35

"And He sat down, called the twelve, and said to them, 'If anyone desires to be first, he shall be last of all and servant of all.' "

2 Corinthians 10:17,18

"But 'he who glories, let him glory in the Lord.' For not he who commends himself is approved, but whom the Lord commends."

Scriptures on Confidence

Proverbs 3:26

For the Lord will be your confidence and will keep your foot from being caught.

Isaiah 41:10

Fear not, for I am with you; be not dismayed, for I am your God; I will strengthen you, I will help you, I will uphold you with my righteous right hand.

2 Corinthians 3:5

Not that we are sufficient in ourselves to claim anything as coming from us, but our sufficiency is from God,

1 John 3:20-21

For whenever our heart condemns us, God is greater than our heart, and he knows everything. Beloved, if our heart does not condemn us, we have confidence before God;

Hebrews 13:6

So we can confidently say, "The Lord is my helper; I will not fear; what can man do to me?"

Philippians 4:13

I can do all things through him who strengthens me.

Romans 15:13

May the God of hope fill you with all joy and peace in believing, so that by the power of the Holy Spirit you may abound in hope.

1 John 4:18

There is no fear in love, but perfect love casts out fear. For fear has to do with punishment, and whoever fears has not been perfected in love.

1 John 3:22

And whatever we ask we receive from him, because we keep his commandments and do what pleases him.

Proverbs 28:26

Whoever trusts in his own mind is a fool, but he who walks in wisdom will be delivered.

Psalm 20:7

Some trust in chariots and some in horses, but we trust in the name of the Lord our God.

James 4:13-15

Come now, you who say, "Today or tomorrow we will go into such and such a town and spend a year there and trade and make a profit"— yet you do not know what tomorrow will bring. What is your life? For you are a mist that appears for a little time and then vanishes. Instead you ought to say, "If the Lord wills, we will live and do this or that."

Psalm 27:1-3

Of David. The Lord is my light and my salvation; whom shall I fear? The Lord is the stronghold of my life; of whom shall I be afraid? When evildoers assail me to eat up my flesh, my adversaries and foes, it is they who stumble and fall. Though an army encamp against me, my heart shall not fear; though war arise against me, yet I will be confident.

2 Corinthians 1:9

Indeed, we felt that we had received the sentence of death. But that was to make us rely not on ourselves but on God who raises the dead.

Hebrews 10:35-36

Therefore do not throw away your confidence, which has a great reward. For you have need of endurance, so that when you have done the will of God you may receive what is promised.

1 Timothy 6:17

As for the rich in this present age, charge them not to be haughty, nor to set their hopes on the uncertainty of riches, but on God, who richly provides us with everything to enjoy.

Proverbs 14:26

In the fear of the Lord one has strong confidence, and his children will have a refuge.

Scriptures on Confusion

1 Corinthians 14:33

For God is not a God of confusion but of peace. As in all the churches of the saints,

2 Timothy 2:7

Think over what I say, for the Lord will give you understanding in everything.

1 John 4:1

Beloved, do not believe every spirit, but test the spirits to see whether they are from God, for many false prophets have gone out into the world.

1 Peter 5:8

Be sober-minded; be watchful. Your adversary the devil prowls around like a roaring lion, seeking someone to devour.

Philippians 4:8-9

Finally, brothers, whatever is true, whatever is honorable, whatever is just, whatever is pure, whatever is lovely, whatever is commendable, if there is any excellence, if there is anything worthy of praise, think about these things. What you have learned and received and heard and seen in me—practice these things, and the God of peace will be with you.

Psalm 119:169

Let my cry come before you, O Lord; give me understanding according to your word!

Psalm 119:34

Give me understanding, that I may keep your law and observe it with my whole heart.

Matthew 7:7

"Ask, and it will be given to you; seek, and you will find; knock, and it will be opened to you.

John 16:13

When the Spirit of truth comes, he will guide you into all the truth, for he will not speak on his own authority, but whatever he hears he will speak, and he will declare to you the things that are to come.

Hebrews 13:8

Jesus Christ is the same yesterday and today and forever.

Isaiah 40:31

But they who wait for the Lord shall renew their strength; they shall mount up with wings like eagles; they shall run and not be weary; they shall walk and not faint.

2 Corinthians 4:8

We are afflicted in every way, but not crushed; perplexed, but not driven to despair;

Proverbs 3:5-6 ESV / 179 helpful votes

Trust in the Lord with all your heart, and do not lean on your own understanding. In all your ways acknowledge him, and he will make straight your paths.

Jeremiah 17:9

The heart is deceitful above all things, and desperately sick; who can understand it?

Psalm 119:125

I am your servant; give me understanding, that I may know your testimonies!

Scriptures on Contentment

Hebrew 13:5

Keep your life free from love of money, and be content with what you have, for he has said, "I will never leave you nor forsake you."

Proverbs 17:22

"A merry heart does good, like medicine, But a broken spirit dries the bones."

Hebrews 13:5

"Let your conduct be without covetousness; be content with such things as you have. For He Himself has said, 'I will never leave you nor forsake you.' "

Proverbs 15:15

"All the days of the afflicted are evil, But he who is of a merry heart has a continual feast."

Proverbs 14:30

"A sound heart is life to the body, But envy is rottenness to the bones."

1 Timothy 6:6

"Now godliness with contentment is great gain."

Proverbs 23:17, 18

"Do not let your heart envy sinners, But be zealous for the fear of the Lord all the day; For surely there is a hereafter, And your hope will not be cut off.

Scriptures on Correction

Proverbs 3:11-12

My son, do not despise the Lord's discipline or be weary of his reproof, for the Lord reproves him whom he loves, as a father the son in whom he delights.

Proverbs 12:1

Whoever loves discipline loves knowledge, but he who hates reproof is stupid.

Hebrews 12:11

For the moment all discipline seems painful rather than pleasant, but later it yields the peaceful fruit of righteousness to those who have been trained by it.

2 Timothy 3:16

All Scripture is breathed out by God and profitable for teaching, for reproof, for correction, and for training in righteousness,

Proverbs 15:32

Whoever ignores instruction despises himself, but he who listens to reproof gains intelligence.

Proverbs 29:15

The rod and reproof give wisdom, but a child left to himself brings shame to his mother.

Hebrews 12:5-11

And have you forgotten the exhortation that addresses you as sons? "My son, do not regard lightly the discipline of the Lord, nor be weary when reproved by him. For the Lord disciplines the one he loves, and chastises every son whom he receives." It is for discipline that you have to endure. God is treating you as sons. For what son is there whom his father does not discipline? If you are left without discipline, in which all have participated, then you are illegitimate children and not sons. Besides this, we have had earthly fathers who disciplined us and we respected them. Shall we not much more be subject to the Father of spirits and live? ...

Proverbs 8:33

Hear instruction and be wise, and do not neglect it.

2 Timothy 3:16-17

All Scripture is breathed out by God and profitable for teaching, for reproof, for correction, and for training in righteousness, that the man of God may be competent, equipped for every good work.

Proverbs 9:7-9

Whoever corrects a scoffer gets himself abuse, and he who reproves a wicked man incurs injury. Do not reprove a scoffer, or he will hate you; reprove a wise man, and he will love you. Give instruction to a wise man, and he will be still wiser; teach a righteous man, and he will increase in learning.

Proverbs 13:24

Whoever spares the rod hates his son, but he who loves him is diligent to discipline him.

Proverbs 6:23

For the commandment is a lamp and the teaching a light, and the reproofs of discipline are the way of life,

James 5:19-20

My brothers, if anyone among you wanders from the truth and someone brings him back, let him know that whoever brings back a sinner from his wandering will save his soul from death and will cover a multitude of sins.

Hebrews 4:12

For the word of God is living and active, sharper than any two-edged sword, piercing to the division of soul and of spirit, of joints and of marrow, and discerning the thoughts and intentions of the heart.

Romans 15:4

For whatever was written in former days was written for our instruction, that through endurance and through the encouragement of the Scriptures we might have hope.

Proverbs 22:15

Folly is bound up in the heart of a child, but the rod of discipline drives it far from him.

Ephesians 6:4

Fathers, do not provoke your children to anger, but bring them up in the discipline and instruction of the Lord.

John 14:15

"If you love me, you will keep my commandments.

Matthew 18:15-17

"If your brother sins against you, go and tell him his fault, between you and him alone. If he listens to you, you have gained your brother. But if he does not listen, take one or two others along with you, that every charge may be established by the evidence of two or three witnesses. If he refuses to listen to them, tell it to the church. And if he refuses to listen even to the church, let him be to you as a Gentile and a tax collector.

Galatians 6:1

Brothers, if anyone is caught in any transgression, you who are spiritual should restore him in a spirit of gentleness. Keep watch on yourself, lest you too be tempted.

Revelation 3:19

Those whom I love, I reprove and discipline, so be zealous and repent.

Romans 13:4

For he is God's servant for your good. But if you do wrong, be afraid, for he does not bear the sword in vain. For he is the servant of God, an avenger who carries out God's wrath on the wrongdoer.

Romans 12:19

Beloved, never avenge yourselves, but leave it to the wrath of God, for it is written, "Vengeance is mine, I will repay, says the Lord."

Job 5:17

"Behold, blessed is the one whom God reproves; therefore despise not the discipline of the Almighty.

Proverbs 10:17

Whoever heeds instruction is on the path to life, but he who rejects reproof leads others astray.

Proverbs 3:12

For the Lord reproves him whom he loves, as a father the son in whom he delights.

Psalm 144:1

Of David. Blessed be the Lord, my rock, who trains my hands for war, and my fingers for battle;

2 Timothy 4:2

Preach the word; be ready in season and out of season; reprove, rebuke, and exhort, with complete patience and teaching.

Proverbs 29:17

Discipline your son, and he will give you rest; he will give delight to your heart.

Proverbs 19:18

Discipline your son, for there is hope; do not set your heart on putting him to death.

Proverbs 12:1

Whoever loves discipline loves knowledge, but he who hates reproof is stupid.

Proverbs 23:13

Do not withhold discipline from a child; if you strike him with a rod, he will not die.

Proverbs 1:7

The fear of the Lord is the beginning of knowledge; fools despise wisdom and instruction.

Psalm 94:12

Blessed is the man whom you discipline, O Lord, and whom you teach out of your law,

Scriptures on Courage:

Joshua 1:9

Have I not commanded you? Be strong and courageous. Do not be frightened, and do not be dismayed, for the Lord your God is with you wherever you go."

Proverbs 28:1

The wicked flee when no one pursues, but the righteous are bold as a lion.

John 16:33

I have said these things to you, that in me you may have peace. In the world you will have tribulation. But take heart; I have overcome the world."

Psalms 27:14

"Wait on the Lord; be of good courage, And He shall strengthen your heart; Wait, I say, on the Lord!"

Psalms 37:28

"For the Lord loves justice, and does not forsake His saints; they are preserved forever, but the descendants of the wicked shall be cut off."

Isaiah 43:1

" But now, thus says the Lord, who created you, O Jacob, And He who formed you, O Israel: ' Fear not, for I have redeemed you; I have called you by your name; you are Mine.

2 Kings 6:16

"So he answered, 'Do not fear, for those who are with us are more than those who are with them.' "

Psalms 37:3

"Trust in the Lord, and do good; dwell in the land, and feed on His faithfulness."

Isaiah 40:29

"He gives power to the weak, And to those who have no might He increases strength."

Psalms 31:24

"Be of good courage, And He shall strengthen your heart, all you who hope in the Lord."

Philippians 4:12, 13

"I know how to be abased, and I know how to abound. Everywhere and in all things I have learned both to be full and to be hungry, both to abound and to suffer need. I can do all things through Christ who strengthens me."

Scriptures on Dating

1 Corinthians 15:33

Do not be deceived: "Bad company ruins good morals."

2 Timothy 2:22

So flee youthful passions and pursue righteousness, faith, love, and peace, along with those who call on the Lord from a pure heart.

2 Corinthians 6:14-15

Do not be unequally yoked with unbelievers. For what partnership has righteousness with lawlessness? Or what fellowship has light with darkness? What accord has Christ with Belial? Or what portion does a believer share with an unbeliever?

1 Corinthians 13:4-7

Love is patient and kind; love does not envy or boast; it is not arrogant or rude. It does not insist on its own way; it is not irritable or resentful; it does not rejoice at wrongdoing, but rejoices with the truth. Love bears all things, believes all things, hopes all things, endures all things.

Genesis 2:18

Then the Lord God said, "It is not good that the man should be alone; I will make him a helper fit for him."

1 Corinthians 6:18

Flee from sexual immorality. Every other sin a person commits is outside the body, but the sexually immoral person sins against his own body.

Genesis 2:24

Therefore a man shall leave his father and his mother and hold fast to his wife, and they shall become one flesh.

Song of Solomon 2:7

I adjure you, O daughters of Jerusalem, by the gazelles or the does of the field, that you not stir up or awaken love until it pleases.

Hebrews 13:4

Let marriage be held in honor among all, and let the marriage bed be undefiled, for God will judge the sexually immoral and adulterous.

Proverbs 18:22

He who finds a wife finds a good thing and obtains favor from the Lord.

Proverbs 4:23

Keep your heart with all vigilance, for from it flow the springs of life.

1 Thessalonians 4:3-5

For this is the will of God, your sanctification: that you abstain from sexual immorality; that each one of you know how to control his own body in holiness and honor, not in the passion of lust like the Gentiles who do not know God;

Proverbs 31:30

Charm is deceitful, and beauty is vain, but a woman who fears the Lord is to be praised.

Romans 12:9-10

Let love be genuine. Abhor what is evil; hold fast to what is good. Love one another with brotherly affection. Outdo one another in showing honor.

Matthew 19:5

And said, 'Therefore a man shall leave his father and his mother and hold fast to his wife, and the two shall become one flesh'?

Amos 3:3

"Do two walk together, unless they have agreed to meet?

Proverbs 19:14

House and wealth are inherited from fathers, but a prudent wife is from the Lord.

Scriptures on Death

Romans 8:38,39

"For I am persuaded that neither death nor life, nor angels nor principalities nor powers, nor things present nor things to come, nor height nor depth, nor any other created thing, shall be able to separate us from the love of God which is in Christ Jesus our Lord."

Psalms 23:4

"Yea, though I walk through the valley of the shadow of death, I will fear no evil; For You are with me; Your rod and Your staff, they comfort me."

John 8:51

"Most assuredly, I say to you, if anyone keeps My word he shall never see death."

Psalms 48:14

"For this is God, Our God forever and ever, He will be our guide even to death."

1 Corinthians 15:55

"O Death, where is your sting? O Hades, where is your victory?"

Proverbs 14:32

"The wicked is banished in his wickedness, but the righteous has a refuge in his death."

Romans 5:9

"Much more then, having now been justified by His blood, we shall be saved from wrath through Him."

Hebrews 2:14, 15

"Inasmuch then as the children have partaken of flesh and blood, He Himself likewise shared in the same, that through death He might destroy him who had the power of death, that is, the devil, and release those who through fear of death were all their lifetime subject to bondage."

Psalms 73:26

"My flesh and my heart fail; But God is the strength of my heart and my portion forever."

Psalms 49:15

"But God will redeem my soul from the power of the grave, For He shall receive me. Selah"

Isaiah 25:8

"He will swallow up death forever, And the Lord God will wipe away tears from all faces; The rebuke of His people He will take away from all the earth; For the Lord has spoken. "

Hosea 13:14

"I will ransom them from the power of the grave; I will redeem them from death. O Death, I will be your plagues! O Grave, I will be your destruction! Pity is hidden from My eyes."

Psalms 37:37

"Mark the blameless man, and observe the upright; for the future of that man is peace."

2 Corinthians 4:16

"Therefore we do not lose heart. Even though our outward man is perishing, yet the inward man is being renewed day by day."

John 3:16

"For God so loved the world, that he gave his only Son, that whoever believes in him should not perish but have eternal life.

Scriptures on Enemies

Isaiah 54:17

"'No weapon formed against you shall prosper, and every tongue which rises against you in judgment You shall condemn. This is the heritage of the servants of the Lord, and their righteousness is from Me," Says the Lord.' "

Psalms 37:40

"And the Lord shall help them and deliver them; He shall deliver them from the wicked, And save them, because they trust in Him."

Job 8:22

"Those who hate you will be clothed with shame, and the dwelling place of the wicked will come to nothing."

Deuteronomy 28:7

"The Lord will cause your enemies who rise against you to be defeated before your face; they shall come out against you one way and flee before you seven ways."

Deuteronomy 20:4

"For the Lord your God is He who goes with you, to fight for you against your enemies, to save you."

Job 5:20

"In famine He shall redeem you from death, And in war from the power of the sword."

Psalms 60:12

"Through God we will do valiantly, for it is He who shall tread down our enemies."

Psalms 118:7

"The Lord is for me among those who help me; therefore I shall see my desire on those who hate me."

Luke 1:74

"To grant us that we, Being delivered from the hand of our enemies, Might serve Him without fear,"

Psalms 125:3

"For the scepter of wickedness shall not rest on the land allotted to the righteous, lest the righteous reach out their hands to iniquity."

Psalms 27:5, 6

"For in the time of trouble He shall hide me in His pavilion; in the secret place of His tabernacle He shall hide me; He shall set me high upon a rock. And now my head shall be lifted up above my enemies all around me; therefore I will offer sacrifices of joy in His tabernacle; I will sing, yes, I will sing praises to the Lord. "

Proverbs 16:7

"When a man's ways please the Lord, He makes even his enemies to be at peace with him."

Psalms 112:8

"His heart is established; He will not be afraid, until he sees his desire upon his enemies."

Luke 18:7

"And shall God not avenge His own elect who cry out day and night to Him, though He bears long with them?"

Isaiah 54:15

"Indeed they shall surely assemble, but not because of Me. Whoever assembles against you shall fall for your sake."

Psalms 97:10

"You who love the Lord, hate evil! He preserves the souls of His saints; He delivers them out of the hand of the wicked."

Jeremiah 39:17, 18

"'But I will deliver you in that day,' says the Lord, 'and you shall not be given into the hand of the men of whom you are afraid. For I will surely deliver you, and you shall not fall by the sword; but your life shall be as a prize to you, because you have put your trust in Me,' says the Lord."

2 Kings 17:39

"But the Lord your God you shall fear; and He will deliver you from the hand of all your enemies."

2 Kings 6:16

"So he answered, 'Do not fear, for those who are with us are more than those who are with them.' "

Proverbs 3:25, 26

"Do not be afraid of sudden terror, Nor of trouble from the wicked when it comes; For the Lord will be your confidence, And will keep your foot from being caught."

Isaiah 41:11, 12

"Behold, all those who were incensed against you shall be ashamed and disgraced; they shall be as nothing, and those who strive with you shall perish. You shall seek them and not find them - Those who contended with you. Those who war against you shall be as nothing, As a nonexistent thing."

Luke 1:71

"That we should be saved from our enemies And from the hand of all who hate us,"

Acts 18:10

"for I am with you, and no one will attack you to hurt you; for I have many people in this city."

Hebrews 13:6

"So we may boldly say: ' The Lord is my helper; I will not fear. What can man do to me?' " (see Psalm 118:6)

Scriptures on Depression

Psalm 143:7-8

Answer me quickly, O Lord! My spirit fails! Hide not your face from me, lest I be like those who go down to the pit. Let me hear in the morning of your steadfast love, for in you I trust. Make me know the way I should go, for to you I lift up my soul.

Psalm 34:17-18

When the righteous cry for help, the Lord hears and delivers them out of all their troubles. The Lord is near to the brokenhearted and saves the crushed in spirit.

Isaiah 41:10

Fear not, for I am with you; be not dismayed, for I am your God; I will strengthen you, I will help you, I will uphold you with my righteous right hand.

1 Peter 5:7

Casting all your anxieties on him, because he cares for you.

Matthew 11:28

Come to me, all who labor and are heavy laden, and I will give you rest.

Jeremiah 29:11

For I know the plans I have for you, declares the Lord, plans for welfare and not for evil, to give you a future and a hope.

Proverbs 3:5-6

Trust in the Lord with all your heart, and do not lean on your own understanding. In all your ways acknowledge him, and he will make straight your paths.

Psalm 30:5

For his anger is but for a moment, and his favor is for a lifetime. Weeping may tarry for the night, but joy comes with the morning.

Philippians 4:6-7

Do not be anxious about anything, but in everything by prayer and supplication with thanksgiving let your requests be made known to God. And the peace of God, which surpasses all understanding, will guard your hearts and your minds in Christ Jesus.

Psalm 23:4

Even though I walk through the valley of the shadow of death, I will fear no evil, for you are with me; your rod and your staff, they comfort me.

Proverbs 12:25

Anxiety in a man's heart weighs him down, but a good word makes him glad.

Psalm 9:9

The Lord is a stronghold for the oppressed, a stronghold in times of trouble.

Psalm 34:18

The Lord is near to the brokenhearted and saves the crushed in spirit.

2 Timothy 1:7

For God gave us a spirit not of fear but of power and love and self-control.

Revelation 21:4 ESV / 302 helpful votes

He will wipe away every tear from their eyes, and death shall be no more, neither shall there be mourning, nor crying, nor pain anymore, for the former things have passed away."

John 10:10

The thief comes only to steal and kill and destroy. I came that they may have life and have it abundantly.

Isaiah 40:31

But they who wait for the Lord shall renew their strength; they shall mount up with wings like eagles; they shall run and not be weary; they shall walk and not faint.

Deuteronomy 31:8

It is the Lord who goes before you. He will be with you; he will not leave you or forsake you. Do not fear or be dismayed."

Psalm 3:3

But you, O Lord, are a shield about me, my glory, and the lifter of my head.

Psalm 30:11

You have turned for me my mourning into dancing; you have loosed my sackcloth and clothed me with gladness,

Isaiah 26:3

You keep him in perfect peace whose mind is stayed on you, because he trusts in you.

Scriptures on Emotions

Philippians 4:6-7

Do not be anxious about anything, but in everything by prayer and supplication with thanksgiving let your requests be made known to God. And the peace of God, which surpasses all understanding, will guard your hearts and your minds in Christ Jesus.

Proverbs 29:11

A fool gives full vent to his spirit, but a wise man quietly holds it back.

Proverbs 15:18

A hot-tempered man stirs up strife, but he who is slow to anger quiets contention.

Romans 12:2

Do not be conformed to this world, but be transformed by the renewal of your mind, that by testing you may discern what is the will of God, what is good and acceptable and perfect.

Galatians 5:16-24

But I say, walk by the Spirit, and you will not gratify the desires of the flesh. For the desires of the flesh are against the Spirit, and the desires of the Spirit are against the flesh, for these are opposed to each other, to keep you from doing the things you want to do. But if you are led by the Spirit, you are not under the law. Now the works of the flesh are evident: sexual immorality, impurity, sensuality, idolatry, sorcery, enmity, strife, jealousy, fits of anger, rivalries, dissensions, divisions, ...

Ecclesiastes 3:4

A time to weep, and a time to laugh; a time to mourn, and a time to dance;

Joshua 1:9

Have I not commanded you? Be strong and courageous. Do not be frightened, and do not be dismayed, for the Lord your God is with you wherever you go."

Romans 12:15

Rejoice with those who rejoice, weep with those who weep.

Romans 8:28

And we know that for those who love God all things work together for good, for those who are called according to his purpose.

Romans 12:9

Let love be genuine. Abhor what is evil; hold fast to what is good.

2 Corinthians 10:5

We destroy arguments and every lofty opinion raised against the knowledge of God, and take every thought captive to obey Christ,

Proverbs 15:13

A glad heart makes a cheerful face, but by sorrow of heart the spirit is crushed.

Ephesians 4:26-27

Be angry and do not sin; do not let the sun go down on your anger, and give no opportunity to the devil.

2 Timothy 1:7

For God gave us a spirit not of fear but of power and love and self-control.

John 11:35

Jesus wept.

Philippians 4:13

I can do all things through him who strengthens me.

Colossians 2:8

See to it that no one takes you captive by philosophy and empty deceit, according to human tradition, according to the elemental spirits of the world, and not according to Christ.

Matthew 10:28

And do not fear those who kill the body but cannot kill the soul. Rather fear him who can destroy both soul and body in hell.

1 John 4:16

So we have come to know and to believe the love that God has for us. God is love, and whoever abides in love abides in God, and God abides in him.

Proverbs 25:28

A man without self-control is like a city broken into and left without walls.

Ephesians 6:13

Therefore take up the whole armor of God, that you may be able to withstand in the evil day, and having done all, to stand firm.

Galatians 5:22-23

But the fruit of the Spirit is love, joy, peace, patience, kindness, goodness, faithfulness, gentleness, self-control; against such things there is no law.

Isaiah 30:15

For thus said the Lord God, the Holy One of Israel, "In returning and rest you shall be saved; in quietness and in trust shall be your strength." But you were unwilling,

Scriptures on Envy

Proverbs 23:17,18

"Do not let your heart envy sinners, but be zealous for the fear of the Lord all the day! For surely there is a hereafter, and your hope will not be cut off. "

Proverbs 14:30

"A sound heart is life to the body, But envy is rottenness to the bones."

James 4:5

"Or do you think that the Scripture says in vain, 'The Spirit who dwells in us yearns jealously?' "

Deuteronomy 5:2

"You shall not covet your neighbor's wife; and you shall not desire your neighbor's house, his field, his male servant, his female servant, his ox, his donkey, or anything that is your neighbor's."

James 3:16

"For where envy and self-seeking exist, confusion and every evil thing are there."

Psalms 37:7

"Rest in the Lord, and wait patiently for Him; Do not fret because of him who prospers in his way, Because of the man who brings wicked schemes to pass."

Psalms 10:3

"For the wicked boasts of his heart's desire; He blesses the greedy and renounces the Lord."

Proverbs 3:31

"Do not envy the oppressor, and choose none of his ways;"

Proverbs 24:1

"Do not be envious of evil men, nor desire to be with them;"

Proverbs 27:4

"Wrath is cruel and anger a torrent, but who is able to stand before jealousy?"

Galatians 5:26

"Let us not become conceited, provoking one another, envying one another."

Luke 12:22, 23

"Then He said to His disciples, 'Therefore I say to you, do not worry about your life, what you will eat; nor about the body, what you will put on. Life is more than food, and the body is more than clothing.' "

James 3:14

"But if you have bitter envy and self-seeking in your hearts, do not boast and lie against the truth."

1 Corinthians 10:24

"Let no one seek his own, but each one the other's well-being."

Ecclesiastes 4:4

"Again, I saw that for all toil and every skillful work a man is envied by his neighbor. This also is vanity and grasping for the wind."

Scriptures on Eternal Life

John 6:47

"Most assuredly, I say to you, he who believes in Me has everlasting life."

John 11:25, 26

"Jesus said to her, 'I am the resurrection and the life. He who believes in Me, though he may die, he shall live. And whoever lives and believes in Me shall never die. Do you believe this?' "

1 Corinthians 15:51-54

"Behold, I tell you a mystery: We shall not all sleep, but we shall all be changed in a moment, in the twinkling of an eye, at the last trumpet. For the trumpet will sound, and the dead will be raised incorruptible, and we shall be changed. For this corruptible must put on incorruption, and this mortal must put on immortality. So when this corruptible has put on incorruption, and this mortal has put on immortality, then shall be brought to pass the saying that is written: 'Death is swallowed up in victory.' "

1 John 2:25

"And this is the promise that He has promised us - eternal life."

1 Corinthians 15:21

"For since by man came death, by Man also came the resurrection of the dead."

1 John 5:13

"These things I have written to you who believe in the name of the Son of God, that you may know that you have eternal life, and that you may continue to believe in the name of the Son of God."

John 5:28, 29

"Do not marvel at this; for the hour is coming in which all who are in the graves will hear His voice and come forth - those who have done good, to the resurrection of life, and those who have done evil, to the resurrection of condemnation."

1 Thessalonians 4:16

"For the Lord Himself will descend from heaven with a shout, with the voice of an archangel, and with the trumpet of God. And the dead in Christ will rise first."

Revelation 7:15-17

"Therefore they are before the throne of God, and serve Him day and night in His temple. And He who sits on the throne will dwell among them. They shall neither hunger anymore nor thirst anymore; the sun shall not strike them, nor any heat; for the Lamb who is in the midst of the throne will shepherd them and lead them to living fountains of waters. And God will wipe away every tear from their eyes"

John 3:16

"For God so loved the world that He gave His only begotten Son, that whoever believes in Him should not perish but have everlasting life."

1 Corinthians 15:42 - 44

"So also is the resurrection of the dead. The body is sown in corruption, it is raised in incorruption. It is sown in dishonor, it is raised in glory. It is sown in weakness, it is raised in power. It is sown a natural body, it is raised a spiritual body. There is a natural body, and there is a spiritual body."

Romans 8:11

"But if the Spirit of Him who raised Jesus from the dead dwells in you, He who raised Christ from the dead will also give life to your mortal bodies (emphasis added) through His Spirit who dwells in you."

Revelation 21:4

"And God will wipe away every tear from their eyes; there shall be no more death, nor sorrow, nor crying. There shall be no more pain, for the former things have passed away."

Romans 6:23

"For the wages of sin is death, but the gift of God is eternal life in Christ Jesus our Lord."

Job 19:26 , 27

"And after my skin is destroyed, this I know, that in my flesh I shall see God, Whom I shall see for myself, and my eyes shall behold, and not another. How my heart yearns within me!"

Galatians 6:8

"For he who sows to his flesh will of the flesh reap corruption, but he who sows to the Spirit will of the Spirit reap everlasting life."

Daniel 12:2

"And many of those who sleep in the dust of the earth shall awake, some to everlasting life, some to shame and everlasting contempt."

Isaiah 26:19

"Your dead shall live; Together with my dead body they shall arise. Awake and sing, you who dwell in dust; for your dew is like the dew of herbs, and the earth shall cast out the dead."

Psalms 16:10

"For You will not leave my soul in Sheol, Nor will You allow Your Holy One to see corruption."

2 Timothy 1:10

"but has now been revealed by the appearing of our Savior Jesus Christ, who has abolished death and brought life and immortality to light through the gospel"

1 John 5:11

"And this is the testimony: that God has given us eternal life, and this life is in His Son."

2 Corinthians 5:1

"For we know that if our earthly house, this tent, is destroyed, we have a building from God, a house not made with hands, eternal in the heavens."

John 14:2, 3

"In My Father's house are many mansions; if it were not so, I would have told you. I go to prepare a place for you. And if I go and prepare a place for you, I will come again and receive you to Myself; that where I am, there you may be also."

John 6:39, 40

"This is the will of the Father who sent Me, that of all He has given Me I should lose nothing, but should raise it up at the last day. And this is the will of Him who sent Me, that everyone who sees the Son and believes in Him may have everlasting life; and I will raise him up at the last day."

John 10:27, 28

"My sheep hear My voice, and I know them, and they follow Me. And I give them eternal life, and they shall never perish; neither shall anyone snatch them out of My hand."

John 6:54

"Whoever eats My flesh and drinks My blood has eternal life, and I will raise him up at the last day." (Metaphoric meaning)

Scriptures on Faith

Hebrews 11:1

"Now faith is the substance of things hoped for, the evidence of things not seen."

Romans 10:17

"So then faith comes by hearing, and hearing by the word of God."

2 Corinthians 5:7

"For we walk by faith, not by sight."

Hebrews 11:6

"But without faith it is impossible to please Him, for he who comes to God must believe that He is, and that He is a rewarder of those who diligently seek Him. "

Psalms 31:23

"Oh, love the Lord, all you His saints! For the Lord preserves the faithful, and fully repays the proud person."

Matthew 17:20

So Jesus said to them, 'Because of your unbelief; for assuredly, I say to you, if you have faith as a mustard seed, you will say to this mountain, 'Move from here to there,' and it will move; and nothing will be impossible for you.' "

Galatians 5:6

"For in Christ Jesus neither circumcision nor uncircumcision avails anything, but faith working through love."

Mark 11:23,24

"For assuredly, I say to you, whoever says to this mountain, 'Be removed and be cast into the sea,' and does not doubt in his heart, but believes that those things he says will be done, he will have whatever he says. Therefore I say to you, whatever things you ask when you pray, believe that you receive them, and you will have them."

James 1:5,6

"If any of you lacks wisdom, let him ask of God, who gives to all liberally and without reproach, and it will be given to him. But let him ask in faith, with no doubting, for he who doubts is like a wave of the sea driven and tossed by the wind."

Colossians 2:6,7

"As you therefore have received Christ Jesus the Lord, so walk in Him, rooted and built up in Him and established in the faith, as you have been taught, abounding in it with thanksgiving."

Ephesians 2:8

"For by grace you have been saved through faith, and that not of yourselves; it is the gift of God,"

Galatians 3:26

"For you are all sons of God through faith in Christ Jesus."

2 Timothy 3:14,15

"But you must continue in the things which you have learned and been assured of, knowing from whom you have learned them, and that from childhood you have known the Holy Scriptures, which are able to make you wise for salvation through faith which is in Christ Jesus."

1 Corinthians 16:13

"Watch, stand fast in the faith, be brave, be strong."

Galatians 5:22

"But the fruit of the Spirit is love, joy, peace, longsuffering, kindness, goodness, faithfulness,"

Galatians 2:20

"I have been crucified with Christ; it is no longer I who live, but Christ lives in me; and the life which I now live in the flesh I live by faith in the Son of God, who loved me and gave Himself for me."

Ephesians 3:17-19

"That Christ may dwell in your hearts through faith; that you, being rooted and grounded in love, may be able to comprehend with all the saints what is the width and length and depth and height - to know the love of Christ which passes knowledge; that you may be filled with all the fullness of God."

Hebrews 12:1,2

"Therefore we also, since we are surrounded by so great a cloud of witnesses, let us lay aside every weight, and the sin which so easily ensnares us, and let us run with endurance the race that is set before us, looking unto Jesus, the author and finisher of our faith, who for the joy that was set before Him endured the cross, despising the shame, and has sat down at the right hand of the throne of God."

Scriptures on Fasting

Matthew 6:16

"Moreover, when you fast, do not be like the hypocrites, with a sad countenance. For they disfigure their faces that they may appear to men to be fasting. Assuredly, I say to you, they have their reward."

Matthew 6:17, 18

"But you, when you fast, anoint your head and wash your face, so that you do not appear to men to be fasting, but to your Father who is in the secret place; and your Father who sees in secret will reward you openly."

Isaiah 58:4-11

"Indeed you fast for strife and debate, And to strike with the fist of wickedness. You will not fast as you do this day, To make your voice heard on high.

Is it a fast that I have chosen, A day for a man to afflict his soul? Is it to bow down his head like a bulrush, And to spread out sackcloth and ashes? Would you call this a fast, And an acceptable day to the Lord?

'Is this not the fast that I have chosen: To loose the bonds of wickedness, To undo the heavy burdens, To let the oppressed go free, And that you break every yoke?

Is it not to share your bread with the hungry, And that you bring to your house the poor who are cast out; When you see the naked, that you cover him, And not hide yourself from your own flesh?

Then your light shall break forth like the morning, Your healing shall spring forth speedily, And your righteousness shall go before you; The glory of the Lord shall be your rear guard.

Then you shall call, and the Lord will answer; You shall cry, and He will say, 'Here I am.' 'If you take away the yoke from your midst, The pointing of the finger, and speaking wickedness,

If you extend your soul to the hungry And satisfy the afflicted soul, Then your light shall dawn in the darkness, And your darkness shall be as the noonday.

The Lord will guide you continually, And satisfy your soul in drought, And strengthen your bones; You shall be like a watered garden, And like a spring of water, whose waters do not fail."

Daniel 9:3

"Then I set my face toward the Lord God to make request by prayer and supplications, with fasting, sackcloth, and ashes."

Joel 2:12

"Now, therefore," says the Lord, Turn to Me with all your heart, With fasting, with weeping, and with mourning."

Luke 2:37

"And this woman was a widow of about eighty-four years, who did not depart from the temple, but served God with fastings and prayers night and day."

Acts 13:2

"As they ministered to the Lord and fasted, the Holy Spirit said, "Now separate to Me Barnabas and Saul for the work to which I have called them."

Acts 14:23

"So when they had appointed elders in every church, and prayed with fasting, they commended them to the Lord in whom they had believed."

Scriptures on Fear and Worry

2 Timothy 1:7

"For God has not given us a spirit of fear, but of power and of love and of a sound mind."

Romans 8:37- 39

"Yet in all these things we are more than conquerors through Him who loved us. For I am persuaded that neither death nor life, nor angels nor principalities nor powers, nor things present nor things to come, nor height nor depth, nor any other created thing, shall be able to separate us from the love of God which is in Christ Jesus our Lord."

Psalms 27:1

"The Lord is my light and my salvation; whom shall I fear? The Lord is the strength of my life; of whom shall I be afraid?"

Psalms 27

The Lord is my light and my salvation;

   whom shall I fear?

The Lord is the stronghold of my life;

   of whom shall I be afraid?

2 When evildoers assail me

   to eat up my flesh,

my adversaries and foes,

   it is they who stumble and fall.

3 Though an army encamp against me,

   my heart shall not fear;

though war arise against me,

   yet I will be confident.

4 One thing have I asked of the Lord,

    that will I seek after:

that I may dwell in the house of the Lord

    all the days of my life,

to gaze upon the beauty of the Lord

    and to inquire in his temple.

5 For he will hide me in his shelter

    in the day of trouble;

he will conceal me under the cover of his tent;

    he will lift me high upon a rock.

6 And now my head shall be lifted up

    above my enemies all around me,

and I will offer in his tent

    sacrifices with shouts of joy;

I will sing and make melody to the Lord.

Isaiah 41:13

"For I, the Lord your God, will hold your right hand, Saying to you, 'Fear not, I will help you.'"

Proverbs 1:33

"But whoever listens to me will dwell safely, and will be secure, without fear of evil."

Luke 12:32

"Do not fear, little flock, for it is your Father's good pleasure to give you the kingdom."

Matthew 10:28

"And do not fear those who kill the body but cannot kill the soul. But rather fear Him who is able to destroy both soul and body in hell."

Proverbs 3:25,26

"Do not be afraid of sudden terror, nor of trouble from the wicked when it comes; For the Lord will be your confidence, and will keep your foot from being caught."

Isaiah 14:3

"It shall come to pass in the day the Lord gives you rest from your sorrow, and from your fear and the hard bondage in which you were made to serve,"

Proverbs 3:24

"When you lie down, you will not be afraid; yes, you will lie down and your sleep will be sweet."

1 Peter 3:12-14

"For the eyes of the Lord are on the righteous, and His ears are open to their prayers; but the face of the Lord is against those who do evil. And who is he who will harm you if you become followers of what is good? But even if you should suffer for righteousness' sake, you are blessed. And do not be afraid of their threats, nor be troubled."

Isaiah 54:14

"In righteousness you shall be established; you shall be far from oppression, for you shall not fear; and from terror, for it shall not come near you."

Hebrews 13:6

"So we may boldly say: 'The Lord is my helper; I will not fear. What can man do to me?' "

Psalms 46:1

"God is our refuge and strength, a very present help in trouble."

Proverbs 29:25

"The fear of man brings a snare, but whoever trusts in the Lord shall be safe."

Psalms 91:4-6

"He shall cover you with His feathers, and under His wings you shall take refuge; His truth shall be your shield and buckler. You shall not be afraid of the terror by night, nor of the arrow that flies by day, Nor of the pestilence that walks in darkness, Nor of the destruction that lays waste at noonday."

Isaiah 54:4

"Do not fear, for you will not be ashamed; Neither be disgraced, for you will not be put to shame; For you will forget the shame of your youth, And will not remember the reproach of your widowhood anymore."

Isaiah 43:2

"When you pass through the waters, I will be with you; And through the rivers, they shall not overflow you. When you walk through the fire, you shall not be burned, nor shall the flame scorch you. "

John 14:27

"Peace I leave with you, My peace I give to you; not as the world gives do I give to you. Let not your heart be troubled, neither let it be afraid."

Psalms 23:4,5

"Yea, though I walk through the valley of the shadow of death, I will fear no evil; For You are with me; Your rod and Your staff, they comfort me. You prepare a table before me in the presence of my enemies; You anoint my head with oil; My cup runs over."

Luke 12:7

"But the very hairs of your head are all numbered. Do not fear therefore; you are of more value than many sparrows."

Luke 8:50

"But when Jesus heard it, He answered him, saying, "Do not be afraid; only believe, and she will be made well.""

Scriptures on Food and Clothing

Psalms 111:5

"He has given food to those who fear Him; He will ever be mindful of His covenant."

Matthew 6:31- 34

"Therefore do not worry, saying, 'What shall we eat?' or 'What shall we drink?' or 'What shall we wear?' For after all these things the Gentiles (heathen) seek. For your heavenly Father knows that you need all these things. But seek first the kingdom of God and His righteousness, and all these things shall be added to you. Therefore do not worry about tomorrow, for tomorrow will worry about its own things. Sufficient for the day is its own trouble."

Psalms 147:14

"He makes peace in your borders, and fills you with the finest wheat."

Joel 2:26

"You shall eat in plenty and be satisfied, and praise the name of the Lord your God, Who has dealt wondrously with you; and My people shall never be put to shame."

Proverbs 13:25

"The righteous eats to the satisfying of his soul, but the stomach of the wicked shall be in want."

Psalms 132:15

"I will abundantly bless her provision; I will satisfy her poor with bread."

Scriptures on Forgiveness

Matthew 5:44, 45

"But I say to you, love your enemies, bless those who curse you, do good to those who hate you, and pray for those who spitefully use you and persecute you, that you may be sons of your Father in heaven; for He makes His sun rise on the evil and on the good, and sends rain on the just and on the unjust."

1 John 1:9

"If we confess our sins, He is faithful and just to forgive us our sins and to cleanse us from all unrighteousness."

Mark 11:25, 26

"And whenever you stand praying, if you have anything against anyone, forgive him, that your Father in heaven may also forgive you your trespasses. But if you do not forgive, neither will your Father in heaven forgive your trespasses."

Ephesians 4:32

Be kind to one another, tenderhearted, forgiving one another, as God in Christ forgave you.

Matthew 18:21

Then Peter came up and said to him, "Lord, how often will my brother sin against me, and I forgive him? As many as seven times?" Jesus said to him, "I do not say to you seven times, but seventy times seven.

Matthew 6:14

"For if you forgive men their trespasses, your heavenly Father will also forgive you."

Romans 12:20

"Therefore ' If your enemy is hungry, feed him; If he is thirsty, give him a drink; for in so doing you will heap coals of fire on his head."

Luke 6:35-38

"But love your enemies, do good, and lend, hoping for nothing in return; and your reward will be great, and you will be sons of the Most High. For He is kind to the unthankful and evil. Therefore be merciful, just as your Father also is merciful. Judge not, and you shall not be judged. Condemn not, and you shall not be condemned. Forgive, and you will be forgiven. Give, and it will be given to you: good measure, pressed down, shaken together, and running over will be put into your bosom. For with the same measure that you use, it will be measured back to you."

Proverbs 20:22

"Do not say, "I will recompense evil"; Wait for the Lord, and He will save you."

Scriptures on Freedom from Sin

Romans 6:6,7

"Knowing this, that our old man was crucified with Him, that the body of sin might be done away with, that we should no longer be slaves of sin. For he who has died has been freed from sin."

Ezekiel 36:25,26

"Then I will sprinkle clean water on you, and you shall be clean; I will cleanse you from all your filthiness and from all your idols. I will give you a new heart and put a new spirit within you; I will take the heart of stone out of your flesh and give you a heart of flesh."

Acts 10:43

"To Him all the prophets witness that, through His name, whoever believes in Him will receive remission of sins."

2 Corinthians 5:17

"Therefore, if anyone is in Christ, he is a new creation; old things have passed away; behold, all things have become new."

Romans 6:1, 2

"What shall we say then? Shall we continue in sin that grace may abound? Certainly not! How shall we who died to sin live any longer in it?"

Romans 6:11

"Likewise you also, reckon yourselves to be dead indeed to sin, but alive to God in Christ Jesus our Lord."

Romans 6:14

"For sin shall not have dominion over you, for you are not under law but under grace."

Scriptures on Fruitfulness

Psalms 1:3

"He shall be like a tree Planted by the rivers of water, that brings forth its fruit in its season, whose leaf also shall not wither; and whatever he does shall prosper."

John 15:1- 5

"I am the true vine, and My Father is the vinedresser. Every branch in Me that does not bear fruit He takes away; and every branch that bears fruit He prunes, that it may bear more fruit. You are already clean because of the word which I have spoken to you. Abide in Me, and I in you. As the branch cannot bear fruit of itself, unless it abides in the vine, neither can you, unless you abide in Me. I am the vine, you are the branches. He who abides in Me, and I in him, bears much fruit; for without Me you can do nothing."

Matthew 7:15-17

"Beware of false prophets, who come to you in sheep's clothing, but inwardly they are ravenous wolves. You will know them by their fruits. Do men gather grapes from thorn bushes or figs from thistles? Even so, every good tree bears good fruit, but a bad tree bears bad fruit."

Psalms 92:14

"They shall still bear fruit in old age; they shall be fresh and flourishing,"

Hosea 14:5

"I will be like the dew to Israel; He shall grow like the lily, and lengthen his roots like Lebanon."

2 Peter 1:8

"For if these things are yours and abound, you will be neither barren nor unfruitful in the knowledge of our Lord Jesus Christ."

Jeremiah 31:12

"Therefore they shall come and sing in the height of Zion, Streaming to the goodness of the Lord - For wheat and new wine and oil, For the young of the flock and the herd; Their souls shall be like a well-watered garden, And they shall sorrow no more at all."

John 15:16

You did not choose me, but I chose you and appointed you that you should go and bear fruit and that your fruit should abide, so that whatever you ask the Father in my name, he may give it to you.

Galatians 5:22-23

But the fruit of the Spirit is love, joy, peace, patience, kindness, goodness, faithfulness, gentleness, self-control; against such things there is no law.

2 Peter 1:5-9

For this very reason, make every effort to supplement your faith with virtue, and virtue with knowledge, and knowledge with self-control, and self-control with steadfastness, and steadfastness with godliness, and godliness with brotherly affection, and brotherly affection with love. For if these qualities are yours and are increasing, they keep you from being ineffective or unfruitful in the knowledge of our Lord Jesus Christ. For whoever lacks these qualities is so nearsighted that he is blind, having forgotten that he was cleansed from his former sins.

John 15:8

By this my Father is glorified, that you bear much fruit and so prove to be my disciples.

Philippians 1:6

And I am sure of this, that he who began a good work in you will bring it to completion at the day of Jesus Christ.

Matthew 3:8

Bear fruit in keeping with repentance.

Scriptures on Friendship

Proverbs 18:24

A man of many companions may come to ruin, but there is a friend who sticks closer than a brother.

John 15:13

Greater love has no one than this that someone lay down his life for his friends.

Proverbs 17:17

A friend loves at all times, and a brother is born for adversity.

Proverbs 27:17

Iron sharpens iron, and one man sharpens another.

Ecclesiastes 4:9-12

Two are better than one, because they have a good reward for their toil. For if they fall, one will lift up his fellow. But woe to him who is alone when he falls and has not another to lift him up! Again, if two lie together, they keep warm, but how can one keep warm alone? And though a man might prevail against one who is alone, two will withstand him—a threefold cord is not quickly broken.

1 Corinthians 15:33

Do not be deceived: "Bad company ruins good morals."

1 Thessalonians 5:11

Therefore encourage one another and build one another up, just as you are doing.

Proverbs 27:9

Oil and perfume make the heart glad, and the sweetness of a friend comes from his earnest counsel.

Proverbs 27:6

Faithful are the wounds of a friend; profuse are the kisses of an enemy.

Job 6:14

"He who withholds kindness from a friend forsakes the fear of the Almighty.

Proverbs 16:28

A dishonest man spreads strife, and a whisperer separates close friends.

Proverbs 13:20

Whoever walks with the wise becomes wise, but the companion of fools will suffer harm.

Hebrews 10:24-25

And let us consider how to stir up one another to love and good works, not neglecting to meet together, as is the habit of some, but encouraging one another, and all the more as you see the Day drawing near.

1 Peter 4:8-10

Above all, keep loving one another earnestly, since love covers a multitude of sins. Show hospitality to one another without grumbling. As each has received a gift, use it to serve one another, as good stewards of God's varied grace:

Ecclesiastes 4:9-10

Two are better than one, because they have a good reward for their toil. For if they fall, one will lift up his fellow. But woe to him who is alone when he falls and has not another to lift him up!

Proverbs 22:24-25

Make no friendship with a man given to anger, nor go with a wrathful man, lest you learn his ways and entangle yourself in a snare.

Scriptures for Giving

Psalms 41:1,2

"Blessed is he who considers the poor; The Lord will deliver him in time of trouble. The Lord will preserve him and keep him alive, and he will be blessed on the earth; you will not deliver him to the will of his enemies."

Proverbs 19:17

"He who has pity on the poor lends to the Lord, and He will pay back what he has given."

Luke 14:13,14

"But when you give a feast, invite the poor, the maimed, the lame, and the blind. And you will be blessed, because they cannot repay you; for you shall be repaid at the resurrection of the just."

Luke 12:33

"Sell what you have and give alms; provide yourselves money bags which do not grow old, a treasure in the heavens that does not fail, where no thief approaches nor moth destroys."

Proverbs 14:21

"He who despises his neighbor sins; But he who has mercy on the poor, happy is he."

Ecclesiastes 11:1

"Cast your bread upon the waters, for you will find it after many days."

Psalms 112:9

"He has dispersed abroad, He has given to the poor; His righteousness endures forever; His horn will be exalted with honor."

Proverbs 22:9

"He who has a generous eye will be blessed, for he gives of his bread to the poor."

Luke 6:38

"Give, and it will be given to you: good measure, pressed down, shaken together, and running over will be put into your bosom. For with the same measure that you use, it will be measured back to you."

Proverbs 28:27

"He who gives to the poor will not lack, but he who hides his eyes will have many curses."

2 Corinthians 9:7

"So let each one give as he purposes in his heart, not grudgingly or of necessity; for God loves a cheerful giver."

Proverbs 11:24,25

"There is one who scatters, yet increases more; and there is one who withholds more than is right, but it leads to poverty. The generous soul will be made rich, And he who waters will also be watered himself."

Psalms 37:25, 26

"I have been young, and now am old; yet I have not seen the righteous forsaken, nor his descendants begging bread. He is ever merciful, and lends; And his descendants are blessed."

Isaiah 58:10

"If you extend your soul to the hungry and satisfy the afflicted soul, then your light shall dawn in the darkness, and your darkness shall be as the noonday."

1 Timothy 6:17,18

"Command those who are rich in this present age not to be haughty, nor to trust in uncertain riches but in the living God, who gives us richly all things to enjoy. Let them do good, that they be rich in good works, ready to give, willing to share..."

Isaiah 58:7,8

"Is it not to share your bread with the hungry, and that you bring to your house the poor who are cast out; when you see the naked, that you cover him, And not hide yourself from your own flesh? Then your light shall break forth like the morning, Your healing shall spring forth speedily, And your righteousness shall go before you; The glory of the Lord shall be your rear guard."

Mark 10:21

"Then Jesus, looking at him, loved him, and said to him, 'One thing you lack: Go your way, sell whatever you have and give to the poor, and you will have treasure in heaven; and come, take up the cross, and follow Me.' "

Matthew 6:1- 4

"Take heed that you do not do your charitable deeds before men, to be seen by them. Otherwise you have no reward from your Father in heaven. Therefore, when you do a charitable deed, do not sound a trumpet before you as the hypocrites do in the synagogues and in the streets, that they may have glory from men. Assuredly, I say to you, they have their reward. But when you do a charitable deed, do not let your left hand know what your right hand is doing, that your charitable deed may be in secret; and your Father who sees in secret will Himself reward you openly."

Scriptures on God's Correction

Proverbs 3:12

"For whom the Lord loves He corrects, just as a father the son in whom he delights."

Job 5:17, 1

"Behold, happy is the man whom God corrects; Therefore do not despise the chastening of the Almighty. For He bruises, but He binds up; He wounds, but His hands make whole."

Psalms 94:12, 13

"Blessed is the man whom You instruct, O Lord, And teach out of Your law, That You may give him rest from the days of adversity, Until the pit is dug for the wicked."

1 Corinthians 11:32

"But when we are judged, we are chastened by the Lord, that we may not be condemned with the world."

2 Corinthians 4:16 ,17

"Therefore we do not lose heart. Even though our outward man is perishing, yet the inward man is being renewed day by day. For our light affliction, which is but for a moment, is working for us a far more exceeding and eternal weight of glory,"

Hebrews 12:6, 7

"For whom the Lord loves He chastens, And scourges every son whom He receives. If you endure chastening, God deals with you as with sons; for what son is there whom a father does not chasten?"

Hebrews 12:10, 11

"For they indeed for a few days chastened us as seemed best to them, but He for our profit, that we may be partakers of His holiness. Now no chastening seems to be joyful for the present, but painful; nevertheless, afterward it yields the peaceable fruit of righteousness to those who have been trained by it.

Scriptures on God's Protection

Psalms 91 He who dwells in the shelter of the Most High

    will abide in the shadow of the Almighty.

2 I will say to the Lord, "My refuge and my fortress,

    my God, in whom I trust."

3 For he will deliver you from the snare of the fowler

    and from the deadly pestilence.

4 He will cover you with his pinions,

    and under his wings you will find refuge;

    his faithfulness is a shield and buckler.

5 You will not fear the terror of the night,

    nor the arrow that flies by day,

6 nor the pestilence that stalks in darkness,

    nor the destruction that wastes at noonday.

7 A thousand may fall at your side,

    ten thousand at your right hand,

    but it will not come near you.

8 You will only look with your eyes

    and see the recompense of the wicked.

9 Because you have made the Lord your dwelling place—

    the Most High, who is my refuge—

10 no evil shall be allowed to befall you,

    no plague come near your tent.

11 For he will command his angels concerning you

    to guard you in all your ways.

12 On their hands they will bear you up,

lest you strike your foot against a stone.

13 You will tread on the lion and the adder;

the young lion and the serpent you will trample underfoot.

14 "Because he holds fast to me in love, I will deliver him;

I will protect him, because he knows my name.

15 When he calls to me, I will answer him;

I will be with him in trouble;

I will rescue him and honor him.

16 With long life I will satisfy him

and show him my salvation."

Psalms 27:1- 5

"The Lord is my light and my salvation; Whom shall I fear? The Lord is the strength of my life; Of whom shall I be afraid? When the wicked came against me To eat up my flesh, My enemies and foes, They stumbled and fell. Though an army may encamp against me, My heart shall not fear; Though war may rise against me, In this I will be confident.

Psalms 27:4-5

One thing I have desired of the Lord, That will I seek: That I may dwell in the house of the Lord All the days of my life, To behold the beauty of the Lord, And to inquire in His temple.

For in the time of trouble He shall hide me in His pavilion; In the secret place of His tabernacle He shall hide me; He shall set me high upon a rock."

Proverbs 3:24

"When you lie down, you will not be afraid; Yes, you will lie down and your sleep will be sweet."

Proverbs 18:10

"The name of the Lord is a strong tower; The righteous run to it and are safe."

Job 5:22

"You shall laugh at destruction and famine, And you shall not be afraid of the beasts of the earth."

Psalms 112:7

"He will not be afraid of evil tidings; His heart is steadfast, trusting in the Lord."

Psalms 91:9,10

"Because you have made the Lord, who is my refuge, Even the Most High, your dwelling place, No evil shall befall you, Nor shall any plague come near your dwelling;"

Isaiah 43:1,2

"...Fear not, for I have redeemed you; I have called you by your name; You are Mine. When you pass through the waters, I will be with you; And through the rivers, they shall not overflow you. When you walk through the fire, you shall not be burned, Nor shall the flame scorch you."

Ezekiel 34:28

"And they shall no longer be a prey for the nations, nor shall beasts of the land devour them; but they shall dwell safely, and no one shall make them afraid."

Proverbs 1:33

"But whoever listens to me will dwell safely, And will be secure, without fear of evil."

Job 11:18,19

"And you would be secure, because there is hope; Yes, you would dig around you, and take your rest in safety. You would also lie down, and no one would make you afraid; Yes, many would court your favor."

Psalms 121:7,8

"The Lord shall preserve you from all evil; He shall preserve your soul. The Lord shall preserve your going out and your coming in From this time forth, and even forevermore."

1 Peter 3:13

"And who is he who will harm you if you become followers of what is good?"

Deuteronomy 33:12

"Of Benjamin he said: 'The beloved of the Lord shall dwell in safety by Him, Who shelters him all the day long; And he shall dwell between His shoulders."

Psalms 4:8

"I will both lie down in peace, and sleep; For You alone, O Lord, make me dwell in safety."

Scriptures on Gossip and Rumors

Leviticus 19:16

"You shall not go about as a talebearer among your people; nor shall you take a stand against the life of your neighbor: I am the Lord."

Proverbs 18:8

"The words of a talebearer are like tasty trifles (wounds), and they go down into the inmost body."

Proverbs 20:19

"He who goes about as a talebearer reveals secrets; therefore do not associate with one who flatters with his lips."

Proverbs 11:13

"A talebearer reveals secrets, but he who is of a faithful spirit conceals a matter."

Proverbs 16:28

"A perverse man sows strife, and a whisperer separates the best of friends."

Psalms 52:2

"Your tongue devises destruction, like a sharp razor, working deceitfully."

Proverbs 25:23

"The north wind brings forth rain, And a backbiting tongue an angry countenance."

Proverbs 26:20,21

"Where there is no wood, the fire goes out; and where there is no talebearer, strife ceases. As charcoal is to burning coals, and wood to fire, so is a contentious man to kindle strife."

Psalms 34:13

"Keep your tongue from evil, And your lips from speaking deceit."

Scriptures on Growing in Grace

2 Corinthians 12:9

But he said to me, "My grace is sufficient for you, for my power is made perfect in weakness." Therefore I will boast all the more gladly of my weaknesses, so that the power of Christ may rest upon me.

Ephesians 2:8-9

For by grace you have been saved through faith. And this is not your own doing; it is the gift of God, not a result of works, so that no one may boast.

Romans 6:14

For sin will have no dominion over you, since you are not under law but under grace.

Romans 11:6

But if it is by grace, it is no longer on the basis of works; otherwise grace would no longer be grace.

James 4:6

But he gives more grace. Therefore it says, "God opposes the proud, but gives grace to the humble."

Ephesians 2:8

For by grace you have been saved through faith. And this is not your own doing; it is the gift of God,

Hebrews 4:16

Let us then with confidence draw near to the throne of grace, that we may receive mercy and find grace to help in time of need.

1 Corinthians 15:10

But by the grace of God I am what I am, and his grace toward me was not in vain. On the contrary, I worked harder than any of them, though it was not I, but the grace of God that is with me.

John 1:16

And from his fullness we have all received, grace upon grace.

Romans 5:8

But God shows his love for us in that while we were still sinners, Christ died for us.

John 15:8

"By this My Father is glorified, that you bear much fruit; so you will be my disciples."

Philippians 1:9

"And this I pray, that your love may abound still more and more in knowledge and all discernment,"

2 Thessalonians 1:3

"We are bound to thank God always for you, brethren, as it is fitting, because your faith grows exceedingly, and the love of every one of you all abounds toward each other,"

1 Thessalonians 4:1

"Finally then, brethren, we urge and exhort in the Lord Jesus that you should abound more and more, just as you received from us how you ought to walk and to please God;"

Philippians 1:11

"being filled with the fruits of righteousness which are by Jesus Christ, to the glory and praise of God."

2 Peter 1:5

"But also for this very reason, giving all diligence, add to your faith virtue, to virtue knowledge,"

Job 17:9

"Yet the righteous will hold to his way, and he who has clean hands will be stronger and stronger."

2 Corinthians 3:18

"But we all, with unveiled face, beholding as in a mirror the glory of the Lord, are being transformed into the same image from glory to glory, just as by the Spirit of the Lord."

Psalms 138:8

"The Lord will perfect that which concerns me; Your mercy, O Lord, endures forever; Do not forsake the works of Your hands."

Colossians 1:6

"which has come to you, as it has also in all the world, and is bringing forth fruit, as it is also among you since the day you heard and knew the grace of God in truth;"

Philippians 3:14-16

"I press toward the goal for the prize of the upward call of God in Christ Jesus. Therefore let us, as many as are mature, have this mind; and if in anything you think otherwise, God will reveal even this to you. Nevertheless, to the degree that we have already attained, let us walk by the same rule, let us be of the same mind"

Proverbs 4:18

"But the path of the just is like the shining sun, That shines ever brighter unto the perfect day."

Scriptures on Guidance

Isaiah 30:21

"Your ears shall hear a word behind you, saying, 'This is the way, walk in it,' whenever you turn to the right hand or whenever you turn to the left."

Psalms 48:14

"For this is God, Our God forever and ever; He will be our guide even to death."

Proverbs 16:9

"A man's heart plans his way, But the Lord directs his steps."

Psalms 37:23

"The steps of a good man are ordered by the Lord, And He delights in his way."

Isaiah 28:26

"For He instructs him in right judgment, His God teaches him."

Proverbs 11:5

"The righteousness of the blameless will direct his way aright, But the wicked will fall by his own wickedness."

Proverbs 3:6

"In all your ways acknowledge Him, And He shall direct your paths."

Isaiah 42:16

"I will bring the blind by a way they did not know; I will lead them in paths they have not known. I will make darkness light before them, And crooked places straight. These things I will do for them, And not forsake them."

Psalms 73:23,24

"Nevertheless I am continually with You; You hold me by my right hand. You will guide me with Your counsel, And afterward receive me to glory. "

Psalms 32:8

"I will instruct you and teach you in the way you should go; I will guide you with My eye."

Psalm 119:105

Your word is a lamp to my feet and a light to my path.

John 16:13

When the Spirit of truth comes, he will guide you into all the truth, for he will not speak on his own authority, but whatever he hears he will speak, and he will declare to you the things that are to come.

Proverbs 3:5-6

Trust in the Lord with all your heart, and do not lean on your own understanding. In all your ways acknowledge him, and he will make straight your paths.

Scriptures on Healing

Psalm 118:17

"I shall not die but live and declare the works of the Lord."

Jeremiah 17:14

Heal me, O Lord, and I shall be healed; save me, and I shall be saved, for you are my praise.

1 Peter 2:24

"Who himself bore our sins in his own body on the tree, that we, having died to sins, might live for righteousness-by whose stripes you were healed."

James 5:14-16

"Is anyone among you sick? Let him call for the elders of the church, and let them pray over him, anointing him with oil in the name of the Lord. And the prayer of faith will save the sick, and if he has committed sins, he will be forgiven."

Psalm 105:37

"He also brought them out with silver and gold, And there was none feeble among his tribes."

Isaiah 53:4-5

"Surely he has borne our griefs and carried our sorrows; yet we esteemed him stricken, smitten by God, and afflicted. But he was wounded for our transgressions, He was crushed for our iniquities; the chastisement for our peace was upon him, and by his stripes we are healed."

Jeremiah 30:17

"For I will restore health to you and heal you of your wounds, says the Lord."

Proverbs 4:20-24

"My son, give attention to my words; Incline your ear to my sayings. Do not let them depart from your eyes; Keep them in the midst of your heart; for they are life to those who find them, and health to all their flesh. Keep your heart with all diligence, for out of it spring the issues of life. And put away from you a deceitful mouth, and out perverse lips far from you."

Psalm 107:19-21

"Then they cried out to the Lord in their trouble, and he saved them out of their distresses. He sent his word and healed them from their destruct ions Oh that men would give thanks to the Lord for his goodness, and for his wonderful works to the children of men."

3 John 2

"Beloved I pray that you may prosper in all things and be in health, just as your soul prospers."

Deuteronomy 30:19-20

"I call heaven and earth as witnesses today against you, that I have set before you life and death, blessings and cursing; therefore choose life, that both you and your descendants may live; that you may love the lord your God, that you may obey him, for he is your life and the length of your days; and that you may dwell in the land which the Lord swore to your fathers, to Abraham, Isaac, and Jacob, to give them."

Deuteronomy 7:14-15

"You shall be blessed above all peoples; there shall not be a male or female barren among you or among your livestock. And the Lord will take away from you all sickness, and will afflict you with none of the terrible diseases of Egypt which you have known, but will lay them on a;; those who hate you."

Exodus 15:26

"If you diligently heed the voice of the Lord your God and do what is right in his sight, give ear to his commandments and keep all his statutes, I will put none of the diseases on you which I have brought on the Egyptians. For I am the Lord who heals you."

Exodus 23:25

"So you shall serve the Lord your God and he will bless your bread and your water. And I will take sickness away from the midst of you."

Matthew:8:16-17

"When evening had come, they brought to him many who were demon-possessed. And he cast out the spirits with a word, and healed all who were sick, that it might be fulfilled which was spoken by Isaiah the prophet,, saying "He himself took our infirmities and bore our sicknesses"

Scriptures on the Heart

Psalm 51:10

Create in me a clean heart, O God, and renew a right spirit within me.

Ezekiel 36:26

And I will give you a new heart, and a new spirit I will put within you. And I will remove the heart of stone from your flesh and give you a heart of flesh.

Jeremiah 17:9

The heart is deceitful above all things, and desperately sick; who can understand it?

Proverbs 4:23

Keep your heart with all vigilance, for from it flow the springs of life.

Matthew 5:8

"Blessed are the pure in heart, for they shall see God.

Psalm 34:18

The Lord is near to the brokenhearted and saves the crushed in spirit.

Jeremiah 17:10

"I the Lord search the heart and test the mind, to give every man according to his ways, according to the fruit of his deeds."

Hebrews 4:12

For the word of God is living and active, sharper than any two-edged sword, piercing to the division of soul and of spirit, of joints and of marrow, and discerning the thoughts and intentions of the heart.

Proverbs 3:5-6

Trust in the Lord with all your heart, and do not lean on your own understanding. In all your ways acknowledge him, and he will make straight your paths.

Proverbs 21:2

Every way of a man is right in his own eyes, but the Lord weighs the heart.

Ezekiel 11:19

And I will give them one heart, and a new spirit I will put within them. I will remove the heart of stone from their flesh and give them a heart of flesh,

1 Samuel 16:7

But the Lord said to Samuel, "Do not look on his appearance or on the height of his stature, because I have rejected him. For the Lord sees not as man sees: man looks on the outward appearance, but the Lord looks on the heart."

Matthew 15:18-20

But what comes out of the mouth proceeds from the heart, and this defiles a person. For out of the heart come evil thoughts, murder, adultery, sexual immorality, theft, false witness, slander. These are what defile a person. But to eat with unwashed hands does not defile anyone."

James 4:8

Draw near to God, and he will draw near to you. Cleanse your hands, you sinners, and purify your hearts, you double-minded.

Luke 12:33-34

Sell your possessions, and give to the needy. Provide yourselves with moneybags that do not grow old, with a treasure in the heavens that does not fail, where no thief approaches and no moth destroys. For where your treasure is, there will your heart be also.

1 Timothy 1:5

The aim of our charge is love that issues from a pure heart and a good conscience and a sincere faith.

Matthew 22:37

And he said to him, "You shall love the Lord your God with all your heart and with all your soul and with all your mind.

Psalm 26:2

Prove me, O Lord, and try me; test my heart and my mind.

Psalm 112:7

He is not afraid of bad news; his heart is firm, trusting in the Lord.

Romans 2:5

But because of your hard and impenitent heart you are storing up wrath for yourself on the day of wrath when God's righteous judgment will be revealed.

Psalm 119:10

With my whole heart I seek you; let me not wander from your commandments!

Hebrews 10:22

Let us draw near with a true heart in full assurance of faith, with our hearts sprinkled clean from an evil conscience and our bodies washed with pure water.

John 14:27

Peace I leave with you; my peace I give to you. Not as the world gives do I give to you. Let not your hearts be troubled, neither let them be afraid.

Romans 10:10

For with the heart one believes and is justified, and with the mouth one confesses and is saved.

Romans 1:21

For although they knew God, they did not honor him as God or give thanks to him, but they became futile in their thinking, and their foolish hearts were darkened.

Proverbs 3:5

Trust in the Lord with all your heart, and do not lean on your own understanding.

Jeremiah 17:9-10

The heart is deceitful above all things, and desperately sick; who can understand it? "I the Lord search the heart and test the mind, to give every man according to his ways, according to the fruit of his deeds."

Psalm 51:17

The sacrifices of God are a broken spirit; a broken and contrite heart, O God, you will not despise.

2 Timothy 2:22

So flee youthful passions and pursue righteousness, faith, love, and peace, along with those who call on the Lord from a pure heart.

Psalm 119:11

I have stored up your word in my heart, that I might not sin against you.

John 14:1

"Let not your hearts be troubled. Believe in God; believe also in me.

Proverbs 28:14

Blessed is the one who fears the Lord always, but whoever hardens his heart will fall into calamity.

Philippians 4:7

And the peace of God, which surpasses all understanding, will guard your hearts and your minds in Christ Jesus.

Psalm 24:4

He who has clean hands and a pure heart, who does not lift up his soul to what is false and does not swear deceitfully.

Ephesians 6:6

Not by the way of eye-service, as people-pleasers, but as servants of Christ, doing the will of God from the heart,

Psalm 37:4

Delight yourself in the Lord, and he will give you the desires of your heart.

Psalm 97:11

Light is sown for the righteous, and joy for the upright in heart.

Scriptures on Help in Trouble

John 16:33

"These things I have spoken to you, that in Me you may have peace. In the world you will have tribulation; but be of good cheer, I have overcome the world."

Psalms 37:39

"But the salvation of the righteous is from the Lord; He is their strength in the time of trouble."

Psalms 146:8

"The Lord opens the eyes of the blind; The Lord raises those who are bowed down; The Lord loves the righteous."

Nahum 1:7

"The Lord is good, A stronghold in the day of trouble; And He knows those who trust in Him."

Psalm 37:24

"Though he fall, he shall not be utterly cast down; For the Lord upholds him with His hand."

Psalms 32:7

"You are my hiding place; You shall preserve me from trouble; You shall surround me with songs of deliverance. Selah"

Psalms 71:20

"You, who have shown me great and severe troubles, Shall revive me again, and bring me up again from the depths of the earth."

Psalms 42:11

"Why are you cast down, O my soul? And why are you disquieted within me? Hope in God; for I shall yet praise Him, The help of my countenance and my God."

Psalms 73:26

"My flesh and my heart fail; But God is the strength of my heart and my portion forever."

Psalms 91:10, 11

"No evil shall befall you, nor shall any plague come near your dwelling; For He shall give His angels charge over you, to keep you in all your ways."

Psalms 126:5, 6

"Those who sow in tears shall reap in joy. He who continually goes forth weeping, Bearing seed for sowing, Shall doubtless come again with rejoicing, bringing his sheaves with him."

Psalms 31:23

"Oh, love the Lord, all you His saints! For the Lord preserves the faithful, and fully repays the proud person."

Psalms 68:13

"Though you lie down among the sheepfolds, you will be like the wings of a dove covered with silver, and her feathers with yellow gold."

Job 8:20, 21

"Behold, God will not cast away the blameless, nor will He uphold the evildoers. He will yet fill your mouth with laughing, and your lips with rejoicing."

Psalms 22:24

"For He has not despised nor abhorred the affliction of the afflicted; Nor has He hidden His face from Him; But when He cried to Him, He heard. "

Job 5:19 - 23

"He shall deliver you in six troubles, yes, in seven no evil shall touch you. In famine He shall redeem you from death, And in war from the power of the sword. You shall be hidden from the scourge of the tongue, And you shall not be afraid of destruction when it comes. You shall laugh at destruction and famine, And you shall not be afraid of the beasts of the earth. For you shall have a covenant with the stones of the field, And the beasts of the field shall be at peace with you."

Psalms 9:9

"The Lord also will be a refuge for the oppressed, A refuge in times of trouble."

Psalms 138:7

"Though I walk in the midst of trouble, You will revive me; You will stretch out Your hand Against the wrath of my enemies, And Your right hand will save me."

Psalm 18:28

"For You will light my lamp; The Lord my God will enlighten my darkness."

Psalms 34:19

"Many are the afflictions of the righteous, But the Lord delivers him out of them all."

Psalms 18:2

"The Lord is my rock and my fortress and my deliverer; My God, my strength, in whom I will trust; My shield and the horn of my salvation, my stronghold."

Micah 7:8,9

"Do not rejoice over me, my enemy; when I fall, I will arise; when I sit in darkness, The Lord will be a light to me. I will bear the indignation of the Lord, because I have sinned against Him, Until He pleads my case and executes justice for me. He will bring me forth to the light; I will see His righteousness."

Scriptures on the Holy Spirit

John 14:16,17

"And I will pray the Father, and He will give you another Helper, that He may abide with you forever - the Spirit of truth, whom the world cannot receive, because it neither sees Him nor knows Him; but you know Him, for He dwells with you and will be in you."

John 7: 38,39

"He who believes in Me, as the Scripture has said, out of his heart will flow rivers of living water. But this He spoke concerning the Spirit, whom those believing in Him would receive; for the Holy Spirit was not yet given, because Jesus was not yet glorified."

John 16:13

"However, when He, the Spirit of truth, has come, He will guide you into all truth; for He will not speak on His own authority, but whatever He hears He will speak; and He will tell you things to come."

Isaiah 59:21

" 'As for Me,' says the Lord, 'this is My covenant with them: My Spirit who is upon you, and My words which I have put in your mouth, shall not depart from your mouth, nor from the mouth of your descendants, nor from the mouth of your descendants' descendants,' says the Lord, 'from this time and forevermore. ' "

Luke 11:13

"If you then, being evil, know how to give good gifts to your children, how much more will your heavenly Father give the Holy Spirit to those who ask Him."

John 4:14

"but whoever drinks of the water that I shall give him will never thirst. But the water that I shall give him will become in him a fountain of water springing up into everlasting life."

Ezekiel 36:27

"I will put My Spirit within you and cause you to walk in My statutes, and you will keep My judgments and do them."

Galatians 3:14

"that the blessing of Abraham might come upon the Gentiles in Christ Jesus, that we might receive the promise of the Spirit through faith."

1 John 2:27

"But the anointing which you have received from Him abides in you, and you do not need that anyone teach you; but as the same anointing teaches you concerning all things, and is true, and is not a lie, and just as it has taught you, you will abide in Him."

Romans 8:26,27

"Likewise the Spirit also helps in our weaknesses. For we do not know what we should pray for as we ought, but the Spirit Himself makes intercession for us with groanings which cannot be uttered. Now He who searches the hearts knows what the mind of the Spirit is, because He makes intercession for the saints according to the will of God."

Romans 14:17

"for the kingdom of God is not eating and drinking, but righteousness and peace and joy in the Holy Spirit."

1 Corinthians 2:12

"Now we have received, not the spirit of the world, but the Spirit who is from God, that we might know the things that have been freely given to us by God."

Romans 8:15

"For you did not receive the spirit of bondage again to fear, but you received the Spirit of adoption by whom we cry out, 'Abba, Father.' "

Scriptures on Homosexuality

Mark 10:6-9

"But from the beginning of the creation, God 'made them male and female.' For this reason a man shall leave his father and mother and be joined to his wife, and the two shall become one flesh'; then they are no longer two, but one flesh. Therefore what God has joined together, let not man separate."

1 John 1:9

"If we confess our sins, He is faithful and just to forgive us our sins and to cleanse us from all unrighteousness."

1 Corinthians 6:9, 10

"Do you not know that the unrighteous will not inherit the kingdom of God? Do not be deceived. Neither fornicators, nor idolaters, nor adulterers, nor homosexuals, nor sodomites, nor thieves, nor covetous, nor drunkards, nor revilers, nor extortioners will inherit the kingdom of God."

Romans 1:26, 27

"For this reason God gave them up to vile passions. For even their women exchanged the natural use for what is against nature. Likewise also the men, leaving the natural use of the woman, burned in their lust for one another, men with men committing what is shameful, and receiving in themselves the penalty of their error which was due."

Jude 1:7

"as Sodom and Gomorrah, and the cities around them in a similar manner to these, having given themselves over to sexual immorality and gone after strange flesh, are set forth as an example, suffering the vengeance of eternal fire."

Leviticus 18:22

"You shall not lie with a male as with a woman. It is an abomination."

Genesis 19:4-8

"Now before they lay down, the men of the city, the men of Sodom, both old and young, all the people from every quarter, surrounded the house. And they called to Lot and said to him, 'Where are the men who came to you tonight? Bring them out to us that we may know them carnally.' So Lot went out to them through the doorway, shut the door behind him, and said, 'Please, my brethren, do not do so wickedly! See now, I have two daughters who have not known a man; please, let me bring them out to you, and you may do to them as you wish; only do nothing to these men, since this is the reason they have come under the shadow of my roof.' "

Scriptures on Honesty

Colossians 3:9,10

"Do not lie to one another, since you have put off the old man with his deeds, and have put on the new man who is renewed in knowledge according to the image of Him who created him,"

Proverbs 12:22

Lying lips are an abomination to the Lord, but those who act faithfully are his delight.

Proverbs 19:1

Better is a poor person who walks in his integrity than one who is crooked in speech and is a fool.

2 Corinthians 8:21

For we aim at what is honorable not only in the Lord's sight but also in the sight of man.

Proverbs 3:27

"Do not withhold good from those to whom it is due when it is in the power of your hand to do so."

Leviticus 19:11

"You shall not steal, nor deal falsely, nor lie to one another."

Micah 6:10-12

"Are there yet the treasures of wickedness In the house of the wicked, And the short measure that is an abomination? Shall I count pure those with the wicked scales, And with the bag of deceitful weights? For her rich men are full of violence, Her inhabitants have spoken lies, And their tongue is deceitful in their mouth."

Leviticus 19:35

"You shall do no injustice in judgment, in measurement of length, weight, or volume."

Proverbs 11:1

"Dishonest scales are an abomination to the Lord, But a just weight is His delight."

Deuteronomy 25:15,16

"You shall have a perfect and just weight, a perfect and just measure, that your days may be lengthened in the land which the Lord your God is giving you. For all who do such things, all who behave unrighteously, are an abomination to the Lord your God." 1

1 Peter 3:10-12

For "Whoever desires to love life and see good days, let him keep his tongue from evil and his lips from speaking deceit; let him turn away from evil and do good; let him seek peace and pursue it. For the eyes of the Lord are on the righteous, and his ears are open to their prayer. But the face of the Lord is against those who do evil."

Thessalonians 4:6,7

"that no one should take advantage of and defraud his brother in this matter, because the Lord is the avenger of all such, as we also forewarned you and testified. For God did not call us to uncleanness, but in holiness."

Psalms 37:21

"The wicked borrows and does not repay, but the righteous shows mercy and gives."

Leviticus 25:14

"And if you sell anything to your neighbor or buy from your neighbor's hand, you shall not oppress one another."

Leviticus 25:17

"Therefore you shall not oppress one another, but you shall fear your God; for I am the Lord your God."

Proverbs 16:8

"Better is a little with righteousness, than vast revenues without justice."

Proverbs 6:16-20

There are six things that the Lord hates, seven that are an abomination to him: haughty eyes, a lying tongue, and hands that shed innocent blood, a heart that devises wicked plans, feet that make haste to run to evil, a false witness who breathes out lies, and one who sows discord among brothers. My son, keep your father's commandment, and forsake not your mother's teaching.

Isaiah 33:15,16

"He who walks righteously and speaks uprightly, He who despises the gain of oppressions, Who gestures with his hands, refusing bribes, Who stops his ears from hearing of bloodshed, And shuts his eyes from seeing evil: He will dwell on high; His place of defense will be the fortress of rocks; Bread will be given him, His water will be sure."

Scriptures on Hope

Psalms 71:5

"For You are my hope, O Lord God; You are my trust from my youth."

Psalms 42:11

"Why are you cast down, O my soul? And why are you disquieted within me? Hope in God; for I shall yet praise Him, The help of my countenance and my God."

1 Peter 1:13

"Therefore gird up the loins of your mind, be sober, and rest your hope fully upon the grace that is to be brought to you at the revelation of Jesus Christ;"

Romans 15:13

May the God of hope fill you with all joy and peace in believing, so that by the power of the Holy Spirit you may abound in hope.

1 John 3:3

"And everyone who has this hope in Him purifies himself, just as He is pure."

Proverbs 14:32

"The wicked is banished in his wickedness, But the righteous has a refuge in his death."

Romans 12:12

Rejoice in hope, be patient in tribulation, be constant in prayer.

Romans 8:24-25

For in this hope we were saved. Now hope that is seen is not hope. For who hopes for what he sees? But if we hope for what we do not see, we wait for it with patience.

Isaiah 40:31

But they who wait for the Lord shall renew their strength; they shall mount up with wings like eagles; they shall run and not be weary; they shall walk and not faint.

1 Peter 1:3

"Blessed be the God and Father of our Lord Jesus Christ, who according to His abundant mercy has begotten us again to a living hope through the resurrection of Jesus Christ from the dead"

Proverbs 13:12

Hope deferred makes the heart sick, but when the desire comes, it is a tree of life.

Psalm 39:7

"And now, O Lord, for what do I wait? My hope is in you.

Scriptures on Humiliation and Shame

Romans 10:11

"For the Scripture says, 'Whoever believes on Him will not be put to shame.' "

Psalms 119:6

"Then I would not be ashamed, When I look into all Your commandments."

Romans 5:5

"Now hope does not disappoint, because the love of God has been poured out in our hearts by the Holy Spirit who was given to us."

2 Timothy 1:12

"For this reason I also suffer these things; nevertheless I am not ashamed, for I know whom I have believed and am persuaded that He is able to keep what I have committed to Him until that Day."

Romans 9:33

"Behold, I lay in Zion a stumbling stone and rock of offense, And whoever believes on Him will not be put to shame."

2 Timothy 2:15

"Be diligent to present yourself approved to God, a worker who does not need to be ashamed, rightly dividing the word of truth."

Psalms 119:80

"Let my heart be blameless regarding Your statutes, That I may not be ashamed."

1 Peter 4:16

"Yet if anyone suffers as a Christian, let him not be ashamed, but let him glorify God in this matter."

Scriptures on Humility

Proverbs 22:4

"By humility and the fear of the Lord Are riches and honor and life."

Matthew 18:4

"Therefore whoever humbles himself as this little child is the greatest in the kingdom of heaven."

Psalms 10:17

"Lord, You have heard the desire of the humble; You will prepare their heart; You will cause Your ear to hear"

Proverbs 29:23

"A man's pride will bring him low, But the humble in spirit will retain honor."

1 Peter 5:6

"Therefore humble yourselves under the mighty hand of God, that He may exalt you in due time"

Matthew 23:12

"And whoever exalts himself will be humbled, and he who humbles himself will be exalted."

Job 22:29

"When they cast you down, and you say, 'Exaltation will come!' Then He will save the humble person."

Proverbs 16:19

"Better to be of a humble spirit with the lowly, Than to divide the spoil with the proud."

Proverbs 3:34

"Surely He scorns the scornful, But gives grace to the humble."

Psalms 9:12

"When He avenges blood, He remembers them; He does not forget the cry of the humble."

James 4:6

"But He gives more grace. Therefore He says: 'God resists the proud, But gives grace to the humble.' "

Proverbs 15:33

"The fear of the Lord is the instruction of wisdom, And before honor is humility."

Scriptures for Husbands

Colossians 3:19

Husbands, love your wives, and do not be harsh with them.

1 Peter 3:7

Likewise, husbands, live with your wives in an understanding way, showing honor to the woman as the weaker vessel, since they are heirs with you of the grace of life, so that your prayers may not be hindered.

Ephesians 5:25

Husbands, love your wives, as Christ loved the church and gave himself up for her,

Ephesians 5:28

In the same way husbands should love their wives as their own bodies. He who loves his wife loves himself.

1 Timothy 5:8

But if anyone does not provide for his relatives, and especially for members of his household, he has denied the faith and is worse than an unbeliever.

Ephesians 5:22-33

Wives, submit to your own husbands, as to the Lord. For the husband is the head of the wife even as Christ is the head of the church, his body, and is himself its Savior. Now as the church submits to Christ, so also wives should submit in everything to their husbands. Husbands, love your wives, as Christ loved the church and gave himself up for her, that he might sanctify her, having cleansed her by the washing of water with the word, ...

Ephesians 5:31

"Therefore a man shall leave his father and mother and hold fast to his wife, and the two shall become one flesh."

Ecclesiastes 9:9

Enjoy life with the wife whom you love, all the days of your vain life that he has given you under the sun, because that is your portion in life and in your toil at which you toil under the sun.

1 Corinthians 11:3

But I want you to understand that the head of every man is Christ, the head of a wife is her husband, and the head of Christ is God.

Hebrews 13:4

Let marriage be held in honor among all, and let the marriage bed be undefiled, for God will judge the sexually immoral and adulterous.

Ephesians 5:33

However, let each one of you love his wife as himself, and let the wife see that she respects her husband.

Genesis 2:24

Therefore a man shall leave his father and his mother and hold fast to his wife, and they shall become one flesh.

Matthew 5:28

But I say to you that everyone who looks at a woman with lustful intent has already committed adultery with her in his heart.

Scriptures on Healing

Jeremiah 17:14

Heal me, O Lord, and I shall be healed; save me, and I shall be saved, for you are my praise.

Isaiah 41:10

Fear not, for I am with you; be not dismayed, for I am your God; I will strengthen you, I will help you, I will uphold you with my righteous right hand.

1 Peter 2:24

He himself bore our sins in his body on the tree, that we might die to sin and live to righteousness. By his wounds you have been healed.

Jeremiah 33:6

Behold, I will bring to it health and healing, and I will heal them and reveal to them abundance of prosperity and security.

Isaiah 53:5

But he was wounded for our transgressions; he was crushed for our iniquities; upon him was the chastisement that brought us peace, and with his stripes we are healed.

Psalm 103:2-4

Bless the Lord, O my soul, and forget not all his benefits, who forgives all your iniquity, who heals all your diseases, who redeems your life from the pit, who crowns you with steadfast love and mercy,

Psalm 41:3

The Lord sustains him on his sickbed; in his illness you restore him to full health.

Psalm 147:3

He heals the brokenhearted and binds up their wounds.

James 5:15

And the prayer of faith will save the one who is sick, and the Lord will raise him up. And if he has committed sins, he will be forgiven.

3 John 1:2

Beloved, I pray that all may go well with you and that you may be in good health, as it goes well with your soul.

James 5:16

Therefore, confess your sins to one another and pray for one another, that you may be healed. The prayer of a righteous person has great power as it is working.

Proverbs 17:22

A joyful heart is good medicine, but a crushed spirit dries up the bones.

Matthew 10:1

And he called to him his twelve disciples and gave them authority over unclean spirits, to cast them out, and to heal every disease and every affliction.

James 5:14

Is anyone among you sick? Let him call for the elders of the church, and let them pray over him, anointing him with oil in the name of the Lord.

Jeremiah 30:17

For I will restore health to you, and your wounds I will heal, declares the Lord, because they have called you an outcast: 'It is Zion, for whom no one cares!'

Proverbs 4:20-22

My son, be attentive to my words; incline your ear to my sayings. Let them not escape from your sight; keep them within your heart. For they are life to those who find them, and healing to all their flesh.

Deuteronomy 7:15

And the Lord will take away from you all sickness, and none of the evil diseases of Egypt, which you knew, will he inflict on you, but he will lay them on all who hate you.

Matthew 10:8

Heal the sick, raise the dead, cleanse lepers, cast out demons. You received without paying; give without pay.

Exodus 15:26

Saying, "If you will diligently listen to the voice of the Lord your God, and do that which is right in his eyes, and give ear to his commandments and keep all his statutes, I will put none of the diseases on you that I put on the Egyptians, for I am the Lord, your healer."

Philippians 4:19

And my God will supply every need of yours according to his riches in glory in Christ Jesus.

Psalm 103:2-3

Bless the Lord, O my soul, and forget not all his benefits, who forgives all your iniquity, who heals all your diseases,

Psalm 6:2

Be gracious to me, O Lord, for I am languishing; heal me, O Lord, for my bones are troubled.

Philippians 4:6-7

Do not be anxious about anything, but in everything by prayer and supplication with thanksgiving let your requests be made known to God. And the peace of God, which surpasses all understanding, will guard your hearts and your minds in Christ Jesus.

Scriptures on Impatience

James 5:7-8

Be patient, therefore, brothers, until the coming of the Lord. See how the farmer waits for the precious fruit of the earth, being patient about it, until it receives the early and the late rains. You also, be patient. Establish your hearts, for the coming of the Lord is at hand.

Galatians 5:22

But the fruit of the Spirit is love, joy, peace, patience, kindness, goodness, faithfulness,

Colossians 1:11

May you be strengthened with all power, according to his glorious might, for all endurance and patience with joy,

Psalm 27:14

Wait for the Lord; be strong, and let your heart take courage; wait for the Lord!

Isaiah 40:31

But they who wait for the Lord shall renew their strength; they shall mount up with wings like eagles; they shall run and not be weary; they shall walk and not faint.

Romans 5:3

More than that, we rejoice in our sufferings, knowing that suffering produces endurance,

Ephesians 4:2-3

With all humility and gentleness, with patience, bearing with one another in love, eager to maintain the unity of the Spirit in the bond of peace.

Scriptures on Increased Life

Proverbs 9:11

"For by me your days will be multiplied, and years of life will be added to you."

Psalms 91:16

"With long life I will satisfy him, and show him My salvation."

Proverbs 10:27

"The fear of the Lord prolongs days, but the years of the wicked will be shortened."

Deuteronomy 6:2

"that you may fear the Lord your God, to keep all His statutes and His commandments which I command you, you and your son and your grandson, all the days of your life, and that your days may be prolonged."

Proverbs 20:29

"The glory of young men is their strength, and the splendor of old men is their gray head."

Isaiah 46:4

"Even to your old age, I am He, and even to gray hairs I will carry you! I have made, and I will bear; even I will carry, and will deliver you."

Job 11:17

"And your life would be brighter than noonday. Though you were dark, you would be like the morning."

Titus 2:1- 5

"But as for you, speak the things which are proper for sound doctrine: that the older men be sober, reverent, temperate, sound in faith, in love, in patience; the older women likewise, that they be reverent in behavior, not slanderers, not given to much wine, teachers of good things - that they admonish the young women to love their husbands, to love their children, to be discreet, chaste, homemakers, good, obedient to their own husbands, that the word of God may not be blasphemed."

Psalms 71:17,18

"O God, You have taught me from my youth; and to this day I declare your wondrous works. Now also when I am old and gray headed, O God, do not forsake me, Until I declare Your strength to this generation, Your power to everyone who is to come."

Job 12:12,13

"Wisdom is with aged men, And with length of days, understanding.' With Him are wisdom and strength, He has counsel and understanding.' "

Job 5:26

"You shall come to the grave at a full age, as a sheaf of grain ripens in its season."

Psalms 71:9

"Do not cast me off in the time of old age; do not forsake me when my strength fails."

Psalms 39:4,5

"Lord, make me to know my end, and what is the measure of my days, that I may know how frail I am. Indeed, You have made my days as handbreadths, And my age is as nothing before You; Certainly every man at his best state is but vapor. Selah "

Deuteronomy 5:33

"You shall walk in all the ways which the Lord your God has commanded you, that you may live and that it may be well with you, and that you may prolong your days in the land which you shall possess."

Proverbs 3:1,2

"My son, do not forget my law, But let your heart keep my commands; for length of days and long life and peace they will add to you."

Scriptures on Integrity

Proverbs 10:9

Whoever walks in integrity walks securely, but he who makes his ways crooked will be found out.

Proverbs 28:6

Better is a poor man who walks in his integrity than a rich man who is crooked in his ways.

Proverbs 11:3

The integrity of the upright guides them, but the crookedness of the treacherous destroys them.

1 John 4:7-10

Beloved, let us love one another, for love is from God, and whoever loves has been born of God and knows God. Anyone who does not love does not know God, because God is love. In this the love of God was made manifest among us, that God sent his only Son into the world, so that we might live through him. In this is love, not that we have loved God but that he loved us and sent his Son to be the propitiation for our sins.

Proverbs 19:1

Better is a poor person who walks in his integrity than one who is crooked in speech and is a fool.

Proverbs 20:7

The righteous who walks in his integrity— blessed are his children after him!

1 Peter 3:16

Having a good conscience, so that, when you are slandered, those who revile your good behavior in Christ may be put to shame.

Proverbs 12:22

Lying lips are an abomination to the Lord, but those who act faithfully are his delight.

Luke 16:10

"One who is faithful in a very little is also faithful in much, and one who is dishonest in a very little is also dishonest in much.

Colossians 3:23

Whatever you do, work heartily, as for the Lord and not for men,

Proverbs 21:3

To do righteousness and justice is more acceptable to the Lord than sacrifice.

2 Corinthians 8:21

For we aim at what is honorable not only in the Lord's sight but also in the sight of man.

Proverbs 4:25-27

Let your eyes look directly forward, and your gaze be straight before you. Ponder the path of your feet; then all your ways will be sure. Do not swerve to the right or to the left; turn your foot away from evil.

Philippians 4:8

Finally, brothers, whatever is true, whatever is honorable, whatever is just, whatever is pure, whatever is lovely, whatever is commendable, if there is any excellence, if there is anything worthy of praise, think about these things.

Luke 6:31

And as you wish that others would do to you, do so to them.

Psalm 25:21

May integrity and uprightness preserve me, for I wait for you.

Psalm 41:11-12

By this I know that you delight in me: my enemy will not shout in triumph over me. But you have upheld me because of my integrity, and set me in your presence forever.

Titus 2:1-14

But as for you, teach what accords with sound doctrine. Older men are to be sober-minded, dignified, self-controlled, sound in faith, in love, and in steadfastness. Older women likewise are to be reverent in behavior, not slanderers or slaves to much wine. They are to teach what is good, and so train the young women to love their husbands and children, to be self-controlled, pure, working at home, kind, and submissive to their own husbands, that the word of God may not be reviled. ...

Job 27:4-6

My lips will not speak falsehood, and my tongue will not utter deceit. Far be it from me to say that you are right; till I die I will not put away my integrity from me. I hold fast my righteousness and will not let it go; my heart does not reproach me for any of my days.

1 Peter 2:12

Keep your conduct among the Gentiles honorable, so that when they speak against you as evildoers, they may see your good deeds and glorify God on the day of visitation.

Hebrews 13:18

Pray for us, for we are sure that we have a clear conscience, desiring to act honorably in all things.

Titus 2:7

Show yourself in all respects to be a model of good works, and in your teaching show integrity, dignity,

Scriptures on Joy and Happiness

Philippians 4:4

Rejoice in the Lord always; again I will say, Rejoice.

Romans 15:13

May the God of hope fill you with all joy and peace in believing, so that by the power of the Holy Spirit you may abound in hope.

Psalms 126:5,6

"Those who sow in tears shall reap in joy. He who continually goes forth weeping, bearing seed for sowing, shall doubtless come again with rejoicing, bringing his sheaves with him."

Psalms 64:10

"The righteous shall be glad in the Lord, and trust in Him. And all the upright in heart shall glory."

Psalms 63:5

"My soul shall be satisfied as with marrow and fatness, and my mouth shall praise You with joyful lips."

Isaiah 55:12

"For you shall go out with joy, and be led out with peace; The mountains and the hills Shall break forth into singing before you, And all the trees of the field shall clap their hands."

Psalms 118:15

"The voice of rejoicing and salvation Is in the tents of the righteous; The right hand of the Lord does valiantly."

Psalms 4:7

"You have put gladness in my heart, More than in the season that their grain and wine increased."

Psalms 89:15,16

"Blessed are the people who know the joyful sound! They walk, O Lord, in the light of Your countenance. In Your name they rejoice all day long, And in Your righteousness they are exalted."

Psalms 97:11,12

"Light is sown for the righteous, And gladness for the upright in heart. Rejoice in the Lord, you righteous, And give thanks at the remembrance of His holy name."

Job 22:26

"For then you will have your delight in the Almighty, And lift up your face to God."

John 15:11

"These things I have spoken to you, that My joy may remain in you, and that your joy may be full."

Habakkuk 3:18

"Yet I will rejoice in the Lord, I will joy in the God of my salvation."

Isaiah 51:11

"So the ransomed of the Lord shall return, And come to Zion with singing, With everlasting joy on their heads. They shall obtain joy and gladness; Sorrow and sighing shall flee away."

Psalms 33:21

"For our heart shall rejoice in Him, Because we have trusted in His holy name."

1 Peter 1:8

"whom having not seen you love. Though now you do not see Him, yet believing, you rejoice with joy inexpressible and full of glory"

Isaiah 41:16

"You shall winnow them, the wind shall carry them away, And the whirlwind shall scatter them; You shall rejoice in the Lord, And glory in the Holy One of Israel."

Psalms 68:3

"But let the righteous be glad; Let them rejoice before God; Yes, let them rejoice exceedingly."

John 16:22

"Therefore you now have sorrow; but I will see you again and your heart will rejoice, and your joy no one will take from you."

Isaiah 61:10

"I will greatly rejoice in the Lord, My soul shall be joyful in my God; For He has clothed me with the garments of salvation, He has covered me with the robe of righteousness, As a bridegroom decks himself with ornaments, And as a bride adorns herself with her jewels."

Nehemiah 8:10

"Then he said to them, 'Go your way, eat the fat, drink the sweet, and send portions to those for whom nothing is prepared; for this day is holy to our Lord. Do not sorrow, for the joy of the Lord is your strength.' "

Scriptures on Kindness

2 Corinthians 8:13,14

"For I do not mean that others should be eased and you burdened; but by an equality, that now at this time your abundance may supply their lack, that their abundance also may supply your lack - that there may be equality."

Romans 12:13

"distributing to the needs of the saints, given to hospitality."

1 Peter 4:9,10

"Be hospitable to one another without grumbling. As each one has received a gift, minister it to one another, as good stewards of the manifold grace of God."

Matthew 25:35,36

"for I was hungry and you gave Me food; I was thirsty and you gave Me drink; I was a stranger and you took Me in; I was naked and you clothed Me; I was sick and you visited Me; I was in prison and you came to Me."

Hebrews 13:2

"Do not forget to entertain strangers, for by so doing some have unwittingly entertained angels."

James 2:15,16

"If a brother or sister is naked and destitute of daily food, and one of you says to them, "Depart in peace, be warmed and filled," but you do not give them the things which are needed for the body, what does it profit?"

Mark 9:41

"For whoever gives you a cup of water to drink in My name, because you belong to Christ, assuredly, I say to you, he will by no means lose his reward."

Acts 20:35

"I have shown you in every way, by laboring like this, that you must support the weak. And remember the words of the Lord Jesus, that He said, 'It is more blessed to give than to receive.' "

1 John 3:17

"But whoever has this world's goods, and sees his brother in need, and shuts up his heart from him, how does the love of God abide in him?"

Scriptures on Laziness

Proverbs 10:4,5

"He who has a slack hand becomes poor, But the hand of the diligent makes rich. He who gathers in summer is a wise son; He who sleeps in harvest is a son who causes shame."

Proverbs 20:13

"Do not love sleep, lest you come to poverty; Open your eyes, and you will be satisfied with bread."

1 Thessalonians 4:11,12

"that you also aspire to lead a quiet life, to mind your own business, and to work with your own hands, as we commanded you, that you may walk properly toward those who are outside, and that you may lack nothing."

Proverbs 15:19

"The way of the lazy man is like a hedge of thorns, But the way of the upright is a highway."

Proverbs 21:5

"The plans of the diligent lead surely to plenty, But those of everyone who is hasty, surely to poverty."

Romans 12:11

"not lagging in diligence, fervent in spirit, serving the Lord;"

Proverbs 28:19

"He who tills his land will have plenty of bread, But he who follows frivolity will have poverty enough!"

Proverbs 13:4

"The soul of a lazy man desires, and has nothing; But the soul of the diligent shall be made rich."

Proverbs 13:18

"Poverty and shame will come to him who disdains correction, But he who regards a rebuke will be honored."

2 Thessalonians 3:10-12

"For even when we were with you, we commanded you this: If anyone will not work, neither shall he eat. For we hear that there are some who walk among you in a disorderly manner, not working at all, but are busybodies. Now those who are such we command and exhort through our Lord Jesus Christ that they work in quietness and eat their own bread."

Proverbs 27:23

"Be diligent to know the state of your flocks, And attend to your herds;"

Proverbs 27:27

"You shall have enough goats' milk for your food, For the food of your household, And the nourishment of your maidservants."

Ecclesiastes 5:18,19

"Here is what I have seen: It is good and fitting for one to eat and drink, and to enjoy the good of all his labor in which he toils under the sun all the days of his life which God gives him; for it is his heritage. As for every man to whom God has given riches and wealth, and given him power to eat of it, to receive his heritage and rejoice in his labor - this is the gift of God."

Proverbs 13:23

"Much food is in the fallow ground of the poor, And for lack of justice there is waste." 2

Timothy 2:6

"The hardworking farmer must be first to partake of the crops."

Ephesians 4:28

"Let him who stole steal no longer, but rather let him labor, working with his hands what is good, that he may have something to give him who has need."

Proverbs 24:30-34

"I went by the field of the lazy man, And by the vineyard of the man devoid of understanding; And there it was, all overgrown with thorns; Its surface was covered with nettles; Its stone wall was broken down. When I saw it, I considered it well; I looked on it and received instruction: A little sleep, a little slumber, A little folding of the hands to rest; So shall your poverty come like a prowler, And your need like an armed man."

Proverbs 12:11

"He who tills his land will be satisfied with bread, But he who follows frivolity is devoid of understanding."

Scriptures on Loneliness

2 Corinthians 6:18

"I will be a Father to you, And you shall be My sons and daughters, Says the Lord Almighty." (Also see 2 Samuel 7:14)

Genisis 28:15

"Behold, I am with you and will keep you wherever you go, and will bring you back to this land; for I will not leave you until I have done what I have spoken to you."

Colossians 2:10

"and you are complete in Him, who is the head of all principality and power."

John 14:18

"I will not leave you orphans; I will come to you."

Isaiah 58:9

"Then you shall call, and the Lord will answer; You shall cry, and He will say, 'Here I am.'..."

Isaiah 43:4

"Since you were precious in My sight, You have been honored, And I have loved you; Therefore I will give men for you, And people for your life."

Psalms 40:17

"But I am poor and needy; Yet the Lord thinks upon me. You are my help and my deliverer; Do not delay, O my God."

Scriptures on Love

1 Corinthians 13:4 - 7

"Love suffers long and is kind; love does not envy; love does not parade itself, is not puffed up; does not behave rudely, does not seek its own, is not provoked, thinks no evil; does not rejoice in iniquity, but rejoices in the truth; bears all things, believes all things, hopes all things, endures all things."

Matthew 5:44 - 48

"But I say to you, love your enemies, bless those who curse you, do good to those who hate you, and pray for those who spitefully use you and persecute you, that you may be sons of your Father in heaven; for He makes His sun rise on the evil and on the good, and sends rain on the just and on the unjust. For if you love those who love you, what reward have you? Do not even the tax collectors do the same? And if you greet your brethren only, what do you do more than others? Do not even the tax collectors do so? Therefore you shall be perfect, just as your Father in heaven is perfect."

Matthew 19:19

"...You shall love your neighbor as yourself."

Matthew 22:37 - 39

"Jesus said to him, 'You shall love the Lord your God with all your heart, with all your soul, and with all your mind.' This is the first and great commandment. And the second is like it: 'You shall love your neighbor as yourself.'"

Luke 7:47

"Therefore I say to you, her sins, which are many, are forgiven, for she loved much. But to whom little is forgiven, the same loves little."

John 3:16

"For God so loved the world that He gave His only begotten Son, that whoever believes in Him should not perish but have everlasting life."

John 14:15

" 'If you love Me, keep My commandments.' "

John 13:34, 35

"A new commandment I give to you, that you love one another; as I have loved you, that you also love one another. By this all will know that you are My disciples, if you have love for one another."

John 15:13

"Greater love has no one than this, than to lay down one's life for his friends."

Romans 12:9 - 21

"Let love be without hypocrisy. Abhor what is evil. Cling to what is good. Be kindly affectionate to one another with brotherly love, in honor giving preference to one another; not lagging in diligence, fervent in spirit, serving the Lord; rejoicing in hope, patient in tribulation, continuing steadfastly in prayer; distributing to the needs of the saints, given to hospitality. Bless those who persecute you; bless and do not curse. Rejoice with those who rejoice, and weep with those who weep. Be of the same mind toward one another. Do not set your mind on high things, but associate with the humble. Do not be wise in your own opinion. Repay no one evil for evil. Have regard for good things in the sight of all men. If it is possible, as much as depends on you, live peaceably with all men. Beloved, do not avenge yourselves, but rather give place to wrath; for it is written, 'Vengeance is Mine, I will repay,' says the Lord. Therefore 'If your enemy is hungry, feed him; If he is thirsty, give him a drink; For in so doing you will heap coals of fire on his head.' Do not be overcome by evil, but overcome evil with good.' "

Romans 13:8

"Owe no one anything except to love one another, for he who loves another has fulfilled the law."

Romans 13:10

"Love does no harm to a neighbor; therefore love is the fulfillment of the law."

Galatians 5:22

"But the fruit of the Spirit is love, joy, peace, longsuffering, kindness, goodness, faithfulness"

Ephesians 5:25

"Husbands, love your wives, just as Christ also loved the church and gave Himself for her"

Colossians 3:19

" Husbands, love your wives and do not be bitter toward them."

1 Timothy 6:10

"For the love of money is a root of all kinds of evil, for which some have strayed from the faith in their greediness, and pierced themselves through with many sorrows."

2 Timothy 1:7

"For God has not given us a spirit of fear, but of power and of love and of a sound mind."

Hebrews 13:1

"Let brotherly love continue."

1 John 2:10

"He who loves his brother abides in the light, and there is no cause for stumbling in him."

1 John 2:25

"And this is the promise that He has promised us - eternal life."

1 John 3:11

"For this is the message that you heard from the beginning, that we should love one another,"

1 John 3:14

"We know that we have passed from death to life, because we love the brethren. He who does not love his brother abides in death."

1 John 3:18

"My little children, let us not love in word or in tongue, but in deed and in truth."

1 John 4:8

"He who does not love does not know God, for God is love."

1 John 4:12

"No one has seen God at any time. If we love one another, God abides in us, and His love has been perfected in us."

1 John 4:18

"There is no fear in love; but perfect love casts out fear, because fear involves torment. But he who fears has not been made perfect in love."

1 John 4:19

"We love Him because He first loved us."

Ephesians 5:1, 2

"Therefore be imitators of God as dear children. And walk in love, as Christ also has loved us and given Himself for us, an offering and a sacrifice to God for a sweet-smelling aroma."

1 John 2:15-17

Do not love the world or the things in the world. If anyone loves the world, the love of the Father is not in him. For all that is in the world—the desires of the flesh and the desires of the eyes and pride in possessions—is not from the Father but is from the world. And the world is passing away along with its desires, but whoever does the will of God abides forever.

Scriptures on Loving God

Matthew 22:27,28

"You shall love the Lord your God with all your heart, with all your soul, and with all your mind. This is the first and great commandment."

Deuteronomy 11:13-15

"And it shall be that if you earnestly obey My commandments which I command you today, to love the Lord your God and serve Him with all your heart and with all your soul, then I will give you the rain for your land in its season, the early rain and the latter rain, that you may gather in your grain, your new wine, and your oil. And I will send grass in your fields for your livestock, that you may eat and be filled."

John 14:21

"He who has My commandments and keeps them, it is he who loves Me. And he who loves Me will be loved by My Father, and I will love him and manifest Myself to him."

Deuteronomy 7:9

"Therefore know that the Lord your God, He is God, the faithful God who keeps covenant and mercy for a thousand generations with those who love Him and keep His commandments"

Proverbs 8:17

"I love those who love me, And those who seek me diligently will find me."

Psalms 145:20

"The Lord preserves all who love Him, But all the wicked He will destroy."

Psalms 91:14

"Because he has set his love upon Me, therefore I will deliver him; I will set him on high, because he has known My name."

Proverbs 8:21

"That I may cause those who love me to inherit wealth, That I may fill their treasuries."

Psalms 37:4

"Delight yourself also in the Lord, And He shall give you the desires of your heart. "

1 Corinthians 2:9

"But as it is written: 'Eye has not seen, nor ear heard, Nor have entered into the heart of man The things which God has prepared for those who love Him.' "

Ephesians 6:24

"Grace be with all those who love our Lord Jesus Christ in sincerity. Amen."

Scriptures on Lust

Romans 6:11- 13

"Likewise you also, reckon yourselves to be dead indeed to sin, but alive to God in Christ Jesus our Lord. Therefore do not let sin reign in your mortal body, that you should obey it in its lusts. And do not present your members as instruments of unrighteousness to sin, but present yourselves to God as being alive from the dead, and your members as instruments of righteousness to God."

Proverbs 6:25 - 29

"Do not lust after her beauty in your heart, Nor let her allure you with her eyelids. For by means of a harlot A man is reduced to a crust of bread; And an adulteress will prey upon his precious life. Can a man take fire to his bosom, And his clothes not be burned? Can one walk on hot coals, And his feet not be seared? So is he who goes in to his neighbor's wife; Whoever touches her shall not be innocent."

James 4:7,8

"Therefore submit to God. Resist the devil and he will flee from you. Draw near to God and He will draw near to you. Cleanse your hands, you sinners; and purify your hearts, you double-minded."

James 4:1 - 4

"Where do wars and fights come from among you? Do they not come from your desires for pleasure that war in your members? You lust and do not have. You murder and covet and cannot obtain. You fight and war. Yet you do not have because you do not ask. You ask and do not receive, because you ask amiss, that you may spend it on your pleasures. Adulterers and adulteresses! Do you not know that friendship with the world is enmity with God? Whoever therefore wants to be a friend of the world makes himself an enemy of God." 1 John 2:16,17

"For all that is in the world - the lust of the flesh, the lust of the eyes, and the pride of life - is not of the Father but is of the world. And the world is passing away, and the lust of it; but he who does the will of God abides forever."

Matthew 5:27,28

"You have heard that it was said to those of old, 'You shall not commit adultery.' But I say to you that whoever looks at a woman to lust for her has already committed adultery with her in his heart."

1 Peter 2:11

"Beloved, I beg you as sojourners and pilgrims, abstain from fleshly lusts which war against the soul,"

1 Peter 1:14 - 16

"as obedient children, not conforming yourselves to the former lusts, as in your ignorance; but as He who called you is holy, you also be holy in all your conduct, because it is written, 'Be holy, for I am holy.' "

2 Timothy 2:22

"Flee also youthful lusts; but pursue righteousness, faith, love, peace with those who call on the Lord out of a pure heart."

Titus 3:3 - 5

"For we ourselves were also once foolish, disobedient, deceived, serving various lusts and pleasures, living in malice and envy, hateful and hating one another. But when the kindness and the love of God our Savior toward man appeared, not by works of righteousness which we have done, but according to His mercy He saved us, through the washing of regeneration and renewing of the Holy Spirit,"

Jude 1:18 - 21

"how they told you that there would be mockers in the last time who would walk according to their own ungodly lusts. These are sensual persons, who cause divisions, not having the Spirit. But you, beloved, building yourselves up on your most holy faith, praying in the Holy Spirit, keep yourselves in the love of God, looking for the mercy of our Lord Jesus Christ unto eternal life."

Galatians 5:16,16

"I say then: Walk in the Spirit, and you shall not fulfill the lust of the flesh."

2 Peter 1:4

"by which have been given to us exceedingly great and precious promises, that through these you may be partakers of the divine nature, having escaped the corruption that is in the world through lust."

Ephesians 2:3 - 6

"among whom also we all once conducted ourselves in the lusts of our flesh, fulfilling the desires of the flesh and of the mind, and were by nature children of wrath, just as the others. But God, who is rich in mercy, because of His great love with which He loved us, even when we were dead in trespasses, made us alive together with Christ (by grace you have been saved), and raised us up together, and made us sit together in the heavenly places in Christ Jesus,"

Titus 2:11,12

"For the grace of God that brings salvation has appeared to all men, teaching us that, denying ungodliness and worldly lusts, we should live soberly, righteously, and godly in the present age,"

Galatians 5:24

"And those who are Christ's have crucified the flesh with its passions and desires."

James 1:13

"Let no one say when he is tempted, 'I am tempted by God'; for God cannot be tempted by evil, nor does He Himself tempt anyone.

Scriptures on Lying

Revelation 21:8

"But the cowardly, unbelieving, abominable, murderers, sexually immoral, sorcerers, idolaters, and all liars shall have their part in the lake which burns with fire and brimstone, which is the second death."

Colossians 3:9,10

"Do not lie to one another, since you have put off the old man with his deeds, and have put on the new man who is renewed in knowledge according to the image of Him who created him"

Leviticus 19:12

"And you shall not swear by My name falsely, nor shall you profane the name of your God: I am the Lord."

Proverbs 25:18

"A man who bears false witness against his neighbor Is like a club, a sword, and a sharp arrow."

Zechariah 8:17

"Let none of you think evil in your heart against your neighbor; And do not love a false oath. For all these are things that I hate,' Says the Lord."

Proverbs 14:5

"A faithful witness does not lie, But a false witness will utter lies."

1 Kings 22:16

"So the king said to him, 'How many times shall I make you swear that you tell me nothing but the truth in the name of the Lord?' "

Proverbs 19:5

"A false witness will not go unpunished, And he who speaks lies will not escape."

Proverbs 24:28

"Do not be a witness against your neighbor without cause, For would you deceive with your lips?"

Psalms 58:3

"The wicked are estranged from the womb; They go astray as soon as they are born, speaking lies."

Exodus 23:1

"You shall not circulate a false report. Do not put your hand with the wicked to be an unrighteous witness."

James 3:14

"But if you have bitter envy and self-seeking in your hearts, do not boast and lie against the truth."

Proverbs 12:19

"The truthful lip shall be established forever, But a lying tongue is but for a moment."

Scriptures on Marriage

Ecclesiastes 9:9

"Live joyfully with the wife whom you love all the days of your vain life which He has given you under the sun, all your days of vanity; for that is your portion in life, and in the labor which you perform under the sun."

Proverbs 5:15

"Drink water from your own cistern, And running water from your own well."

Proverbs 5:18-20

"Let your fountain be blessed, And rejoice with the wife of your youth. As a loving deer and a graceful doe, Let her breasts satisfy you at all times; And always be enraptured with her love. For why should you, my son, be enraptured by an immoral woman, And be embraced in the arms of a seductress?"

1 Corinthians 7:3

"Let the husband render to his wife the affection due her, and likewise also the wife to her husband."

Ephesians 5:22,23

"Wives, submit to your own husbands, as to the Lord. For the husband is head of the wife, as also Christ is head of the church; and He is the Savior of the body."

Ephesians 5:25

"Husbands, love your wives, just as Christ also loved the church and gave Himself for her"

Ephesians 5:28

"So husbands ought to love their own wives as their own bodies; he who loves his wife loves himself."

Ephesians 5:31

"For this reason a man shall leave his father and mother and be joined to his wife, and the two shall become one flesh." (Also see Genesis 2:24)

Ephesians 5:33

"Nevertheless let each one of you in particular so love his own wife as himself, and let the wife see that she respects her husband."

1 Timothy 5:8

"But if anyone does not provide for his own, and especially for those of his household, he has denied the faith and is worse than an unbeliever."

Colossians 3:18,19

"Wives, submit to your own husbands, as is fitting in the Lord. Husbands, love your wives and do not be bitter toward them."

1 Peter 3:7

"Husbands, likewise, dwell with them with understanding, giving honor to the wife, as to the weaker vessel, and as being heirs together of the grace of life, that your prayers may not be hindered."

Titus 2:4,5

"that they admonish the young women to love their husbands, to love their children, to be discreet, chaste, homemakers, good, obedient to their own husbands, that the word of God may not be blasphemed."

Scriptures on Meekness

Matthew 5:5

"Blessed are the meek, For they shall inherit the earth."

Isaiah 11:4

"But with righteousness He shall judge the poor, And decide with equity for the meek of the earth; He shall strike the earth with the rod of His mouth, And with the breath of His lips He shall slay the wicked."

Psalms 22:26

"The poor shall eat and be satisfied; Those who seek Him will praise the Lord. Let your heart live forever!"

Psalms 149:4

"For the Lord takes pleasure in His people; He will beautify the humble with salvation."

Isaiah 29:19

"The humble also shall increase their joy in the Lord, And the poor among men shall rejoice In the Holy One of Israel."

Psalms 147:6

"The Lord lifts up the humble; He casts the wicked down to the ground."

Psalms 25:9

"The humble He guides in justice, And the humble He teaches His way."

Zephaniah 2:3

"Seek the Lord, all you meek of the earth, Who have upheld His justice. Seek righteousness, seek humility. It may be that you will be hidden In the day of the Lord's anger."

1 Peter 3:4

"rather let it be the hidden person of the heart, with the incorruptible beauty of a gentle and quiet spirit, which is very precious in the sight of God."

Psalms 37:11

"But the meek shall inherit the earth, And shall delight themselves in the abundance of peace."

Proverbs 15:1

"A soft answer turns away wrath, But a harsh word stirs up anger."

Scriptures on Mercy

Isaiah 30:18

"Therefore the Lord will wait, that He may be gracious to you; And therefore He will be exalted, that He may have mercy on you. For the Lord is a God of justice; Blessed are all those who wait for Him."

Job 11:6

"That He would show you the secrets of wisdom! For they would double your prudence. Know therefore that God exacts from you Less than your iniquity deserves."

Psalms 103:13

"As a father pities his children, So the Lord pities those who fear Him."

Psalms 103:17

"But the mercy of the Lord is from everlasting to everlasting On those who fear Him, And His righteousness to children's children"

Exodus 33:19

"Then He said, 'I will make all My goodness pass before you, and I will proclaim the name of the Lord before you. I will be gracious to whom I will be gracious, and I will have compassion on whom I will have compassion.' "

Hosea 2:23

"Then I will sow her for Myself in the earth, And I will have mercy on her who had not obtained mercy; Then I will say to those who were not My people, 'You are My people!' And they shall say, 'You are my God!' "

Isaiah 60:10

"The sons of foreigners shall build up your walls, And their kings shall minister to you; For in My wrath I struck you, But in My favor I have had mercy on you."

Isaiah 48:9

"For My name's sake I will defer My anger, And for My praise I will restrain it from you, So that I do not cut you off.

Scriptures on Money

Deuteronomy 8:18

"And you shall remember the Lord your God, for it is He who gives you power to get wealth, that He may establish His covenant which He swore to your fathers, as it is this day."

Proverbs 23:4,5

"Do not overwork to be rich; Because of your own understanding, cease! Will you set your eyes on that which is not? For riches certainly make themselves wings; They fly away like an eagle toward heaven."

Psalms 37:16

"A little that a righteous man has Is better than the riches of many wicked."

James 2:5

"Listen, my beloved brethren: Has God not chosen the poor of this world to be rich in faith and heirs of the kingdom which He promised to those who love Him?"

Ecclesiastes 4:6

"Better a handful with quietness Than both hands full, together with toil and grasping for the wind."

Psalms 12:5

" 'For the oppression of the poor, for the sighing of the needy, Now I will arise,' says the Lord; 'I will set him in the safety for which he yearns.' "

Proverbs 17:5

"He who mocks the poor reproaches his Maker; He who is glad at calamity will not go unpunished."

Proverbs 22:22

"Do not rob the poor because he is poor, Nor oppress the afflicted at the gate;"

1 Timothy 6:17-19

"Command those who are rich in this present age not to be haughty, nor to trust in uncertain riches but in the living God, who gives us richly all things to enjoy. Let them do good, that they be rich in good works, ready to give, willing to share, storing up for themselves a good foundation for the time to come, that they may lay hold on eternal life."

Ecclesiastes 5:12-14

"The sleep of a laboring man is sweet, Whether he eats little or much; But the abundance of the rich will not permit him to sleep. There is a severe evil which I have seen under the sun: Riches kept for their owner to his hurt. But those riches perish through misfortune; When he begets a son, there is nothing in his hand."

Job 5:15,16

"But He saves the needy from the sword, From the mouth of the mighty, And from their hand. So the poor have hope, And injustice shuts her mouth."

Psalms 9:18

"For the needy shall not always be forgotten; The expectation of the poor shall not perish forever."

Proverbs 11:28

"He who trusts in his riches will fall, But the righteous will flourish like foliage."

Proverbs 28:20

"A faithful man will abound with blessings, But he who hastens to be rich will not go unpunished. "

Proverbs 11:4

"Riches do not profit in the day of wrath, But righteousness delivers from death. "

Ezekiel 7:19

"They will throw their silver into the streets, And their gold will be like refuse; Their silver and their gold will not be able to deliver them In the day of the wrath of the Lord; They will not satisfy their souls, Nor fill their stomachs, Because it became their stumbling block of iniquity."

Proverbs 13:7

"There is one who makes himself rich, yet has nothing; And one who makes himself poor, yet has great riches."

Ecclesiastes 5:10

"He who loves silver will not be satisfied with silver; Nor he who loves abundance, with increase. This also is vanity."

Proverbs 22:16

"He who oppresses the poor to increase his riches, And he who gives to the rich, will surely come to poverty."

Proverbs 28:22

"A man with an evil eye hastens after riches, And does not consider that poverty will come upon him."

Proverbs 22:2

"The rich and the poor have this in common, The Lord is the maker of them all."

Job 36:15

"He delivers the poor in their affliction, And opens their ears in oppression."

Proverbs 15:16

"Better is a little with the fear of the Lord, Than great treasure with trouble."

Proverbs 28:6

"Better is the poor who walks in his integrity Than one perverse in his ways, though he be rich."

Psalms 41:1

"Blessed is he who considers the poor; The Lord will deliver him in time of trouble."

Scriptures on Obedience

Deuteronomy 30:15,16

"See, I have set before you today life and good, death and evil, in that I command you today to love the Lord your God, to walk in His ways, and to keep His commandments, His statutes, and His judgments, that you may live and multiply; and the Lord your God will bless you in the land which you go to possess."

Deuteronomy 6:18

"And you shall do what is right and good in the sight of the Lord, that it may be well with you, and that you may go in and possess the good land of which the Lord swore to your fathers"

Deuteronomy 6:3

"Therefore hear, O Israel, and be careful to observe it, that it may be well with you, and that you may multiply greatly as the Lord God of your fathers has promised you - 'a land flowing with milk and honey.' "

Deuteronomy 7:12

"Then it shall come to pass, because you listen to these judgments, and keep and do them, that the Lord your God will keep with you the covenant and the mercy which He swore to your fathers."

Deuteronomy 29:9

"Therefore keep the words of this covenant, and do them, that you may prosper in all that you do."

Deuteronomy 5:29

"Oh, that they had such a heart in them that they would fear Me and always keep all My commandments, that it might be well with them and with their children forever!"

Philippians 4:9

"The things which you learned and received and heard and saw in me, these do, and the God of peace will be with you."

Matthew 5:19

"Whoever therefore breaks one of the least of these commandments, and teaches men so, shall be called least in the kingdom of heaven; but whoever does and teaches them, he shall be called great in the kingdom of heaven."

Matthew 7:24,25

"Therefore whoever hears these sayings of Mine, and does them, I will liken him to a wise man who built his house on the rock: and the rain descended, the floods came, and the winds blew and beat on that house; and it did not fall, for it was founded on the rock."

Job 36:11

"If they obey and serve Him, They shall spend their days in prosperity, And their years in pleasures."

Romans 8:28

"And we know that all things work together for good to those who love God, to those who are the called according to His purpose."

John 15:10

"If you keep My commandments, you will abide in My love, just as I have kept My Father's commandments and abide in His love."

John 13:17

"If you know these things, blessed are you if you do them."

James 1:25

"But he who looks into the perfect law of liberty and continues in it, and is not a forgetful hearer but a doer of the work, this one will be blessed in what he does."

1 John 3:22

"And whatever we ask we receive from Him, because we keep His commandments and do those things that are pleasing in His sight."

Romans 2:13

"for not the hearers of the law are just in the sight of God, but the doers of the law will be justified"

John 5:24

"Most assuredly, I say to you, he who hears My word and believes in Him who sent Me has everlasting life, and shall not come into judgment, but has passed from death into life."

Matthew 12:50

"For whoever does the will of My Father in heaven is My brother and sister and mother."

1 John 2:17

"And the world is passing away, and the lust of it; but he who does the will of God abides forever."

Matthew 7:21

"Not everyone who says to Me, 'Lord, Lord,' shall enter the kingdom of heaven, but he who does the will of My Father in heaven."

Psalms 106:3

"Blessed are those who keep justice, And he who does righteousness at all times!"

Hebrews 5:9

"And having been perfected, He became the author of eternal salvation to all who obey Him,"

John 8:51

"Most assuredly, I say to you, if anyone keeps My word he shall never see death."

Scriptures on Patience

James 5:7,8

"Therefore be patient, brethren, until the coming of the Lord. See how the farmer waits for the precious fruit of the earth, waiting patiently for it until it receives the early and latter rain. You also be patient. Establish your hearts, for the coming of the Lord is at hand."

1 Peter 2:20

"For what credit is it if, when you are beaten for your faults, you take it patiently? But when you do good and suffer, if you take it patiently, this is commendable before God."

Galatians 6:9

"And let us not grow weary while doing good, for in due season we shall reap if we do not lose heart."

Hebrews 10:23

"Let us hold fast the confession of our hope without wavering, for He who promised is faithful."

Matthew 24:13

"But he who endures to the end shall be saved."

Hebrews 6:12

"that you do not become sluggish, but imitate those who through faith and patience inherit the promises."

Hebrews 10:36

"For you have need of endurance, so that after you have done the will of God, you may receive the promise"

James 1:2-4

"My brethren, count it all joy when you fall into various trials, knowing that the testing of your faith produces patience. But let patience have its perfect work, that you may be perfect and complete, lacking nothing."

Romans 5:3,4

"And not only that, but we also glory in tribulations, knowing that tribulation produces perseverance; and perseverance, character; and character, hope."

Scriptures on Peace

Philippians 4:7

"and the peace of God, which surpasses all understanding, will guard your hearts and minds through Christ Jesus."

Colossians 3:15

"And let the peace of God rule in your hearts, to which also you were called in one body; and be thankful."

Isaiah 57:19

" 'I create the fruit of the lips: Peace, peace to him who is far off and to him who is near,' Says the Lord, 'And I will heal him.' "

Hebrews 12:14

Strive for peace with everyone, and for the holiness without which no one will see the Lord.

Colossians 3:15

And let the peace of Christ rule in your hearts, to which indeed you were called in one body. And be thankful.

Psalms 85:8

"I will hear what God the Lord will speak, For He will speak peace To His people and to His saints; But let them not turn back to folly."

Romans 15:13

May the God of hope fill you with all joy and peace in believing, so that by the power of the Holy Spirit you may abound in hope.

Isaiah 32:17

"The work of righteousness will be peace, and the effect of righteousness, quietness and assurance forever."

Luke 7:50

"Then He said to the woman, 'Your faith has saved you. Go in peace.' "

1 Peter 3:11

Let him turn away from evil and do good; let him seek peace and pursue it.

Psalm 4:8

In peace I will both lie down and sleep; for you alone, O Lord, make me dwell in safety.

Psalms 37:37

"Mark the blameless man, and observe the upright; For the future of that man is peace."

2 Thessalonians 3:16

"Now may the Lord of peace Himself give you peace always in every way. The Lord be with you all."

John 16:33

I have said these things to you, that in me you may have peace. In the world you will have tribulation. But take heart; I have overcome the world."

Romans 12:18

If possible, so far as it depends on you, live peaceably with all.

Matthew 5:9

"Blessed are the peacemakers, for they shall be called sons of God.

John 14:27

"Peace I leave with you, My peace I give to you; not as the world gives do I give to you. Let not your heart be troubled, neither let it be afraid."

Scriptures on Persecution

2 Timothy 3:12

Indeed, all who desire to live a godly life in Christ Jesus will be persecuted,

John 15:18

"If the world hates you, know that it has hated me before it hated you.

Matthew 5:10

"Blessed are those who are persecuted for righteousness' sake, for theirs is the kingdom of heaven.

1 Peter 4:12-14

Beloved, do not be surprised at the fiery trial when it comes upon you to test you, as though something strange were happening to you. But rejoice insofar as you share

Christ's sufferings, that you may also rejoice and be glad when his glory is revealed. If you are insulted for the name of Christ, you are blessed, because the Spirit of glory and of God rests upon you.

Matthew 5:44

But I say to you, Love your enemies and pray for those who persecute you,

2 Corinthians 12:10

For the sake of Christ, then, I am content with weaknesses, insults, hardships, persecutions, and calamities. For when I am weak, then I am strong.

Luke 6:22

"Blessed are you when people hate you and when they exclude you and revile you and spurn your name as evil, on account of the Son of Man!

Matthew 5:10-12

"Blessed are those who are persecuted for righteousness' sake, for theirs is the kingdom of heaven. "Blessed are you when others revile you and persecute you and utter all kinds of evil against you falsely on my account. Rejoice and be glad, for your reward is great in heaven, for so they persecuted the prophets who were before you.

1 Peter 3:17

For it is better to suffer for doing good, if that should be God's will, than for doing evil.

1 Peter 3:14

But even if you should suffer for righteousness' sake, you will be blessed. Have no fear of them, nor be troubled,

1 John 3:13

Do not be surprised, brothers, that the world hates you.

Romans 8:35

Who shall separate us from the love of Christ? Shall tribulation, or distress, or persecution, or famine, or nakedness, or danger, or sword?

Romans 12:14

Bless those who persecute you; bless and do not curse them.

John 15:20

Remember the word that I said to you: 'A servant is not greater than his master.' If they persecuted me, they will also persecute you. If they kept my word, they will also keep yours.

1 Peter 3:16

Having a good conscience, so that, when you are slandered, those who revile your good behavior in Christ may be put to shame.

John 16:33

I have said these things to you, that in me you may have peace. In the world you will have tribulation. But take heart; I have overcome the world."

1 Peter 4:16

Yet if anyone suffers as a Christian, let him not be ashamed, but let him glorify God in that name.

Acts 14:22

Strengthening the souls of the disciples, encouraging them to continue in the faith, and saying that through many tribulations we must enter the kingdom of God.

John 15:19

If you were of the world, the world would love you as its own; but because you are not of the world, but I chose you out of the world, therefore the world hates you.

1 Peter 4:19

Therefore let those who suffer according to God's will entrust their souls to a faithful Creator while doing good.

Scriptures on Prayer

Matthew 6:6

"But you, when you pray, go into your room, and when you have shut your door, pray to your Father who is in the secret place; and your Father who sees in secret will reward you openly."

Matthew 7:7,8

"Ask, and it will be given to you; seek, and you will find; knock, and it will be opened to you. For everyone who asks receives, and he who seeks finds, and to him who knocks it will be opened."

Matthew 21:22

"And whatever things you ask in prayer, believing, you will receive."

1 John 5:14,15

"Now this is the confidence that we have in Him, that if we ask anything according to His will, He hears us. And if we know that He hears us, whatever we ask, we know that we have the petitions that we have asked of Him."

Jeremiah 29:12

"Then you will call upon Me and go and pray to Me, and I will listen to you."

Isaiah 65:24

"It shall come to pass That before they call, I will answer; And while they are still speaking, I will hear."

John 16:23,24

"And in that day you will ask Me nothing. Most assuredly, I say to you, whatever you ask the Father in My name He will give you. Until now you have asked nothing in My name. Ask, and you will receive, that your joy may be full."

James 5:16

"Confess your trespasses to one another, and pray for one another, that you may be healed. The effective, fervent prayer of a righteous man avails much."

Job 22:27

"You will make your prayer to Him, He will hear you, And you will pay your vows."

John 14:13,14

"And whatever you ask in My name, that I will do, that the Father may be glorified in the Son. If you ask anything in My name, I will do it."

John 15:7

"If you abide in Me, and My words abide in you, you will ask what you desire, and it shall be done for you."

Psalms 50:15

"Call upon Me in the day of trouble; I will deliver you, and you shall glorify Me."

Isaiah 58:9

"Then you shall call, and the Lord will answer; You shall cry, and He will say, 'Here I am.' 'If you take away the yoke from your midst, The pointing of the finger, and speaking wickedness ' "

Proverbs 15:29

"The Lord is far from the wicked, But He hears the prayer of the righteous."

Psalms 91:15

"He shall call upon Me, and I will answer him; I will be with him in trouble; I will deliver him and honor him."

Matthew 7:11

"If you then, being evil, know how to give good gifts to your children, how much more will your Father who is in heaven give good things to those who ask Him!"

Psalms 34:17

"The righteous cry out, and the Lord hears, And delivers them out of all their troubles."

Psalms 55:17

"Evening and morning and at noon I will pray, and cry aloud, And He shall hear my voice."

Psalms 145:18 - 21

"The Lord is near to all who call upon Him, To all who call upon Him in truth. He will fulfill the desire of those who fear Him; He also will hear their cry and save them. The Lord preserves all who love Him, But all the wicked He will destroy. My mouth shall speak the praise of the Lord, And all flesh shall bless His holy name Forever and ever."

Zechariah 13:9

"I will bring the one-third through the fire, Will refine them as silver is refined, And test them as gold is tested. They will call on My name, And I will answer them. I will say, 'This is My people'; And each one will say, 'The Lord is my God."

Matthew 6:8

"Therefore do not be like them. For your Father knows the things you have need of before you ask Him."

1 John 3:22

"And whatever we ask we receive from Him, because we keep His commandments and do those things that are pleasing in His sight."

Jeremiah 33:3

"Call to Me, and I will answer you, and show you great and mighty things, which you do not know."

Mark 11:24

"Therefore I say to you, whatever things you ask when you pray, believe that you receive them, and you will have them."

Philippians 4:6

Do not be anxious about anything, but in everything by prayer and supplication with thanksgiving let your requests be made known to God.

1 Thessalonians 5:17

Pray without ceasing,

Romans 8:26

Likewise the Spirit helps us in our weakness. For we do not know what to pray for as we ought, but the Spirit himself intercedes for us with groanings too deep for words.

Matthew 6:6

But when you pray, go into your room and shut the door and pray to your Father who is in secret. And your Father who sees in secret will reward you.

Matthew 6:7

"And when you pray, do not heap up empty phrases as the Gentiles do, for they think that they will be heard for their many words.

1 Peter 3:7

Likewise, husbands, live with your wives in an understanding way, showing honor to the woman as the weaker vessel, since they are heirs with you of the grace of life, so that your prayers may not be hindered.

Scriptures on Prosperity

Psalms 1:3

"He shall be like a tree Planted by the rivers of water, That brings forth its fruit in its season, Whose leaf also shall not wither; And whatever he does shall prosper."

Proverbs 15:6

"In the house of the righteous there is much treasure, But in the revenue of the wicked is trouble."

Proverbs 22:4

"By humility and the fear of the Lord Are riches and honor and life."

Deuteronomy 30:9

"The Lord your God will make you abound in all the work of your hand, in the fruit of your body, in the increase of your livestock, and in the produce of your land for good. For the Lord will again rejoice over you for good as He rejoiced over your fathers"

Isaiah 30:23

"Then He will give the rain for your seed with which you sow the ground, and bread of the increase of the earth; It will be fat and plentiful. In that day your cattle will feed In large pastures."

Deuteronomy 28:11- 13

"And the Lord will grant you plenty of goods, in the fruit of your body, in the increase of your livestock, and in the produce of your ground, in the land of which the Lord swore to your fathers to give you. The Lord will open to you His good treasure, the heavens, to give the rain to your land in its season, and to bless all the work of your hand. You shall lend to many nations, but you shall not borrow. And the Lord will make you the head and not the tail; you shall be above only, and not be beneath, if you heed the commandments of the Lord your God, which I command you today, and are careful to observe them."

Ecclesiastes 3:13

"and also that every man should eat and drink and enjoy the good of all his labor - it is the gift of God."

Job 22:28

"You will also declare a thing, and it will be established for you; so light will shine on your ways."

Proverbs 8:18,19

"Riches and honor are with me, Enduring riches and righteousness. My fruit is better than gold, yes, than fine gold, and my revenue than choice silver."

Psalms 112:3

"Wealth and riches will be in his house, and his righteousness endures forever."

Deuteronomy 11:15

"And I will send grass in your fields for your livestock that you may eat and be filled."

Job 22:24, 25

"Then you will lay your gold in the dust, And the gold of Ophir among the stones of the brooks. Yes, the Almighty will be your gold and your precious silver."

Psalms 128:2

"When you eat the labor of your hands, you shall be happy, and it shall be well with you."

Isaiah 65:21- 23

"They shall build houses and inhabit them; They shall plant vineyards and eat their fruit. They shall not build and another inhabit; They shall not plant and another eat; For as the days of a tree, so shall be the days of My people, And My elect shall long enjoy the work of their hands. They shall not labor in vain, Nor bring forth children for trouble; For they shall be the descendants of the blessed of the Lord, And their offspring with them."

Deuteronomy 28:2- 6

"And all these blessings shall come upon you and overtake you, because you obey the voice of the Lord your God: Blessed shall you be in the city, and blessed shall you be in the country. Blessed shall be the fruit of your body, the produce of your ground and the increase of your herds, the increase of your cattle and the offspring of your flocks. Blessed shall be your basket and your kneading bowl. Blessed shall you be when you come in, and blessed shall you be when you go out."

Scriptures on Purpose

Romans 8:28

And we know that for those who love God all things work together for good, for those who are called according to his purpose.

Jeremiah 29:11

For I know the plans I have for you, declares the Lord, plans for welfare and not for evil, to give you a future and a hope.

Matthew 28:18-20

And Jesus came and said to them, "All authority in heaven and on earth has been given to me. Go therefore and make disciples of all nations, baptizing them in the name of the Father and of the Son and of the Holy Spirit, teaching them to observe all that I have commanded you. And behold, I am with you always, to the end of the age."

Ecclesiastes 12:13-14

The end of the matter; all has been heard. Fear God and keep his commandments, for this is the whole duty of man. For God will bring every deed into judgment, with every secret thing, whether good or evil.

Proverbs 16:4

The Lord has made everything for its purpose, even the wicked for the day of trouble.

Ephesians 2:10

For we are his workmanship, created in Christ Jesus for good works, which God prepared beforehand, that we should walk in them.

1 Peter 2:9

But you are a chosen race, a royal priesthood, a holy nation, a people for his own possession, that you may proclaim the excellencies of him who called you out of darkness into his marvelous light.

Psalm 138:8

The Lord will fulfill his purpose for me; your steadfast love, O Lord, endures forever. Do not forsake the work of your hands.

Colossians 1:16

For by him all things were created, in heaven and on earth, visible and invisible, whether thrones or dominions or rulers or authorities—all things were created through him and for him.

Isaiah 55:11

So shall my word be that goes out from my mouth; it shall not return to me empty, but it shall accomplish that which I purpose, and shall succeed in the thing for which I sent it.

Ecclesiastes 3:1

For everything there is a season, and a time for every matter under heaven:

Proverbs 19:21

Many are the plans in the mind of a man, but it is the purpose of the Lord that will stand.

Isaiah 46:10

Declaring the end from the beginning and from ancient times things not yet done, saying, 'My counsel shall stand, and I will accomplish all my purpose,'

Job 42:2

"I know that you can do all things, and that no purpose of yours can be thwarted.

1 Corinthians 6:19-20

Or do you not know that your body is a temple of the Holy Spirit within you, whom you have from God? You are not your own, for you were bought with a price. So glorify God in your body.

2 Timothy 1:9

Who saved us and called us to a holy calling, not because of our works but because of his own purpose and grace, which he gave us in Christ Jesus before the ages began,

Micah 6:8

He has told you, O man, what is good; and what does the Lord require of you but to do justice, and to love kindness, and to walk humbly with your God?

Ephesians 1:11

In him we have obtained an inheritance, having been predestined according to the purpose of him who works all things according to the counsel of his will,

1 Corinthians 10:31

So, whether you eat or drink, or whatever you do, do all to the glory of God.

Romans 11:36

For from him and through him and to him are all things. To him be glory forever. Amen.

Scriptures on Repentance

Matthew 4:17

From that time Jesus began to preach, saying, "Repent, for the kingdom of heaven is at hand."

2 Peter 3:9

The Lord is not slow to fulfill his promise as some count slowness, but is patient toward you, not wishing that any should perish, but that all should reach repentance.

Acts 2:38

And Peter said to them, "Repent and be baptized every one of you in the name of Jesus Christ for the forgiveness of your sins, and you will receive the gift of the Holy Spirit.

Acts 3:19

Repent therefore, and turn again, that your sins may be blotted out,

Mark 1:15

"and saying, 'The time is fulfilled, and the kingdom of God is at hand. Repent, and believe in the gospel.' "

Romans 2:4

Or do you presume on the riches of his kindness and forbearance and patience, not knowing that God's kindness is meant to lead you to repentance?

Matthew 3:8

Bear fruit in keeping with repentance.

1 John 1:9

If we confess our sins, he is faithful and just to forgive us our sins and to cleanse us from all unrighteousness.

2 Chronicles 7:14

If my people who are called by my name humble themselves, and pray and seek my face and turn from their wicked ways, then I will hear from heaven and will forgive their sin and heal their land.

Acts 17:30

The times of ignorance God overlooked, but now he commands all people everywhere to repent,

Mark 6:12

"So they went out and preached that people should repent."

Psalms 34:18

"The Lord is near to those who have a broken heart, and saves such as have a contrite spirit."

Psalms 147:3

"He heals the brokenhearted and binds up their wounds."

Ezekiel 18:21,22

"But if a wicked man turns from all his sins which he has committed, keeps all My statutes, and does what is lawful and right, he shall surely live; he shall not die. None of the transgressions which he has committed shall be remembered against him; because of the righteousness which he has done, he shall live."

Matthew 9:13

"But go and learn what this means: 'I desire mercy and not sacrifice.' For I did not come to call the righteous, but sinners, to repentance.' "

Scriptures on Righteousness

Matthew 6:33

"But seek first the kingdom of God and His righteousness, and all these things shall be added to you."

2 Timothy 3:16

All Scripture is breathed out by God and profitable for teaching, for reproof, for correction, and for training in righteousness,

Psalms 84:11

"For the Lord God is a sun and shield; The Lord will give grace and glory; No good thing will He withhold from those who walk uprightly."

Psalms 34:10

"The young lions lack and suffer hunger; but those who seek the Lord shall not lack any good thing."

Proverbs 10:24

"The fear of the wicked will come upon him, and the desire of the righteous will be granted."

Proverbs 13:21

"Evil pursues sinners, but to the righteous, good shall be repaid."

Proverbs 12:2

"A good man obtains favor from the Lord, but a man of wicked intentions He will condemn."

Proverbs 11:28

"He who trusts in his riches will fall, but the righteous will flourish like foliage."

Psalms 58:11

"So that men will say, 'Surely there is a reward for the righteous; Surely He is God who judges in the earth.' "

Psalms 5:12

"For You, O Lord, will bless the righteous; with favor You will surround him as with a shield."

Psalms 3:8

"Salvation belongs to the Lord. Your blessing is upon Your people. Selah"

Romans 8:32

"He who did not spare His own Son, but delivered Him up for us all, how shall He not with Him also freely give us all things?"

Isaiah 3:10

"Say to the righteous that it shall be well with them, For they shall eat the fruit of their doings."

Psalms 23:6

"Surely goodness and mercy shall follow me All the days of my life; And I will dwell in the house of the Lord Forever."

Scriptures on Rest and Sleep

Matthew 11:28-30

Come to me, all who labor and are heavy laden, and I will give you rest. Take my yoke upon you, and learn from me, for I am gentle and lowly in heart, and you will find rest for your souls. For my yoke is easy, and my burden is light."

Mark 6:31

And he said to them, "Come away by yourselves to a desolate place and rest a while." For many were coming and going, and they had no leisure even to eat.

Psalm 127:2

It is in vain that you rise up early and go late to rest, eating the bread of anxious toil; for he gives to his beloved sleep.

Exodus 33:14

And he said, "My presence will go with you, and I will give you rest."

Psalm 4:8

In peace I will both lie down and sleep; for you alone, O Lord, make me dwell in safety.

Psalm 37:7

Be still before the Lord and wait patiently for him; fret not yourself over the one who prospers in his way, over the man who carries out evil devices!

Psalm 46:10

"Be still, and know that I am God. I will be exalted among the nations, I will be exalted in the earth!"

Philippians 4:6-7

Do not be anxious about anything, but in everything by prayer and supplication with thanksgiving let your requests be made known to God. And the peace of God, which surpasses all understanding, will guard your hearts and your minds in Christ Jesus.

Genesis 2:2-3

And on the seventh day God finished his work that he had done, and he rested on the seventh day from all his work that he had done. So God blessed the seventh day and made it holy, because on it God rested from all his work that he had done in creation.

Proverbs 3:24

If you lie down, you will not be afraid; when you lie down, your sleep will be sweet.

Psalm 4:8

In peace I will both lie down and sleep; for you alone, O Lord, make me dwell in safety.

Psalm 127:2

It is in vain that you rise up early and go late to rest, eating the bread of anxious toil; for he gives to his beloved sleep.

Proverbs 20:13

Love not sleep, lest you come to poverty; open your eyes, and you will have plenty of bread.

Psalm 3:5

I lay down and slept; I woke again, for the Lord sustained me.

Proverbs 6:10

A little sleep, a little slumber, a little folding of the hands to rest,

Proverbs 6:9

How long will you lie there, O sluggard? When will you arise from your sleep?

Psalm 132:4-5

I will not give sleep to my eyes or slumber to my eyelids, until I find a place for the Lord, a dwelling place for the Mighty One of Jacob."

Psalm 121:3-4

He will not let your foot be moved; he who keeps you will not slumber. Behold, he who keeps Israel will neither slumber nor sleep.

Matthew 8:24

And behold, there arose a great storm on the sea, so that the boat was being swamped by the waves; but he was asleep.

Scriptures on Reputation

Proverbs 22:1

A good name is to be chosen rather than great riches, and favor is better than silver or gold.

Ecclesiastes 7:1

A good name is better than precious ointment, and the day of death than the day of birth.

Philippians 2:7

But made himself nothing, taking the form of a servant, being born in the likeness of men.

1 Peter 2:12

Keep your conduct among the Gentiles honorable, so that when they speak against you as evildoers, they may see your good deeds and glorify God on the day of visitation.

Ecclesiastes 10:1

Dead flies make the perfumer's ointment give off a stench; so a little folly outweighs wisdom and honor.

Matthew 5:16

In the same way, let your light shine before others, so that they may see your good works and give glory to your Father who is in heaven.

Proverbs 10:7

The memory of the righteous is a blessing, but the name of the wicked will rot.

1 Timothy 3:7

Moreover, he must be well thought of by outsiders, so that he may not fall into disgrace, into a snare of the devil.

1 Timothy 3:2-7

Therefore an overseer must be above reproach, the husband of one wife, sober-minded, self-controlled, respectable, hospitable, able to teach, not a drunkard, not violent but gentle, not quarrelsome, not a lover of money. He must manage his own household well, with all dignity keeping his children submissive, for if someone does not know how to manage his own household, how will he care for God's church? He must not be a recent convert, or he may become puffed up with conceit and fall into the condemnation of the devil. ...

Galatians 5:22-23

But the fruit of the Spirit is love, joy, peace, patience, kindness, goodness, faithfulness, gentleness, self-control; against such things there is no law.

Acts 16:2

He was well spoken of by the brothers at Lystra and Iconium.

1 Corinthians 15:33

Do not be deceived: "Bad company ruins good morals."

Philippians 4:5

Let your reasonableness be known to everyone. The Lord is at hand;

Matthew 7:17

So, every healthy tree bears good fruit, but the diseased tree bears bad fruit.

Scriptures on Revenge

Romans 12:19

Beloved, never avenge yourselves, but leave it to the wrath of God, for it is written, "Vengeance is mine, I will repay, says the Lord."

Romans 12:17-21

Repay no one evil for evil, but give thought to do what is honorable in the sight of all. If possible, so far as it depends on you, live peaceably with all. Beloved, never avenge yourselves, but leave it to the wrath of God, for it is written, "Vengeance is mine, I will repay, says the Lord." To the contrary, "if your enemy is hungry, feed him; if he is thirsty, give him something to drink; for by so doing you will heap burning coals on his head." Do not be overcome by evil, but overcome evil with good.

1 Peter 3:9

Do not repay evil for evil or reviling for reviling, but on the contrary, bless, for to this you were called, that you may obtain a blessing.

Matthew 5:38-39

"You have heard that it was said, 'An eye for an eye and a tooth for a tooth.' But I say to you, Do not resist the one who is evil. But if anyone slaps you on the right cheek, turn to him the other also.

Proverbs 24:29

Do not say, "I will do to him as he has done to me; I will pay the man back for what he has done."

Leviticus 19:18

You shall not take vengeance or bear a grudge against the sons of your own people, but you shall love your neighbor as yourself: I am the Lord.

1 Thessalonians 5:15

See that no one repays anyone evil for evil, but always seek to do good to one another and to everyone.

Mark 11:25

And whenever you stand praying, forgive, if you have anything against anyone, so that your Father also who is in heaven may forgive you your trespasses."

Matthew 26:52-54

Then Jesus said to him, "Put your sword back into its place. For all who take the sword will perish by the sword. Do you think that I cannot appeal to my Father, and he will at once send me more than twelve legions of angels? But how then should the Scriptures be fulfilled, that it must be so?"

Romans 13:4

For he is God's servant for your good. But if you do wrong, be afraid, for he does not bear the sword in vain. For he is the servant of God, an avenger who carries out God's wrath on the wrongdoer.

Proverbs 20:22

Do not say, "I will repay evil"; wait for the Lord, and he will deliver you.

James 1:19-20

Know this, my beloved brothers: let every person be quick to hear, slow to speak, slow to anger; for the anger of man does not produce the righteousness of God.

Matthew 5:7

"Blessed are the merciful, for they shall receive mercy.

Deuteronomy 32:35

Vengeance is mine, and recompense, for the time when their foot shall slip; for the day of their calamity is at hand, and their doom comes swiftly.'

Proverbs 10:12

Hatred stirs up strife, but love covers all offenses.

Ephesians 4:31-32

Let all bitterness and wrath and anger and clamor and slander be put away from you, along with all malice. Be kind to one another, tenderhearted, forgiving one another, as God in Christ forgave you.

Hebrews 10:30

For we know him who said, "Vengeance is mine; I will repay." And again, "The Lord will judge his people."

Colossians 3:25

For the wrongdoer will be paid back for the wrong he has done, and there is no partiality.

Proverbs 3:5-6

Trust in the Lord with all your heart, and do not lean on your own understanding. In all your ways acknowledge him, and he will make straight your paths.

Scriptures on Salvation

Ephesians 2:8

"For by grace you have been saved through faith, and that not of yourselves; it is the gift of God"

Romans 10:9

"that if you confess with your mouth the Lord Jesus and believe in your heart that God has raised Him from the dead, you will be saved."

Acts 2:21

"And it shall come to pass that whoever calls on the name of the Lord Shall be saved."

John 3:16

"For God so loved the world that He gave His only begotten Son, that whoever believes in Him should not perish but have everlasting life."

John 14:6

"Jesus said to him, "I am the way, the truth, and the life. No one comes to the Father except through Me."

John 3:3-7

"Jesus answered and said to him, 'Most assuredly, I say to you, unless one is born again, he cannot see the kingdom of God.' Nicodemus said to Him, 'How can a man be born when he is old? Can he enter a second time into his mother's womb and be born?' Jesus answered, 'Most assuredly, I say to you, unless one is born of water and the Spirit, he cannot enter the kingdom of God. That which is born of the flesh is flesh, and that which is born of the Spirit is spirit. Do not marvel that I said to you, You must be born again.' "

2 Corinthians 5:17

"Therefore, if anyone is in Christ, he is a new creation; old things have passed away; behold, all things have become new."

2 Corinthians 5:21

"For He made Him who knew no sin to be sin for us, that we might become the righteousness of God in Him."

Ephesians 2:1

"And you He made alive, who were dead in trespasses and sins"

1 Timothy 2:3,4

"For this is good and acceptable in the sight of God our Savior, who desires all men to be saved and to come to the knowledge of the truth."

1 John 2:1,2

"My little children, these things I write to you, so that you may not sin. And if anyone sins, we have an Advocate with the Father, Jesus Christ the righteous. And He Himself is the propitiation for our sins, and not for ours only but also for the whole world."

Colossians 2:13

"And you, being dead in your trespasses and the uncircumcision of your flesh, He has made alive together with Him, having forgiven you all trespasses"

1 Timothy 4:9,10

"This is a faithful saying and worthy of all acceptance. For to this end we both labor and suffer reproach, because we trust in the living God, who is the Savior of all men, especially of those who believe."

Romans 5:15

"But the free gift is not like the offense. For if by the one man's offense many died, much more the grace of God and the gift by the grace of the one Man, Jesus Christ, abounded to many."

Titus 3:4 - 6

"But when the kindness and the love of God our Savior toward man appeared, not by works of righteousness which we have done, but according to His mercy He saved us, through the washing of regeneration and renewing of the Holy Spirit, whom He poured out on us abundantly through Jesus Christ our Savior"

John 1:12,13

"But as many as received Him, to them He gave the right to become children of God, to those who believe in His name: who were born, not of blood, nor of the will of the flesh, nor of the will of man, but of God."

Titus 3:5

He saved us, not because of works done by us in righteousness, but according to his own mercy, by the washing of regeneration and renewal of the Holy Spirit,

Romans 10:9

Because, if you confess with your mouth that Jesus is Lord and believe in your heart that God raised him from the dead, you will be saved.

Acts 4:12

And there is salvation in no one else, for there is no other name under heaven given among men by which we must be saved."

Scriptures on satan

1 Peter 5:8

Be sober-minded; be watchful. Your adversary the devil prowls around like a roaring lion, seeking someone to devour.

1 John 3:8

Whoever makes a practice of sinning is of the devil, for the devil has been sinning from the beginning. The reason the Son of God appeared was to destroy the works of the devil.

John 8:44

You are of your father the devil, and your will is to do your father's desires. He was a murderer from the beginning, and has nothing to do with the truth, because there is no truth in him. When he lies, he speaks out of his own character, for he is a liar and the father of lies.

2 Corinthians 11:14

And no wonder, for even Satan disguises himself as an angel of light.

James 4:7

Submit yourselves therefore to God. Resist the devil, and he will flee from you.

Revelation 12:9

And the great dragon was thrown down, that ancient serpent, who is called the devil and Satan, the deceiver of the whole world—he was thrown down to the earth, and his angels were thrown down with him.

2 Corinthians 11:3

But I am afraid that as the serpent deceived Eve by his cunning, your thoughts will be led astray from a sincere and pure devotion to Christ.

2 Corinthians 4:4

In their case the god of this world has blinded the minds of the unbelievers, to keep them from seeing the light of the gospel of the glory of Christ, who is the image of God.

Romans 16:20

The God of peace will soon crush Satan under your feet. The grace of our Lord Jesus Christ be with you.

John 10:10

The thief comes only to steal and kill and destroy. I came that they may have life and have it abundantly.

Ephesians 6:11

Put on the whole armor of God, that you may be able to stand against the schemes of the devil.

Luke 10:18

And he said to them, "I saw Satan fall like lightning from heaven.

Ephesians 4:27

And give no opportunity to the devil.

1 John 5:19

We know that we are from God, and the whole world lies in the power of the evil one.

Matthew 16:23

But he turned and said to Peter, "Get behind me, Satan! You are a hindrance to me. For you are not setting your mind on the things of God, but on the things of man."

Isaiah 14:12-15

"How you are fallen from heaven, O Day Star, son of Dawn! How you are cut down to the ground, you who laid the nations low! You said in your heart, 'I will ascend to heaven; above the stars of God I will set my throne on high; I will sit on the mount of assembly in the far reaches of the north; I will ascend above the heights of the clouds; I will make myself like the Most High.' But you are brought down to Sheol, to the far reaches of the pit.

Ephesians 6:12

For we do not wrestle against flesh and blood, but against the rulers, against the authorities, against the cosmic powers over this present darkness, against the spiritual forces of evil in the heavenly places.

Scriptures on Seeking God

Matthew 6:33

"But seek first the kingdom of God and His righteousness, and all these things shall be added to you."

Hosea 10:12

"Sow for yourselves righteousness; Reap in mercy; Break up your fallow ground, For it is time to seek the Lord, Till He comes and rains righteousness on you."

Hebrews 11:6

"But without faith it is impossible to please Him, for he who comes to God must believe that He is, and that He is a rewarder of those who diligently seek Him."

Acts 17:27

"so that they should seek the Lord, in the hope that they might grope for Him and find Him, though He is not far from each one of us"

Lamentations 3:25

"The Lord is good to those who wait for Him, To the soul who seeks Him. "

Amos 5:4

"For thus says the Lord to the house of Israel: 'Seek Me and live' "

Deuteronomy 4:29,30

"But from there you will seek the Lord your God, and you will find Him if you seek Him with all your heart and with all your soul. When you are in distress, and all these things come upon you in the latter days, when you turn to the Lord your God and obey His voice"

Ezra 8:22

"For I was ashamed to request of the king an escort of soldiers and horsemen to help us against the enemy on the road, because we had spoken to the king, saying, "The hand of our God is upon all those for good who seek Him, but His power and His wrath are against all those who forsake Him."

1 Chronicles 28:9

"As for you, my son Solomon, know the God of your father, and serve Him with a loyal heart and with a willing mind; for the Lord searches all hearts and understands all the intent of the thoughts. If you seek Him, He will be found by you; but if you forsake Him, He will cast you off forever."

Job 8:5,6

"If you would earnestly seek God And make your supplication to the Almighty, If you were pure and upright, Surely now He would awake for you, And prosper your rightful dwelling place."

Psalms 9:10

"And those who know Your name will put their trust in You; For You, Lord, have not forsaken those who seek You."

Jeremiah 29:13

"And you will seek Me and find Me, when you search for Me with all your heart."

Scriptures on Self Denial

Titus 2:11-12

For the grace of God has appeared, bringing salvation for all people, training us to renounce ungodliness and worldly passions, and to live self-controlled, upright, and godly lives in the present age,

Matthew 16:24 - 26

"Then Jesus said to His disciples, 'If anyone desires to come after Me, let him deny himself, and take up his cross, and follow Me. For whoever desires to save his life will lose it, but whoever loses his life for My sake will find it. For what profit is it to a man if he gains the whole world, and loses his own soul? Or what will a man give in exchange for his soul?' "

Galatians 5:24

"And those who are Christ's have crucified the flesh with its passions and desires."

Romans 8:12,13

"Therefore, brethren, we are debtors - not to the flesh, to live according to the flesh. For if you live according to the flesh you will die; but if by the Spirit you put to death the deeds of the body, you will live."

Galatians 2:20

I have been crucified with Christ. It is no longer I who live, but Christ who lives in me. And the life I now live in the flesh I live by faith in the Son of God, who loved me and gave himself for me.

Titus 2:11,12

"For the grace of God that brings salvation has appeared to all men, teaching us that, denying ungodliness and worldly lusts, we should live soberly, righteously, and godly in the present age"

Matthew 5:39 - 41

"But I tell you not to resist an evil person. But whoever slaps you on your right cheek, turn the other to him also. If anyone wants to sue you and take away your tunic, let him have your cloak also. And whoever compels you to go one mile, go with him two."

Luke 18:29,30

"So He said to them, 'Assuredly, I say to you, there is no one who has left house or parents or brothers or wife or children, for the sake of the kingdom of God, who shall not receive many times more in this present time, and in the age to come eternal life."

Scriptures on Selfishness

Philippians 2:4

Let each of you look not only to his own interests, but also to the interests of others.

2 Timothy 3:2-4

For people will be lovers of self, lovers of money, proud, arrogant, abusive, disobedient to their parents, ungrateful, unholy, heartless, unappeasable, slanderous, without self-control, brutal, not loving good, treacherous, reckless, swollen with conceit, lovers of pleasure rather than lovers of God,

1 John 3:17

But if anyone has the world's goods and sees his brother in need, yet closes his heart against him, how does God's love abide in him?

1 Corinthians 10:24

Let no one seek his own good, but the good of his neighbor.

Philippians 2:3-4

Do nothing from rivalry or conceit, but in humility count others more significant than yourselves. Let each of you look not only to his own interests, but also to the interests of others.

1 Corinthians 13:4-6

Love is patient and kind; love does not envy or boast; it is not arrogant or rude. It does not insist on its own way; it is not irritable or resentful; it does not rejoice at wrongdoing, but rejoices with the truth.

Philippians 2:21

For they all seek their own interests, not those of Jesus Christ.

Galatians 6:2

Bear one another's burdens, and so fulfill the law of Christ.

James 3:16

For where jealousy and selfish ambition exist, there will be disorder and every vile practice.

James 4:1-2

What causes quarrels and what causes fights among you? Is it not this, that your passions are at war within you? You desire and do not have, so you murder. You covet and cannot obtain, so you fight and quarrel. You do not have, because you do not ask.

Scriptures on Self Righteousness

Job 33:8,9

"Surely you have spoken in my hearing, And I have heard the sound of your words, saying, 'I am pure, without transgression; I am innocent, and there is no iniquity in me."

Job 35:2

"Do you think this is right? Do you say, 'My righteousness is more than God's?' "

Isaiah 5:21

"Woe to those who are wise in their own eyes, And prudent in their own sight! "

Job 35:13

"Surely God will not listen to empty talk, Nor will the Almighty regard it."

Proverbs 26:12

"Do you see a man wise in his own eyes? There is more hope for a fool than for him."

Galatians 6:3

"For if anyone thinks himself to be something, when he is nothing, he deceives himself."

2 Corinthians 10:17,18

" ' But he who glories, let him glory in the Lord.' For not he who commends himself is approved, but whom the Lord commends."

John 9:41

"Jesus said to them, 'If you were blind, you would have no sin; but now you say, 'We see.' Therefore your sin remains.' "

Isaiah 64:4

"For since the beginning of the world Men have not heard nor perceived by the ear, Nor has the eye seen any God besides You, Who acts for the one who waits for Him."

Proverbs 28:25,26

"He who is of a proud heart stirs up strife, But he who trusts in the Lord will be prospered. He who trusts in his own heart is a fool, But whoever walks wisely will be delivered."

Luke 16:15

"And He said to them, 'You are those who justify yourselves before men, but God knows your hearts. For what is highly esteemed among men is an abomination in the sight of God.' "

Proverbs 27:2

"Let another man praise you, and not your own mouth; A stranger, and not your own lips."

Scriptures on Sexual Sins

1 Corinthians 6:18-20

"Flee sexual immorality. Every sin that a man does is outside the body, but he who commits sexual immorality sins against his own body. Or do you not know that your body is the temple of the Holy Spirit who is in you, whom you have from God, and you are not your own? For you were bought at a price; therefore glorify God in your body and in your spirit, which are God's."

1 Thessalonians 4:3

"For this is the will of God, your sanctification: that you should abstain from sexual immorality"

1 Corinthians 10:13

"No temptation has overtaken you except such as is common to man; but God is faithful, who will not allow you to be tempted beyond what you are able, but with the temptation will also make the way of escape, that you may be able to bear it."

1 Corinthians 6:13

"Foods for the stomach and the stomach for foods, but God will destroy both it and them. Now the body is not for sexual immorality but for the Lord, and the Lord for the body."

1 Corinthians 7:1

"Now concerning the things of which you wrote to me: It is good for a man not to touch a woman."

1 Corinthians 7:37

"Nevertheless he who stands steadfast in his heart, having no necessity, but has power over his own will, and has so determined in his heart that he will keep his virgin does well."

Revelation 14:4

"These are the ones who were not defiled with women, for they are virgins. These are the ones who follow the Lamb wherever He goes. These were redeemed from among men, being firstfruits to God and to the Lamb."

Hebrews 13:4

"Marriage is honorable among all, and the bed undefiled; but fornicators and adulterers God will judge."

1 Corinthians 6:15

"Do you not know that your bodies are members of Christ? Shall I then take the members of Christ and make them members of a harlot? Certainly not!"

2 Peter 2:9

"then the Lord knows how to deliver the godly out of temptations and to reserve the unjust under punishment for the day of judgment"

James 1:12

"Blessed is the man who endures temptation; for when he has been approved, he will receive the crown of life which the Lord has promised to those who love Him."

Hebrews 2:18

"For in that He Himself has suffered, being tempted, He is able to aid those who are tempted."

Hebrews 4:15,16

"For we do not have a High Priest who cannot sympathize with our weaknesses, but was in all points tempted as we are, yet without sin. Let us therefore come boldly to the throne of grace, that we may obtain mercy and find grace to help in time of need."

Proverbs 6:32

He who commits adultery lacks sense; he who does it destroys himself.

1 Corinthians 7:2

But because of the temptation to sexual immorality, each man should have his own wife and each woman her own husband.

Scriptures on Shame

Romans 10:11

"For the Scripture says, 'Whoever believes on Him will not be put to shame.' "

Psalms 119:6

"Then I would not be ashamed, when I look into all Your commandments."

Romans 5:5

"Now hope does not disappoint, because the love of God has been poured out in our hearts by the Holy Spirit who was given to us."

2 Timothy 2:15

"Be diligent to present yourself approved to God, a worker who does not need to be ashamed, rightly dividing the word of truth."

Romans 9:33

"As it is written: 'Behold, I lay in Zion a stumbling stone and rock of offense, And whoever believes on Him will not be put to shame.' "

2 Timothy 2:15

"Be diligent to present yourself approved to God, a worker who does not need to be ashamed, rightly dividing the word of truth."

Psalms 119:80

"Let my heart be blameless regarding Your statutes, That I may not be ashamed."

1 Peter 4:16

"Yet if anyone suffers as a Christian, let him not be ashamed, but let him glorify God in this matter."

Scriptures on Sickness and disease

1 Peter 2:24

"who Himself bore our sins in His own body on the tree, that we, having died to sins, might live for righteousness - by whose stripes you were healed."

James 5:14 - 16

"Is anyone among you sick? Let him call for the elders of the church, and let them pray over him, anointing him with oil in the name of the Lord. And the prayer of faith will save the sick, and the Lord will raise him up. And if he has committed sins, he will be forgiven. Confess your trespasses to one another, and pray for one another, that you may be healed. The effective, fervent prayer of a righteous man avails much."

Matthew 9:28 - 30

"And when He had come into the house, the blind men came to Him. And Jesus said to them, 'Do you believe that I am able to do this?' They said to Him, 'Yes, Lord.' Then He touched their eyes, saying, 'According to your faith let it be to you.' And their eyes were opened. And Jesus sternly warned them, saying, 'See that no one knows it.' "

Jeremiah 17:14

"Heal me, O Lord, and I shall be healed; Save me, and I shall be saved, For You are my praise."

Matthew 9:35

"Then Jesus went about all the cities and villages, teaching in their synagogues, preaching the gospel of the kingdom, and healing every sickness and every disease among the people."

Matthew 9:6,7

"But that you may know that the Son of Man has power on earth to forgive sins - then He said to the paralytic, 'Arise, take up your bed, and go to your house.' And he arose and departed to his house."

Jeremiah 30:17

"For I will restore health to you And heal you of your wounds, says the Lord, 'Because they called you an outcast saying: This is Zion; No one seeks her.' "

Exodus 23:25

"So you shall serve the Lord your God, and He will bless your bread and your water. And I will take sickness away from the midst of you."

Isaiah 53:5

"But He was wounded for our transgressions, He was bruised for our iniquities; The chastisement for our peace was upon Him, And by His stripes we are healed."

Scriptures on Sin

James 4:17

So whoever knows the right thing to do and fails to do it, for him it is sin.

Romans 6:23

For the wages of sin is death, but the free gift of God is eternal life in Christ Jesus our Lord.

Romans 3:23

For all have sinned and fall short of the glory of God,

1 John 1:8-10

If we say we have no sin, we deceive ourselves, and the truth is not in us. If we confess our sins, he is faithful and just to forgive us our sins and to cleanse us from all unrighteousness. If we say we have not sinned, we make him a liar, and his word is not in us.

Mark 7:20-23

And he said, "What comes out of a person is what defiles him. For from within, out of the heart of man, come evil thoughts, sexual immorality, theft, murder, adultery, coveting, wickedness, deceit, sensuality, envy, slander, pride, foolishness. All these evil things come from within, and they defile a person."

1 Corinthians 10:13

No temptation has overtaken you that is not common to man. God is faithful, and he will not let you be tempted beyond your ability, but with the temptation he will also provide the way of escape, that you may be able to endure it.

Psalm 51:5

Behold, I was brought forth in iniquity, and in sin did my mother conceive me.

1 John 3:4

Everyone who makes a practice of sinning also practices lawlessness; sin is lawlessness.

Galatians 5:19-21

Now the works of the flesh are evident: sexual immorality, impurity, sensuality, idolatry, sorcery, enmity, strife, jealousy, fits of anger, rivalries, dissensions, divisions, envy, drunkenness, orgies, and things like these. I warn you, as I warned you before, that those who do such things will not inherit the kingdom of God.

James 4:7

Submit yourselves therefore to God. Resist the devil, and he will flee from you.

Galatians 5:16

But I say, walk by the Spirit, and you will not gratify the desires of the flesh.

1 John 5:17

All wrongdoing is sin, but there is sin that does not lead to death.

1 John 1:9

If we confess our sins, he is faithful and just to forgive us our sins and to cleanse us from all unrighteousness.

Genesis 4:7

If you do well, will you not be accepted? And if you do not do well, sin is crouching at the door. Its desire is for you, but you must rule over it."

James 1:15

Then desire when it has conceived gives birth to sin, and sin when it is fully grown brings forth death.

2 Timothy 3:1-5

But understand this that in the last days there will come times of difficulty. For people will be lovers of self, lovers of money, proud, arrogant, abusive, disobedient to their parents, ungrateful, unholy, heartless, unappeasable, slanderous, without self-control, brutal, not loving good, treacherous, reckless, swollen with conceit, lovers of pleasure rather than lovers of God, having the appearance of godliness, but denying its power. Avoid such people.

Matthew 5:48

You therefore must be perfect, as your heavenly Father is perfect.

John 8:34

Jesus answered them, "Truly, truly, I say to you, everyone who commits sin is a slave to sin.

1 John 3:6-10

No one who abides in him keeps on sinning; no one who keeps on sinning has either seen him or known him. Little children, let no one deceive you. Whoever practices righteousness is righteous, as he is righteous. Whoever makes a practice of sinning is of the devil, for the devil has been sinning from the beginning. The reason the Son of God appeared was to destroy the works of the devil. No one born of God makes a practice of sinning, for God's seed abides in him, and he cannot keep on sinning because he has been born of God. By this it is evident who are the children of God, and who are the children of the devil: whoever does not practice righteousness is not of God, nor is the one who does not love his brother.

John 3:16-17

"For God so loved the world, that he gave his only Son, that whoever believes in him should not perish but have eternal life. For God did not send his Son into the world to condemn the world, but in order that the world might be saved through him.

Hebrews 10:26

For if we go on sinning deliberately after receiving the knowledge of the truth, there no longer remains a sacrifice for sins,

Scriptures on Slander

Matthew 5:11,12

"Blessed are you when they revile and persecute you, and say all kinds of evil against you falsely for My sake. Rejoice and be exceedingly glad, for great is your reward in heaven, for so they persecuted the prophets who were before you."

1 Peter 4:14

"If you are reproached for the name of Christ, blessed are you, for the Spirit of glory and of God rests upon you. On their part He is blasphemed, but on your part He is glorified."

Psalms 57:3

"He shall send from heaven and save me; He reproaches the one who would swallow me up. Selah God shall send forth His mercy and His truth."

Isaiah 51:7

"Listen to Me, you who know righteousness, You people in whose heart is My law: Do not fear the reproach of men, Nor be afraid of their insults."

Psalms 31:20

"You shall hide them in the secret place of Your presence From the plots of man; You shall keep them secretly in a pavilion From the strife of tongues."

Job 5:21

"You shall be hidden from the scourge of the tongue, and you shall not be afraid of destruction when it comes."

Psalms 37:6

"He shall bring forth your righteousness as the light, and your justice as the noonday."

Scriptures on Stillness

Psalm 46:10

"Be still, and know that I am God. I will be exalted among the nations, I will be exalted in the earth!"

Exodus 14:14

The Lord will fight for you, and you have only to be silent."

Isaiah 40:31

But they who wait for the Lord shall renew their strength; they shall mount up with wings like eagles; they shall run and not be weary; they shall walk and not faint.

Job 37:14

"Hear this, O Job; stop and consider the wondrous works of God.

2 Chronicles 20:17

You will not need to fight in this battle. Stand firm, hold your position, and see the salvation of the Lord on your behalf, O Judah and Jerusalem.' Do not be afraid and do not be dismayed. Tomorrow go out against them, and the Lord will be with you."

Exodus 14:13

And Moses said to the people, "Fear not, stand firm, and see the salvation of the Lord, which he will work for you today. For the Egyptians whom you see today, you shall never see again.

Psalm 23:1-6

A Psalm of David. The Lord is my shepherd; I shall not want. He makes me lie down in green pastures. He leads me beside still waters. He restores my soul. He leads me in paths of righteousness for his name's sake. Even though I walk through the valley of the shadow of death, I will fear no evil, for you are with me; your rod and your staff, they comfort me. You prepare a table before me in the presence of my enemies; you anoint my head with oil; my cup overflows. ...

Psalm 119:18

Open my eyes, that I may behold wondrous things out of your law.

1 Samuel 12:7

Now therefore stand still that I may plead with you before the Lord concerning all the righteous deeds of the Lord that he performed for you and for your fathers.

Isaiah 30:15

For thus said the Lord God, the Holy One of Israel, "In returning and rest you shall be saved; in quietness and in trust shall be your strength." But you were unwilling,

Psalm 131:1-3

A Song of Ascents. Of David. O Lord, my heart is not lifted up; my eyes are not raised too high; I do not occupy myself with things too great and too marvelous for me. But I have calmed and quieted my soul, like a weaned child with its mother; like a weaned child is my soul within me. O Israel, hope in the Lord from this time forth and forevermore.

Isaiah 26:3

You keep him in perfect peace whose mind is stayed on you, because he trusts in you.

John 16:33

I have said these things to you, that in me you may have peace. In the world you will have tribulation. But take heart; I have overcome the world."

John 14:27

Peace I leave with you; my peace I give to you. Not as the world gives do I give to you. Let not your hearts be troubled, neither let them be afraid.

Mark 4:39

And he awoke and rebuked the wind and said to the sea, "Peace! Be still!" And the wind ceased, and there was a great calm.

1 Kings 19:12

And after the earthquake a fire, but the Lord was not in the fire. And after the fire the sound of a low whisper.

Scriptures on Submission

James 4:7

"Therefore submit to God. Resist the devil and he will flee from you."

1 Peter 5:5,6

"Likewise you younger people, submit yourselves to your elders. Yes, all of you be submissive to one another, and be clothed with humility, for 'God resists the proud, But gives grace to the humble.' "

Ephesians 5:33

"Nevertheless let each one of you in particular so love his own wife as himself, and let the wife see that she respects her husband."

Ephesians 5:21-25,28

"Wives, submit to your own husbands, as to the Lord. For the husband is head of the wife, as also Christ is head of the church; and He is the Savior of the body. Therefore, just as the church is subject to Christ, so let the wives be to their own husbands in everything. Husbands, love your wives, just as Christ also loved the church and gave Himself for her"

1 Peter 3:1-4

"Wives, likewise, be submissive to your own husbands, that even if some do not obey the word, they, without a word, may be won by the conduct of their wives, when they observe your chaste conduct accompanied by fear. Do not let your adornment be merely outward—arranging the hair, wearing gold, or putting on fine apparel—rather let it be the hidden person of the heart, with the incorruptible beauty of a gentle and quiet spirit, which is very precious in the sight of God."

Ephesians 6:5-9

"Bondservants, be obedient to those who are your masters according to the flesh, with fear and trembling, in sincerity of heart, as to Christ; not with eyeservice, as men-pleasers, but as bondservants of Christ, doing the will of God from the heart, with goodwill doing service, as to the Lord, and not to men, knowing that whatever good anyone does, he will receive the same from the Lord, whether he is a slave or free. And you, masters, do the same things to them, giving up threatening, knowing that your own Master also[a] is in heaven, and there is no partiality with Him."

Ephesians 6:1-4

"Children, obey your parents in the Lord, for this is right. 'Honor your father and mother,' which is the first commandment with promise: 'that it may be well with you and you may live long on the earth.' And you, fathers, do not provoke your children to wrath, but bring them up in the training and admonition of the Lord."

Scriptures on Temptation

1 Corinthians 10:13

No temptation has overtaken you that is not common to man. God is faithful, and he will not let you be tempted beyond your ability, but with the temptation he will also provide the way of escape, that you may be able to endure it.

James 4:7

Submit yourselves therefore to God. Resist the devil, and he will flee from you.

Hebrews 2:18

For because he himself has suffered when tempted, he is able to help those who are being tempted.

James 1:13-14

Let no one say when he is tempted, "I am being tempted by God," for God cannot be tempted with evil, and he himself tempts no one. But each person is tempted when he is lured and enticed by his own desire.

Hebrews 13:8

Jesus Christ is the same yesterday and today and forever.

Hebrews 4:15

For we do not have a high priest who is unable to sympathize with our weaknesses, but one who in every respect has been tempted as we are, yet without sin.

Scriptures on the Love of God

John 3:16

"For God so loved the world that He gave His only begotten Son, that whoever believes in Him should not perish but have everlasting life."

Deuteronomy 7:13

"And He will love you and bless you and multiply you; He will also bless the fruit of your womb and the fruit of your land, your grain and your new wine and your oil, the increase of your cattle and the offspring of your flock, in the land of which He swore to your fathers to give you."

Psalms 146:8

"The Lord opens the eyes of the blind; The Lord raises those who are bowed down; The Lord loves the righteous."

Proverbs 15:9

"The way of the wicked is an abomination to the Lord, But He loves him who follows righteousness."

Isaiah 62:5

"For as a young man marries a virgin, So shall your sons marry you; And as the bridegroom rejoices over the bride, So shall your God rejoice over you."

Zephaniah 3:17

"The Lord your God in your midst, The Mighty One, will save; He will rejoice over you with gladness, He will quiet you with His love, He will rejoice over you with singing."

Jeremiah 31:3

"The Lord has appeared of old to me, saying: 'Yes, I have loved you with an everlasting love; Therefore with lovingkindness I have drawn you.' "

Hosea 14:4

"I will heal their backsliding, I will love them freely, For My anger has turned away from him."

Jeremiah 32:41

"Yes, I will rejoice over them to do them good, and I will assuredly plant them in this land, with all My heart and with all My soul."

Ephesians 2:4 - 7

"But God, who is rich in mercy, because of His great love with which He loved us, even when we were dead in trespasses, made us alive together with Christ (by grace you have been saved), and raised us up together, and made us sit together in the heavenly places in Christ Jesus, that in the ages to come He might show the exceeding riches of His grace in His kindness toward us in Christ Jesus."

1 John 4:10

"In this is love, not that we loved God, but that He loved us and sent His Son to be the propitiation for our sins."

1 John 4:16

"And we have known and believed the love that God has for us. God is love, and he who abides in love abides in God, and God in him."

1 John 4:19

"We love Him because He first loved us."

John 17:26

"And I have declared to them Your name, and will declare it, that the love with which You loved Me may be in them, and I in them."

John 17:23

"I in them, and You in Me; that they may be made perfect in one, and that the world may know that You have sent Me, and have loved them as You have loved Me."

John 16:27

"for the Father Himself loves you, because you have loved Me, and have believed that I came forth from God."

2 Thessalonians 2:16,17

"Now may our Lord Jesus Christ Himself, and our God and Father, who has loved us and given us everlasting consolation and good hope by grace, comfort your hearts and establish you in every good word and work."

Scriptures on the Word of God

John 1:1

In the beginning was the Word, and the Word was with God, and the Word was God.

Hebrews 4:12

"For the word of God is living and powerful, and sharper than any two-edged sword, piercing even to the division of soul and spirit, and of joints and marrow, and is a discerner of the thoughts and intents of the heart."

Romans 10:17

"So then faith comes by hearing, and hearing by the word of God."

2 Timothy 3:16-17

All Scripture is breathed out by God and profitable for teaching, for reproof, for correction, and for training in righteousness, that the man of God may be competent, equipped for every good work.

Romans 1:16

"For I am not ashamed of the gospel of Christ, for it is the power of God to salvation for everyone who believes, for the Jew first and also for the Greek."

Revelation 1:3

"Blessed is he who reads and those who hear the words of this prophecy, and keep those things which are written in it; for the time is near."

2 Peter 1:19

"And so we have the prophetic word confirmed, which you do well to heed as a light that shines in a dark place, until the day dawns and the morning star rises in your hearts"

Psalms 119:130

"The entrance of Your words gives light; It gives understanding to the simple."

Proverbs 6:23

"For the commandment is a lamp, And the law a light; Reproofs of instruction are the way of life"

Psalms 119:105

"Your word is a lamp to my feet And a light to my path."

John 5:39

"You search the Scriptures, for in them you think you have eternal life; and these are they which testify of Me."

2 Timothy 3:15,16

"and that from childhood you have known the Holy Scriptures, which are able to make you wise for salvation through faith which is in Christ Jesus. All Scripture is given by inspiration of God, and is profitable for doctrine, for reproof, for correction, for instruction in righteousness"

1 Peter 2:2

"as newborn babes, desire the pure milk of the word, that you may grow thereby"

James 1:21-25

"Therefore lay aside all filthiness and overflow of wickedness, and receive with meekness the implanted word, which is able to save your souls. But be doers of the word, and not hearers only, deceiving yourselves. For if anyone is a hearer of the word and not a doer, he is like a man observing his natural face in a mirror; for he observes himself, goes away, and immediately forgets what kind of man he was. But he who looks into the perfect law of liberty and continues in it, and is not a forgetful hearer but a doer of the work, this one will be blessed in what he does."

Deuteronomy 11:18

"Therefore you shall lay up these words of mine in your heart and in your soul, and bind them as a sign on your hand, and they shall be as frontlets between your eyes."

Joshua 1:8

"This Book of the Law shall not depart from your mouth, but you shall meditate in it day and night, that you may observe to do according to all that is written in it. For then you will make your way prosperous, and then you will have good success."

1 Peter 1:23

"having been born again, not of corruptible seed but incorruptible, through the word of God which lives and abides forever"

Acts 20:32

"So now, brethren, I commend you to God and to the word of His grace, which is able to build you up and give you an inheritance among all those who are sanctified."

Scriptures on Time

Ephesians 5:15-17

Look carefully then how you walk, not as unwise but as wise, making the best use of the time, because the days are evil. Therefore do not be foolish, but understand what the will of the Lord is.

Psalm 90:12

So teach us to number our days that we may get a heart of wisdom.

Colossians 4:5

Walk in wisdom toward outsiders, making the best use of the time.

Matthew 6:33

But seek first the kingdom of God and his righteousness, and all these things will be added to you.

Ecclesiastes 3:8

A time to love, and a time to hate; a time for war, and a time for peace.

Luke 14:28

For which of you, desiring to build a tower, does not first sit down and count the cost, whether he has enough to complete it?

Proverbs 16:9

The heart of man plans his way, but the Lord establishes his steps.

James 4:13-17

Come now, you who say, "Today or tomorrow we will go into such and such a town and spend a year there and trade and make a profit"— yet you do not know what tomorrow will bring. What is your life? For you are a mist that appears for a little time and then vanishes. Instead you ought to say, "If the Lord wills, we will live and do this or that." As it is, you boast in your arrogance. All such boasting is evil. So whoever knows the right thing to do and fails to do it, for him it is sin.

Psalm 39:4-5

"O Lord, make me know my end and what is the measure of my days; let me know how fleeting I am! Behold, you have made my days a few handbreadths, and my lifetime is as nothing before you. Surely all mankind stands as a mere breath! Selah

Psalm 31:14-15

But I trust in you, O Lord; I say, "You are my God." My times are in your hand; rescue me from the hand of my enemies and from my persecutors!

John 9:4

We must work the works of him who sent me while it is day; night is coming, when no one can work.

Psalm 118:24

This is the day that the Lord has made; let us rejoice and be glad in it.

Ephesians 5:15-16

Look carefully then how you walk, not as unwise but as wise, making the best use of the time, because the days are evil.

Ecclesiastes 3:11

He has made everything beautiful in its time. Also, he has put eternity into man's heart, yet so that he cannot find out what God has done from the beginning to the end.

Matthew 24:36

"But concerning that day and hour no one knows, not even the angels of heaven, nor the Son, but the Father only.

Proverbs 3:9

Honor the Lord with your wealth and with the firstfruits of all your produce;

Proverbs 10:4

A slack hand causes poverty, but the hand of the diligent makes rich.

Galatians 4:4

But when the fullness of time had come, God sent forth his Son, born of woman, born under the law,

Ecclesiastes 3:1-8

For everything there is a season, and a time for every matter under heaven: a time to be born, and a time to die; a time to plant, and a time to pluck up what is planted; a time to kill, and a time to heal; a time to break down, and a time to build up; a time to weep, and a time to laugh; a time to mourn, and a time to dance; a time to cast away stones, and a time to gather stones together; a time to embrace, and a time to refrain from embracing;
…

Habakkuk 2:3

For still the vision awaits its appointed time; it hastens to the end—it will not lie. If it seems slow, wait for it; it will surely come; it will not delay.

Galatians 6:9

And let us not grow weary of doing good, for in due season we will reap, if we do not give up.

1 Corinthians 14:40

But all things should be done decently and in order.

Scriptures on Thoughts and the Mind

Colossians 3:2

Set your minds on things that are above, not on things that are on earth.

Romans 8:5-6

For those who live according to the flesh set their minds on the things of the flesh, but those who live according to the Spirit set their minds on the things of the Spirit. For to set the mind on the flesh is death, but to set the mind on the Spirit is life and peace.

Colossians 2:8

See to it that no one takes you captive by philosophy and empty deceit, according to human tradition, according to the elemental spirits of the world, and not according to Christ.

Philippians 4:8

Finally, brothers, whatever is true, whatever is honorable, whatever is just, whatever is pure, whatever is lovely, whatever is commendable, if there is any excellence, if there is anything worthy of praise, think about these things.

2 Corinthians 10:5

We destroy arguments and every lofty opinion raised against the knowledge of God, and take every thought captive to obey Christ,

Hebrews 4:12

For the word of God is living and active, sharper than any two-edged sword, piercing to the division of soul and of spirit, of joints and of marrow, and discerning the thoughts and intentions of the heart.

Romans 12:2

Do not be conformed to this world, but be transformed by the renewal of your mind, that by testing you may discern what is the will of God, what is good and acceptable and perfect.

Romans 12:1-2

I appeal to you therefore, brothers, by the mercies of God, to present your bodies as a living sacrifice, holy and acceptable to God, which is your spiritual worship. Do not be conformed to this world, but be transformed by the renewal of your mind, that by testing you may discern what is the will of God, what is good and acceptable and perfect.

Psalm 139:17

How precious to me are your thoughts, O God! How vast is the sum of them!

Isaiah 26:3

You keep him in perfect peace whose mind is stayed on you, because he trusts in you.

Proverbs 4:23

Keep your heart with all vigilance, for from it flow the springs of life.

Psalm 19:14

Let the words of my mouth and the meditation of my heart be acceptable in your sight, O Lord, my rock and my redeemer.

Scriptures on Trials

James 1:2-4

Count it all joy, my brothers, when you meet trials of various kinds, for you know that the testing of your faith produces steadfastness. And let steadfastness have its full effect, that you may be perfect and complete, lacking in nothing.

Romans 5:3-5

More than that, we rejoice in our sufferings, knowing that suffering produces endurance, and endurance produces character, and character produces hope, and hope does not put us to shame, because God's love has been poured into our hearts through the Holy Spirit who has been given to us.

1 Peter 4:12-13

Beloved, do not be surprised at the fiery trial when it comes upon you to test you, as though something strange were happening to you. But rejoice insofar as you share Christ's sufferings, that you may also rejoice and be glad when his glory is revealed.

James 1:12

Blessed is the man who remains steadfast under trial, for when he has stood the test he will receive the crown of life, which God has promised to those who love him.

2 Corinthians 6:4-8

But as servants of God we commend ourselves in every way: by great endurance, in afflictions, hardships, calamities, beatings, imprisonments, riots, labors, sleepless nights, hunger; by purity, knowledge, patience, kindness, the Holy Spirit, genuine love; by truthful speech, and the power of God; with the weapons of righteousness for the right hand and for the left; through honor and dishonor, through slander and praise. We are treated as impostors, and yet are true;

James 1:1-3

Count it all joy, my brothers, when you meet trials of various kinds, for you know that the testing of your faith produces steadfastness. And let steadfastness have its full effect, that you may be perfect and complete, lacking in nothing.

1 Corinthians 10:13

No temptation has overtaken you that is not common to man. God is faithful, and he will not let you be tempted beyond your ability, but with the temptation he will also provide the way of escape, that you may be able to endure it.

Romans 8:28

And we know that for those who love God all things work together for good, for those who are called according to his purpose.

John 16:33

I have said these things to you, that in me you may have peace. In the world you will have tribulation. But take heart; I have overcome the world."

2 Corinthians 4:16-18

So we do not lose heart. Though our outer self is wasting away, our inner self is being renewed day by day. For this light momentary affliction is preparing for us an eternal weight of glory beyond all comparison, as we look not to the things that are seen but to the things that are unseen. For the things that are seen are transient, but the things that are unseen are eternal.

Revelation 3:19

Those whom I love, I reprove and discipline, so be zealous and repent.

Romans 8:18

For I consider that the sufferings of this present time are not worth comparing with the glory that is to be revealed to us.

Scriptures on Trust

Proverbs 3:5,6

"Trust in the Lord with all your heart, And lean not on your own understanding; In all your ways acknowledge Him, And He shall direct your paths

Psalms 46:1,2

"God is our refuge and strength, A very present help in trouble. Therefore we will not fear, Even though the earth be removed, And though the mountains be carried into the midst of the sea"

Psalms 84:11,12

"For the Lord God is a sun and shield; The Lord will give grace and glory; No good thing will He withhold From those who walk uprightly. O Lord of hosts, Blessed is the man who trusts in You!"

Psalms 37:3-5

"Trust in the Lord, and do good; Dwell in the land, and feed on His faithfulness. Delight yourself also in the Lord, And He shall give you the desires of your heart. Commit your way to the Lord, Trust also in Him, And He shall bring it to pass."

Luke 12:32

"Do not fear, little flock, for it is your Father's good pleasure to give you the kingdom."

Matthew 6:31,32

"Therefore do not worry, saying, 'What shall we eat?' or 'What shall we drink?' or 'What shall we wear?' For after all these things the Gentiles seek. For your heavenly Father knows that you need all these things."

1 Peter 5:7

"casting all your care upon Him, for He cares for you."

Psalms 40:4

"Blessed is that man who makes the Lord his trust, And does not respect the proud, nor such as turn aside to lies."

Psalms 125:1

"Those who trust in the Lord Are like Mount Zion, Which cannot be moved, but abides forever."

Scriptures on Wisdom

James 1:5

"If any of you lacks wisdom, let him ask of God, who gives to all liberally and without reproach, and it will be given to him."

Isaiah 2:3

"Many people shall come and say, 'Come, and let us go up to the mountain of the Lord, To the house of the God of Jacob; He will teach us His ways, And we shall walk in His paths.' For out of Zion shall go forth the law, And the word of the Lord from Jerusalem. "

Psalms 32:8

"I will instruct you and teach you in the way you should go; I will guide you with My eye."

Ecclesiastes 2:26

"For God gives wisdom and knowledge and joy to a man who is good in His sight; but to the sinner He gives the work of gathering and collecting, that he may give to him who is good before God. This also is vanity and grasping for the wind."

Psalms 16:7

"I will bless the Lord who has given me counsel; My heart also instructs me in the night seasons."

Proverbs 2:5-7

"Then you will understand the fear of the Lord, And find the knowledge of God. For the Lord gives wisdom; From His mouth come knowledge and understanding; He stores up sound wisdom for the upright; He is a shield to those who walk uprightly;"

1 John 5:20

"And we know that the Son of God has come and has given us an understanding, that we may know Him who is true; and we are in Him who is true, in His Son Jesus Christ. This is the true God and eternal life."

2 Corinthians 4:6

"For it is the God who commanded light to shine out of darkness, who has shone in our hearts to give the light of the knowledge of the glory of God in the face of Jesus Christ."

Proverbs 28:5

"Evil men do not understand justice, But those who seek the Lord understand all."

Psalms 51:6

"Behold, You desire truth in the inward parts, And in the hidden part You will make me to know wisdom."

James 1:5

If any of you lacks wisdom, let him ask God, who gives generously to all without reproach, and it will be given him.

James 3:17

But the wisdom from above is first pure, then peaceable, gentle, open to reason, full of mercy and good fruits, impartial and sincere.

Proverbs 3:13-18

Blessed is the one who finds wisdom, and the one who gets understanding, for the gain from her is better than gain from silver and her profit better than gold. She is more precious than jewels, and nothing you desire can compare with her. Long life is in her right hand; in her left hand are riches and honor. Her ways are ways of pleasantness, and all her paths are peace. ...

Proverbs 1:7

The fear of the Lord is the beginning of knowledge; fools despise wisdom and instruction.

Ephesians 5:15-17

Look carefully then how you walk, not as unwise but as wise, making the best use of the time, because the days are evil. Therefore do not be foolish, but understand what the will of the Lord is.

Proverbs 19:20

Listen to advice and accept instruction, that you may gain wisdom in the future.

Proverbs 12:15

The way of a fool is right in his own eyes, but a wise man listens to advice.

Proverbs 10:23

Doing wrong is like a joke to a fool, but wisdom is pleasure to a man of understanding.

Colossians 3:16

Let the word of Christ dwell in you richly, teaching and admonishing one another in all wisdom, singing psalms and hymns and spiritual songs, with thankfulness in your hearts to God.

Proverbs 18:15

An intelligent heart acquires knowledge, and the ear of the wise seeks knowledge.

Proverbs 2:6

For the Lord gives wisdom; from his mouth come knowledge and understanding;

Psalm 111:10

The fear of the Lord is the beginning of wisdom; all those who practice it have a good understanding. His praise endures forever!

Proverbs 17:27-28 whoever restrains his words has knowledge, and he who has a cool spirit is a man of understanding. Even a fool who keeps silent is considered wise; when he closes his lips, he is deemed intelligent.

Scriptures on Work

Colossians 3:23

Whatever you do, work heartily, as for the Lord and not for men,

Proverbs 16:3

Commit your work to the Lord, and your plans will be established.

1 Corinthians 10:31

So, whether you eat or drink, or whatever you do, do all to the glory of God.

Proverbs 18:9

Whoever is slack in his work is a brother to him who destroys.

Genesis 2:15

The Lord God took the man and put him in the Garden of Eden to work it and keep it.

Ephesians 4:28

Let the thief no longer steal, but rather let him labor, doing honest work with his own hands, so that he may have something to share with anyone in need.

2 Thessalonians 3:10

For even when we were with you, we would give you this command: If anyone is not willing to work, let him not eat.

Proverbs 14:23

In all toil there is profit, but mere talk tends only to poverty.

Luke 1:37

For nothing will be impossible with God."

John 6:27

Do not labor for the food that perishes, but for the food that endures to eternal life, which the Son of Man will give to you. For on him God the Father has set his seal."

1 Corinthians 15:10

But by the grace of God I am what I am, and his grace toward me was not in vain. On the contrary, I worked harder than any of them, though it was not I, but the grace of God that is with me.

1 Thessalonians 4:11

And to aspire to live quietly, and to mind your own affairs, and to work with your hands, as we instructed you,

Galatians 6:4-5

But let each one test his own work, and then his reason to boast will be in himself alone and not in his neighbor. For each will have to bear his own load.

1 Corinthians 16:14

Let all that you do be done in love.

Proverbs 21:5

The plans of the diligent lead surely to abundance, but everyone who is hasty comes only to poverty.

Matthew 11:28

Come to me, all who labor and are heavy laden, and I will give you rest.

Psalm 90:17

Let the favor of the Lord our God be upon us, and establish the work of our hands upon us; yes, establish the work of our hands!

Colossians 3:23-25

Whatever you do, work heartily, as for the Lord and not for men, knowing that from the Lord you will receive the inheritance as your reward. You are serving the Lord Christ. For the wrongdoer will be paid back for the wrong he has done, and there is no partiality.

Proverbs 22:7

The rich rules over the poor, and the borrower is the slave of the lender.

Colossians 3:17

And whatever you do, in word or deed, do everything in the name of the Lord Jesus, giving thanks to God the Father through him.

Proverbs 12:11

Whoever works his land will have plenty of bread, but he who follows worthless pursuits lacks sense.

Proverbs 24:27

Prepare your work outside; get everything ready for yourself in the field, and after that build your house.

Proverbs 24:30-34

I passed by the field of a sluggard, by the vineyard of a man lacking sense, and behold, it was all overgrown with thorns; the ground was covered with nettles, and its stone wall was broken down. Then I saw and considered it; I looked and received instruction. A little sleep, a little slumber, a little folding of the hands to rest, and poverty will come upon you like a robber, and want like an armed man.

1 Timothy 5:8

But if anyone does not provide for his relatives, and especially for members of his household, he has denied the faith and is worse than an unbeliever.

Proverbs 12:24

The hand of the diligent will rule, while the slothful will be put to forced labor.

Proverbs 13:22

A good man leaves an inheritance to his children's children, but the sinner's wealth is laid up for the righteous.

Proverbs 13:4

The soul of the sluggard craves and gets nothing, while the soul of the diligent is richly supplied.

Proverbs 13:11

Wealth gained hastily will dwindle, but whoever gathers little by little will increase it.

James 2:26

For as the body apart from the spirit is dead, so also faith apart from works is dead.

1 Corinthians 15:58

Therefore, my beloved brothers, be steadfast, immovable, always abounding in the work of the Lord, knowing that in the Lord your labor is not in vain.

Proverbs 10:4

A slack hand causes poverty, but the hand of the diligent makes rich.

James 2:18

But someone will say, "You have faith and I have works." Show me your faith apart from your works, and I will show you my faith by my works.

Ecclesiastes 3:13

Also that everyone should eat and drink and take pleasure in all his toil—this is God's gift to man.

Proverbs 22:29

Do you see a man skillful in his work? He will stand before kings; he will not stand before obscure men.

John 5:17

But Jesus answered them, "My Father is working until now, and I am working."

Luke 14:28

For which of you, desiring to build a tower, does not first sit down and count the cost, whether he has enough to complete it?

Acts 20:35

In all things I have shown you that by working hard in this way we must help the weak and remember the words of the Lord Jesus, how he himself said, 'It is more blessed to give than to receive.'"

Scriptures for Youth

1 Timothy 4:12

Let no one despise you for your youth, but set the believers an example in speech, in conduct, in love, in faith, in purity.

Ecclesiastes 11:9

Rejoice, O young man, in your youth, and let your heart cheer you in the days of your youth. Walk in the ways of your heart and the sight of your eyes. But know that for all these things God will bring you into judgment.

Jeremiah 1:4-8

Now the word of the Lord came to me, saying, "Before I formed you in the womb I knew you, and before you were born I consecrated you; I appointed you a prophet to the nations." Then I said, "Ah, Lord God! Behold, I do not know how to speak, for I am only a youth." But the Lord said to me, "Do not say, 'I am only a youth'; for to all to whom I send you, you shall go, and whatever I command you, you shall speak. Do not be afraid of them, for I am with you to deliver you, declares the Lord."

Ecclesiastes 12:1

Remember also your Creator in the days of your youth, before the evil days come and the years draw near of which you will say, "I have no pleasure in them";

Psalm 119:9

How can a young man keep his way pure? By guarding it according to your word.

2 Timothy 2:22

So flee youthful passions and pursue righteousness, faith, love, and peace, along with those who call on the Lord from a pure heart.

1 Corinthians 10:13

No temptation has overtaken you that is not common to man. God is faithful, and he will not let you be tempted beyond your ability, but with the temptation he will also provide the way of escape, that you may be able to endure it.

Ephesians 6:1-4

Children, obey your parents in the Lord, for this is right. "Honor your father and mother" (this is the first commandment with a promise), "that it may go well with you and that you may live long in the land." Fathers, do not provoke your children to anger, but bring them up in the discipline and instruction of the Lord.

Proverbs 23:26

My son, give me your heart, and let your eyes observe my ways.

Jeremiah 29:11

For I know the plans I have for you, declares the Lord, plans for welfare and not for evil, to give you a future and a hope.

Ephesians 4:29

Let no corrupting talk come out of your mouths, but only such as is good for building up, as fits the occasion, that it may give grace to those who hear.

Psalm 144:12

May our sons in their youth be like plants full grown, our daughters like corner pillars cut for the structure of a palace;

Proverbs 3:5-6

Trust in the Lord with all your heart, and do not lean on your own understanding. In all your ways acknowledge him, and he will make straight your paths.

Romans 12:1-2

I appeal to you therefore, brothers, by the mercies of God, to present your bodies as a living sacrifice, holy and acceptable to God, which is your spiritual worship. Do not be conformed to this world, but be transformed by the renewal of your mind, that by testing you may discern what is the will of God, what is good and acceptable and perfect.

Manufactured by Amazon.ca
Bolton, ON